The Revivifying Word

Studies in German Literature, Linguistics, and Culture

The Revivifying Word

Literature, Philosophy, and the
Theory of Life in Europe's Romantic Age

Clayton Koelb

CAMDEN HOUSE
Rochester, New York

Copyright © 2008 Clayton Koelb

All Rights Reserved. Except as permitted under current legislation,
no part of this work may be photocopied, stored in a retrieval system,
published, performed in public, adapted, broadcast, transmitted,
recorded, or reproduced in any form or by any means,
without the prior permission of the copyright owner.

First published 2008
by Camden House

Camden House is an imprint of Boydell & Brewer Inc.
668 Mt. Hope Avenue, Rochester, NY 14620, USA
www.camden-house.com
and of Boydell & Brewer Limited
PO Box 9, Woodbridge, Suffolk IP12 3DF, UK
www.boydellandbrewer.com

ISBN-13: 978–1–57113–388–5
ISBN-10: 1–57113–388–7

Library of Congress Cataloging-in-Publication Data

Koelb, Clayton, 1942–
    The Revivifying word : literature, philosophy, and the theory of life in europe's romantic age / Clayton Koelb.
    p. cm. — (Studies in German literature, linguistics, and culture.)
Includes bibliographical references and index.
ISBN-13: 978–1–57113–388–5
ISBN-10: 1–57113–388–7
    Literature — History and criticism — Theory, etc. 2. Romanticism.
I. Title. II. Series.

PN441.K64 2008
809′.9145—dc22

2008021901

A catalogue record for this title is available from the British Library.

This publication is printed on acid-free paper.
Printed in the United States of America.

> Call ye these appearances
> Which I beheld of shepherds in my youth,
> This sanctity of nature given to man,
> A shadow, a delusion — ye who are fed
> By the dead letter, not the spirit of things,
> Whose truth is not a motion or a shape
> Instinct with vital functions, but a block
> Or waxen image which yourselves have made
> And ye adore!
> — Wordsworth, *The Prelude* VIII

Contents

Preface	ix
Note on Abbreviations and Translations	xiii

Part I: Letter and Spirit

	Introduction: "The Dead Man's Life": Romantic Reading and Revivification	3
1:	"The Sound Which Echoes in Our Soul": The Romantic Aesthetics of Matter and Spirit	14
2:	"Spirit Thinks Only Through the Body": Materialist Spiritualism in Romantic Europe	30

Part II: The Dead and Living Past

3:	"The Heavenly Revelation of Her Spirit": Goethe's *The Sorrows of Young Werther*	47
4:	"O Read for Pity's Sake!": Keats's *Endymion*	68
5:	"Graecum Est, Non Legitur": Hugo's *Notre-Dame de Paris*	78
6:	"Spiritual Communication": Gautier's *Spirite*	97

Part III: The Incarnate Word

7:	"Eat This Scroll": Kleist's "Michael Kohlhaas"	113
8:	"I Sickened as I Read": Mary Shelley's *Frankenstein*	127
9:	"Those Who, Being Dead, Are Yet Alive": Maturin's *Melmoth the Wanderer*	145
10:	"This Hideous Drama of Revivification": Poe and the Rhetoric of Terror	165

Conclusion	181
Works Cited	185
Index	195

Preface

THIS BOOK EXAMINES A FRUITFUL POINT of intersection between the rhetoric of philosophy and the rhetoric of fiction during the Romantic century: the apostle Paul's well-known proposition that the dead letter can be revivified by the living spirit. This proposition provided the philosophical foundation for an aesthetic theory, and that theory in turn implied a remarkably productive narrative idea. The aesthetic theory focused attention on the mysterious process by which lifeless material objects mediate an interaction between the living minds of artists and their audiences. The narrative application was a set of literary texts in which characters cross the boundary between death and life with the help of some form of reading. Romantic aesthetics thus provided not only the theory but also the principal theme for a persistent genre of Romantic fiction. In both theory and practice, then, Romanticism was frequently a matter of life and death.

The period-concept "Romanticism," though still much contested, is useful for a study like this one, which traces a concept (and a practice derived from that concept) that traveled widely geographically — from Europe to the United States and beyond — and extended in time from the middle of the eighteenth century to the middle of the nineteenth.[1] In this book, therefore, I follow the proposal of William Galperin and Susan Wolfson, who have suggested redefining Romanticism as

> an intellectually and historically coherent century-long category, 1750–1850, which we unabashedly call "The Romantic Century." Our totalizing nomenclature may appear a bit backward-looking, especially for an era of revolutions. But the words and events of romanticism at this category's center are actually quite consistent with the essential monism that lurks (at least teleologically) in the dialectical constitution of romantic studies currently in vogue, where "and" is invariably the keyword: margin "and" center; past "and" present; self "and" society; along with the host of rubrics that begin with "romanticism and...."

This book suggests that another important "and" be added to the list: "matter/letter *and* spirit." The dialectical relation between dead matter and living spirit, it can be argued, is the most significant and persistent of all the Romantic "ands." Its persistence is indeed formidable: fascination with its implications continues to the present day.

It is essential not to lose sight of the fact that behind the impetus for the expansion suggested by Galperin and Wolfson lies a historically significant insight: the Romantic century set the agenda for modernity. That is not all it did, by any means, but it surely did at least that. The important issues that have been contested throughout the modern period (from around 1750 to approximately the present) were first framed, or significantly reframed, by writers who were productive from 1750 to 1850.

Those familiar with my other work will not be surprised to find that this project, too, focuses on reading, which I understand here as the process of reconstructing and construing human discourse that has been embodied as a material artifact. The interaction between the living producers and receivers of such discourse, mediated as it is by lifeless objects, necessarily involves readers in an activity that must, at times, seem like a rite of revivification. It surely seemed so to the writers discussed in this book, who in effect founded their conception of art on the mysterious possibility that potential life inheres in apparently dead matter. In this conception they were undoubtedly abetted by a prominent strain of scientific thought, outlined in the second chapter, arguing for the presence of life even in presumably "dead" things like minerals. The interpenetration of matter and spirit was in fact assumed by an influential sector of the European cultural elite, and in consequence the conceptual boundary between dead matter and living organisms could, in the minds of many, blur and even disappear. The process of reading was the paradigmatic and homely example of precisely how one could — and regularly did — cross the boundary, taking the dead matter of a text and turning it into the living thoughts of a reader.

The study of Romantic culture, particularly of literary culture, has in recent years most frequently been cast in the mode of ideological critique. Artistic endeavors have been regularly understood as epiphenomena that reflect, distort, or attempt to evade the more important political, social, economic conditions of human life. There has been a significant effort to bring to the foreground these allegedly more basic, allegedly more "historical," circumstances of which cultural artifacts like literary texts are supposed to be symptoms. Certainly some very interesting and illuminating work has come out of this approach, and it has appropriately chastened those who might have become inattentive to some of the features of the total historical matrix in which texts are necessarily embedded. One prominent strain of current research, for example, pays particular attention to the material culture of the period, partly out of a desire to investigate something hitherto neglected by scholarship, but partly also out of the conviction that Romantic writers had themselves ignored or devalued material conditions in their quest for a fuller understanding of that intellectual/spiritual quality denoted by the German word *Geist*.

This study takes an approach to cultural history that attempts analysis rather than critique. As D. W. Smith has defined it, cultural analysis "studies the social practices that help to shape or serve as cultural substrate of the various types of mental activity, including conscious experience."

Scholarship in this vein tries to identify in social practices such as literature, philosophy, and science those cultural structures that shape the way participants in that culture experience the world — without taking any stand on the adequacy or inadequacy of those structures. Cultural criticism of Romanticism looks to identify its omissions and distortions; cultural analysis of Romanticism hopes to trace as clearly as possible those cultural constellations that allowed Romantics to see the world as they did. It does not come to any conclusions as to whether or not they saw it correctly. The concepts "omission" and "distortion" do not play a central role in the analysis.

Still, one side effect of closely examining such constellations might be the discovery that some of our assumptions about omissions and distortions were premature. While it is true that Romantic culture placed a very high value on *Geist*, a careful examination of the letter/spirit constellation suggests that there was a significant materialist component in Romantic thought. This book tries to show that Romantic culture was deeply and abidingly concerned about the interdependence of *Geist* with a material vehicle. The process of writing and reading exemplifies every aspect and subtlety of the interaction between matter and spirit. Indeed, it is hardly possible to overstate the theoretical complexity of a process that involves taking thought embodied in a living creature, reembodying such thought in language, and embodying that language yet again in material objects; then, conversely, extracting language from material objects and thought from linguistic structures to reembody them once more in a living organism. Far from evading or suppressing the material, the Romantic century lavished upon matter its most consistent and careful intellectual scrutiny.

Because my overall aim has been to contribute to the cultural history of the Romantic century by looking through the lens of literature, I have had to make certain strategic decisions about the deployment of evidence. As part of my endeavor I have had to examine, to a limited degree and with a very tight focus, the history of philosophy and the history of science: the early chapters offer the results of my investigation in those areas. The political history of the time, important as it was, had primarily indirect effects on the matters relevant to this inquiry and therefore receives less attention. I have chosen for detailed analysis a number works of European fiction that represent both the phenomenon I am describing and its temporal and geographic span. The sample offered here is not meant to be exhaustive but rather illustrative; it seeks to indicate the overall shape of a cultural trend.

* * *

I am grateful to the Johnston family, particularly Margaret and Paul A. Johnston, the donors who generously endowed several professorships at the University of North Carolina, Chapel Hill. Not only did they provide the funds, but they also specified that these endowed chairs be named, not in honor of themselves, but in recognition the achievements made by distinguished Carolina scholars. I therefore also owe a special debt of thanks to the late Guy Benton Johnson, whose important contributions to a field far from my own provided an occasion for the Johnston family's philanthropy. The research fund accompanying the Guy B. Johnson chair, along with a research and study leave provided by Carolina's College of Arts and Sciences, facilitated completion of the book. I benefited from the opportunity to try out portions of the manuscript as talks, first at a panel held at a Modern Language Association convention, and later on the occasion of an invitation to speak at Duke University. The comments I received were very helpful in refocusing my thinking as I revised the text. Chapter 4, "Eat This Scroll," has appeared in print before in somewhat different form, under the title "Incorporating the Text: Kleist's 'Michael Kohlhaas,'" in *PMLA* 105, no. 5 (1990):1098–1107.

The manuscript went though a number of transformations on its way to completion. The last and most important of them was stimulated by the work of Janice Hewlett Koelb in her book *The Poetics of Description* and by the detailed advice she offered me in the final stages of revision. Without her I would not have known many of the things I needed to know and should have known when the project began. It was her suggestion, for example, that I look into the writings of Robinet, a key figure in late eighteenth-century natural philosophy and an essential link in the argument of the early chapters. It is thanks to her that my various drafts finally developed into a book fit to print.

Clayton Koelb
Chapel Hill, North Carolina

Note

[1] For differing points of view on how to understand "Romanticism," see Lovejoy; Wellek; Peckham; Abrams, "English Romanticism"; Eichner, *"Romantic"*; Kroeber; and McFarland (25–49). McGann provides a useful overview (17–56). Reinhart Koselleck has called this period the "Sattelzeit" (saddle period) — that is, the era of transition from the premodern to full-fledged modernity. "This period thematizes the transformation of the premodern usage of language to our usage, and I cannot emphasize strongly enough its heuristic character" (5). Koselleck has vigorously defended the notion that modernity begins in the eighteenth century, most notably perhaps in his essay "The Eighteenth Century as the Beginning of Modernity" (154–69).

Note on Abbreviations and Translations

I USE THE FOLLOWING ABBREVIATIONS to refer to frequently cited works. Although I quote the original French or German for texts written in those languages only when necessary for the analysis, I provide references throughout to standard editions of the original texts, alongside that of the translation, so that readers can easily locate the passages in the original as needed. Translations not otherwise credited are mine.

GE [Gautier English] Gautier, Théophile. *The Works of Théophile Gautier*. Trans. and ed. F. C. de Sumichrast. Vol. 11. New York: George D. Sproul, 1901.

GF [Gautier French] Gautier, Théophile. *Spirite: Nouvelle fantastique*. Paris: Editions A.-G. Nizet, 1970.

GS [Goethe *Sorrows*] Goethe, J. W. *The Sorrows of Young Werther and Selected Writings*. Trans. Catherine Hutter. New York: Signet-New American Library, 1962.

GW [Goethe *Werke*] Goethe, J. W. *Werke. Hamburger Ausgabe in 14 Bänden*. Ed. Erich Trunz. Vol. 6. München: C. H. Beck, 1996.

HE [Hugo English] Hugo, Victor. *Notre-Dame of Paris*. Trans. John Sturrock. Harmondsworth: Penguin, 1978.

HF [Hugo French] Hugo, Victor. *Notre-Dame de Paris. Les Travailleurs de la mer*. Ed. Jacques Seebacher and Yves Gohin. Paris: Gallimard, 1975.

KM [Kleist *Marquise*] Kleist, Heinrich von. *The Marquise of O—and Other Stories*. Ed. and trans. David Luke and Nigel Reeves. Harmondsworth: Penguin, 1978.

KW [Kleist *Werke*] Kleist, Heinrich von. *Sämtliche Werke und Briefe*. Ed. Helmut Sembdner. Vol. 2. München: Hanser, 1961.

MM [Maturin *Melmoth*] Maturin, Charles Robert. *Melmoth the Wanderer*. Ed. Victor Sage. Harmondsworth: Penguin, 2000.

PT [Poe *Tales*] Poe, Edgar Allan. *Selected Tales*. Ed. Julian Symons. Oxford: Oxford UP, 1980.

SF [Shelley *Frankenstein*] Shelley, Mary Wollstonecraft. *Frankenstein; or, The Modern Prometheus. The 1818 Text*. Ed. James Rieger. Chicago: U of Chicago P, 1982.

Part I

Letter and Spirit

Introduction: "The Dead Man's Life": Romantic Reading and Revivification

> But how are we to raise the defunct language of Nature from the dead?
> — Hamann, *Aesthetica in Nuce*

MANY POETS, PHILOSOPHERS, AND SCIENTISTS of Europe's Romantic age struggled to formulate a theory of life that would answer some of the most difficult questions in philosophy. How can we properly characterize and explain the mysterious relation between dead material bodies and living, animate beings? What process causes one to turn into the other? What happens when a living creature ceases to live? And, most puzzling of all, is it possible that life could arise out of lifeless matter? The key that could unlock these mysteries lay surprisingly close at hand: the process by which dead matter could come to life, they imagined, must be something like the process of reading.

In the context of a natural philosophy that suggested the potential presence of life in all material bodies,[1] a novel way of thinking about reading and writing began to develop in the mid-to-late eighteenth century in Germany. Although its basic notions were daring — even a bit alarming — this way of thinking spread steadily across the continent and helped to shape European culture for much of the next century. The new notion of reading was founded upon no less radical a project than the raising of the dead in and through language. Of course I do not mean that the goal of the writers I consider here was to restore life to the dead bodies of actual previously living persons — though their fictional characters sometimes attempted just that. I mean rather that these writers wanted to reanimate cultural materials they thought of as worn-out, decayed, dismembered, or effaced and to find a vital spirit in apparently lifeless material bodies. The aim of their art was revivification of a world filled with objects that were now (or in some cases had always been) devoid of vitality, and their aesthetic theory frequently presents artistic creativity as a spirit that animates otherwise dead matter. Such a fascination with the resurrection of the dead was hardly new in Christian Europe, but during the eighteenth century it took a turn away from the orthodox concern for the promised awakening of the dead at the Last Judgment and indeed away from the death and resurrection of Jesus, toward an urgent and abiding interest in the problem of reading. What follows is an exploration of the ways in which certain late eighteenth-century and early nineteenth-century writers struggled with reading as a life-and-death issue.

Even in its earliest stages, long before the Schlegels made the term "Romantic" the emblem of a particular literary outlook and the focus of a critical debate that goes on to this day, the reaction against Enlightenment rationalism had certain characteristics that we recognize as typical of the Romantic strain of modernity. Nowhere are these roots of Romantic modernity more apparent than in the writings of Johann Georg Hamann and Johann Gottfried Herder, whose influence was great among the *Stürmer und Dränger* who helped set the agenda for the intellectual revolution in Europe that marks the boundary, imprecise though it may be, between the early modern (ca. 1492–1750) and the modern world (1750–?). Hamann and Herder offer an early version of the already complex question of the role of art in bringing the dead back to life.

Hamann's *Aesthetica in Nuce* (1762), though notoriously difficult to interpret, clearly demonstrates such a close relation between reading and revivification that it can serve as an initial landmark in the history of Romantic thought.[2] Hamann understands the entire universe as a text in need of interpretation. God's act of creation, he says, is

> an utterance to created things through created things, for day speaketh unto day, and night proclaimeth unto night. Its word traverses every clime to the ends of the earth, and its voice can be heard in every dialect. The fault may lie where it will (outside us or within us): all we have left in Nature for our use is fragmentary verse and *disjecta membra poetae*. To collect these together is the scholar's modest part; the philosopher's is to interpret them; to imitate them, or — bolder still — to adapt them, the poet's. (141–42)

God is the supreme poet, and His poetic masterpiece is the created world of nature.[3] For reasons that are not clear — the problem may have a cause "outside us or within us" — the great poem of the world appears to us in a fragmented form. The pages of the great book of the world have already been scattered, ripped apart, written over, or simply lost. The language of nature is already, from the limited human perspective, at any rate, "defunct [*ausgestorben*]" (147). Hamann's "cabalistic" voice suggests that human beings may be at least partially responsible for the apparent death of nature: "Behold, the scribes of worldly wisdom, great and small, have overwhelmed the text of Nature [*den Text der Natur*], like the Great Flood" (146). Hamann believed that Enlightenment scholars had done the same thing to God's other great book, Scripture, by paying too much attention to its linguistic surface.

The two great poetic works of the Creator, in this view, are composed in a language now defunct. When Hamann claims that the language of nature is dead, he makes an implicit analogy with the Bible, for it is clear everywhere in the *Aesthetica* that nature and Scripture are two variants of a single great divine enterprise. By means of this analogy one can begin to get a sense of what Hamann means by his claim that the language of nature is now defunct and why he cannot point to a specific cause of death. A "dead" language is one that, over the course of time, has lost its character as mother tongue and can only be understood by complex acts of reconstruction. Such a language no longer has a connection to any living community of speakers, but one cannot pinpoint the exact moment when the connection was severed. So it is with the language of nature, from which the living community of men has become estranged. Death now gapes between the utterance that speaks through created things and those who try to understand it.

The task of poets and philosophers, then, is no different from that of biblical scholars: they must "raise the defunct language of Nature from the dead" (147). As the analogy with Scripture suggests, there is no other way to go about this project of revivification than by *reading*. Though it is not certain what methods we should use in order to obtain the best result, it is certain that we will get no result unless we read, for only by reading can the living spirit return to the dead letter. We must begin, however, with those dead letters, hoping to reanimate them and not merely manipulate and multiply their dead bodies.[4] Hamann directs much of his ironic venom against scholars who paid special attention to the Bible as a textual artifact, like the orientalist and theologian Johann David Michaelis, whom he presents as one of the principal "scribes of worldly wisdom."[5] Hamann's distaste for Michaelis, Voltaire, and the rest of the rationalists is based on his horror at a literal mode of reading that attends to the text itself as a set of verbal signifiers rather than to the spiritual meaning figured by the text. The "literal" reading of the Bible Hamann is objecting to is thus quite different from that advocated by modern evangelical Christians who hold to a belief in the "literal" truth of Scripture. Hamann thinks Michaelis pays too much attention to the letters and not enough to their significance, thus leaving the text as dead at the end of the process of reading as it was at the beginning:

> But if we raise up the whole deserving righteousness of a scribe upon the dead body of the letter [*auf den Leichnam des Buchstabens*], what sayeth the spirit [*Geist*] to that? Shall he be but a groom of the chamber of the dead letter, or perhaps a mere esquire to the deadening letter [*des tödtenden Buchstabens*]? God forbid! (143)

The allusion in these lines to Paul's famous formulation in the Second Epistle to the Corinthians is only one of the scores of biblical allusions in the *Aesthetica*, but it is one of the most revealing — and one of the most important for the history of Romantic aesthetics. It offers the passage from Paul as a concise conceptual foundation, a vocabulary and a set of relationships, upon which may be erected an elaborate structure of thought concerning the connection between reading and writing on the one hand

and living and dying on the other. Hamann himself makes a substantial contribution to the elaboration of that structure in his little "Rhapsody in Cabalistic Prose." The passage in question is this one from Paul's second letter to the Corinthians:

> Do we begin again to commend ourselves? or need we, as some others, epistles of commendation to you, or letters of commendation from you? Ye are our epistle written in our hearts, known and read of all men: forasmuch as ye are manifestly declared to be the epistle of Christ ministered by us, written not with ink, but with the spirit of the living God; not in tables of stone, but in fleshy tablets of the heart. And such trust we have through Christ to God-ward: not that we are sufficient of ourselves to think any thing of ourselves; but our sufficiency is of God; who also hath made us able ministers of the new testament; not of the letter, but of the spirit: for the letter killeth, but the spirit giveth life [τὸ γὰρ γράμμα ἀποκτέννει, τὸ δὲ πνεῦμα ζῳοποιεῖ]. (2 Cor. 3:1–6)

The question that Paul addresses is one that resonates loudly in Romantic thinking, even among those Romantics not at all concerned, as Hamann was, with the preservation of Christianity. For Paul must specify for the Corinthians — and above all for himself — the source of the power and authority that resides in the documents of Scripture. His immediate concern is obviously to establish his own authority, but to do so he has to derive his legitimacy from some source other than written texts, for he has none. He must find a way to account for the power of texts like the Old Testament without undermining his own claim to authority.

His strategy is to take a notion of apparently Greek heritage and use it to undermine the authority of the bare text. It seems likely that Paul knew, directly or by way of an intermediary, the skepticism displayed toward writing by Plato in the *Phaedrus* and elsewhere in the writings attributed to him. In making his distinction between the living spirit and the dead letter, Paul echoes the sentiment upon which Socrates and Phaedrus agree near the end of the dialogue. In response to Socrates' recommendation of a kind of discourse he compares to writing "in the soul [ἐν τῃ ψυχῇ]" rather than on paper, Phaedrus says: "You mean the living, breathing discourse [λόγος ἔμψυχος] of the man who knows, of which the written one can be fairly called an image" (276 A). Paul's distinction between the dead letter (γράμμα) and the living spirit (πνεῦμα) is a significant variation and extension of Plato's distinction between inanimate "written discourse [λόγος γεγραμμένος]" and "animate speech [λόγος ἔμψυχος]." For Plato's Socrates, the written word is inanimate because it is merely an image (εἴδωλον) of the originally animate discourse, and as such it has to function outside the context of the interaction between "living, breathing" persons that Plato calls dialectic. Paul's argument is similar in suggesting that the discourse of the soul or spirit (πνεῦμα) is more powerful than writing and closer to the divine original of all authority. But Paul, a man brought up in a culture that revered the written word in a manner unknown to classical Greece, displays an ambivalence about documents more radical than Plato's. Paul actually shifts this ambivalence onto documents themselves, which he understands to possess both a living and a dead aspect. Documents *can* be a form of living, breathing discourse, but only if their dead letters are animated by the living spirit.

Like Plato's Socrates, who prefers writing "in the soul," Paul prefers writing "in the fleshy tablets of the heart [ἐν πλαξὶν καρδίαις σαρκίναις]" to literal written documents. But Paul is willing to grant a far greater spiritual power to written texts than the very limited role Socrates sees for them in the *Phaedrus*. This becomes clear in lines from 2 Corinthians immediately following those just cited:

> But if the ministration of death, written and engraven in stones, was glorious, so that the children of Israel could not steadily behold the face of Moses for the glory of his countenance; which glory was to be done away: how shall not the ministration of the spirit be rather glorious. For if the ministration of condemnation be glory, much more doth the ministration of righteousness exceed in glory. (2 Cor. 3:7–9)

Although the "ministration of death, written and engraven" (Paul's Greek is "service of death in letters [ἡ διακονία τοῦ θανάτου ἐν γράμμασιν]") gets the worst of the comparison with the "service/ministration of the spirit [διακονίατ οῦ πνεύματος]," it is still acknowledged as "glorious" and worthy of esteem. Paul's rhetoric obviously means to devalue the (written) law of Moses, the old covenant, in order to extol the merits of the new covenant of Jesus, whose testament was as yet unwritten. It was not his intention, however, to dismiss the Torah as devoid of divine authority — quite the contrary. The "glory" he ascribes to the old covenant is a measure of its great worth, of its genuine derivation from God. The coming of Christ and the new covenant, however, sets aside the old, replaces its sentence of death passed on all the children of Adam with the promise of life, and therefore surpasses it in glory.

Paul goes on to explain how it is that the covenant of Moses, though "made in glory," can appear to be nothing but a set of dead letters. It is as if, he says, the veil that Moses had to wear to shield the children of Israel from the splendor of the Lord that shone in the lawgiver's face still clung to the Mosaic law itself. The Old Testament text is hard to understand, "for until this day remaineth the same veil untaken away in the reading of the old testament." Scripture reports, however, that the veil was taken away from Moses' face "whenever he turns to the Lord." Paul glosses this passage from the old Scripture by claiming that "the Lord [in this passage — perhaps Exodus 34:34] is the Spirit [ὁ δὲ κύριος τὸ πνεῦμά ἐστιν]" (2 Cor. 3:17). In the presence of the divine πνεῦμα, then, the dead letters come back to life, the veil is removed, and the old text speaks plainly, even as it seems to do to Paul when he reads Exodus. The surest evidence that Paul believed in the possibility of turning the "service of death in letters" to the service of the living spirit is his own practice of rereading passages from the Old Testament.

Hamann's abhorrence for the dead letter is no less than Paul's; indeed one would have to say that it is even greater, since Hamann is concerned with a far larger text than the apostle was. When Hamann expresses his anger at the possibility of raising "the whole deserving righteousness of a scribe upon the dead body of the letter," his concern is directed not exclusively or even principally at Michaelis and the other philologically oriented readers of Scripture but at the entire project of Enlightenment philosophy. For Hamann this project amounts to nothing less than the transformation of the whole book of creation into a set of dead letters untouched by the spirit, the divine πνεῦμα of which Paul spoke. The threat of rationalism is that the great text, the language of which is now "dead" for us, will remain dead forever, never again receiving the revivifying touch of the spirit, or even the touch of the emotions that constitute the embodiments of the spirit. "If the passions are limbs of dishonor, do they therefore cease to be weapons of virility? Have you a wiser understanding of the letter of reason than that allegorical chamberlain of the Alexandrian Church [Origen] had of the letter of the Scriptures when he castrated himself in order to reach heaven?" (146). Enlightenment philosophy suffers from the same self-destructive literalism that afflicted Origen,[6] but it is directed not toward Scripture alone but toward the entire book of Nature.

Hamann proposes that all intellectual activity — philosophy, scholarship, and poetic art — should be a form of revivification of dead language. "Nature and Scripture then are the materials of the beautiful spirit which creates and imitates [*Natur und Schrift also sind die Materialien des schönen, schaffenden, nachahmenden Geistes*]" (147). The "beautiful spirit" brings vitality to these materials, while literalism leaves them cold and lifeless. Hamann agrees with Augustine's assessment that the prophetic books of the Old Testament are nothing but "insipidity and foolishness" if read literally but are miraculously revitalized and transformed by the power of Christ, just as that power transformed the water into wine at Cana: "the first sign by which He reveals the majesty of His humble figure transforms the holy books of the covenant into fine old wine" (148). One cannot avoid noticing that the creative spirit of revivification is at work in Hamann's reading of the Gospel of John. Hamann simply takes for granted the figurative equation of the jars filled with water with the books of the old covenant, making the story of the miracle at Cana an allegory of Christ's skill at raising the defunct language of an old document from the dead.

Hamann's "aesthetic in a nutshell" is founded on the possibility of endless acts of revivification, made possible by the infinite and ultimately incomprehensible power of the spirit of God. The dark side of Hamann's aesthetic emerges when we face squarely the fact that it assumes that the fundamental "materials" with which the creative spirit has to work are dead and that it takes a miraculous power to bring them back to life. The need for this power is no problem for Hamann, whose faith in the recuperative powers of God through Christ appears to be absolute. Later Romantic writers often will share Hamann's optimism, even when they do not share his faith. But a sense of the troubling presence of death at the origin of creative acts (when understood as Hamann understood them) complicates and darkens the writings of both aestheticians and authors of fiction.

Such a troubling presence can be detected even in the enthusiasm with which Johann Gottfried Herder speaks of the essential vitality of ancient poetry. Herder's love of Ossian and Homer — a taste he helped to form in his younger contemporary, Goethe — is based on a belief that "all the songs of these savage peoples move around objects, actions, events, around a living world!" (160). He cannot muster a similar enthusiasm for modern (that is, eighteenth-century) poetry, which he finds dry, pedantic, and dead: "Our schoolmasters [. . .] raid the scholar's house and come out empty-handed until finally, like Shakespeare's gravediggers, his Lancelot and his Dogberry, they speak in the uncertain inauthentic tones of decline and death" (158). This forceful opposition — ancient, "savage" poetry comes out of life, modern poetry comes out of death — structures the basic argument of his "Correspondence on Ossian and the Songs of Ancient Peoples."

But Herder's discourse also subtly complicates this opposition in the very moment of its inception, precisely because the "living world" of ancient poetry is known to us primarily by way of letters (*Lettern, Buchstaben*). Just as Paul had suggested in 2 Corinthians, letters might be merely dead things, or they might be repositories of the living spirit:

> Know then, that the more barbarous [*je wilder*] a people is — that is, the more alive [*je lebendiger*], the more freely acting (for that is what the word means) — the more barbarous [*desto wilder*], that is, the more alive [*desto lebendiger*], the more free, the closer to the senses, the more lyrically dynamic its songs will be, if songs it has. The more remote a people is from an artificial, scientific manner of thinking, speaking, and writing, the less its songs are made for paper and print, the less its verses are written for the dead letter [*todte Lettern*]. The purpose, the nature, the miraculous power of these songs as the delight, the driving force, the traditional chant and everlasting joy of the people — all this depends on the lyrical, living, dance-like quality of the song, on the living presence of the images [*von lebendiger Gegenwart der Bilder*], and the coherence and, as it were, compulsion of the content, the feelings; on the symmetry of the words and syllables, and sometimes even of the letters [*bey manchen*

sogar die Buchstaben], on the flow of the melody, and on a hundred other things which belong to the living world [*zur lebendigen Welt*], to the gnomic song of the nation, and vanish with it. These are the arrows of this barbarous Apollo with which he pierces our hearts and transfixes soul and memory. (155–56)

Herder pursues an antirationalist line very similar to Hamann's, finding liveliness and dynamic power in inverse relation to the "scientific manner of thinking." He insists forcefully and frequently that the poetry of ancient "barbarous" people derived from a "living presence" untouched by the "dead letter" in the form of what he considers the throttling constraints imposed by writing. At the same time, however, these same letters return (now called by the everyday German word *Buchstaben* instead of the Latinate *Lettern*) as the markers of living, oral form: they stand here for the sounds the letters represent, thus for something vital and fluid rather than for something fixed and dead. The "symmetry [. . .] even of the letters" refers to the patterns of alliteration and assonance that are important features of the oral poetry he admires. We understand, then, that his second use of the term "letters" is a metonymy for "sounds," whereas his first use meant "written letters," and that the one sort is associated with life and the other with death. Herder's argument needs both kinds of letters, those with spirit and those without, as evidence for the power of the poetry he admires and the impotence of the modern verse he despises.

Herder wants to present the "barbarous" poetry he loves as something that originates in a living world and that returns to enhance the life of the world. But his language suggests that such poetry is always tinged with death because it is always a matter of letters, and the same letters that can be infused with spirit might also be devoid of it. Herder's rhetoric thus discloses something his explicit argument does not acknowledge: an ambivalence about the written word similar to what we find in Plato and Paul. For all that he insists that ancient poetry is associated only with the living spirit, his mode of discourse suggests that it, too, is a matter of potentially dead letters.

Herder claims that the poems of Homer and Ossian belong to the realm of a sensuously unfettered nature from which we moderns have become estranged and whose language we no longer understand. This natural world is therefore "defunct" for us (in Hamann's terms), and its remnants can only remind us of its loss. Herder points out that the power of "barbarous" poems depends on various elements that belong to "the living world, to the gnomic song of the nation, and vanish with it." The songs themselves have survived, but cultural institutions essential to their vitality have disappeared. He fears that this process was in his own day rapidly diminishing the vital power of Shakespeare's dramas: "And soon perhaps, as everything gets blurred and tends in different directions, even his drama will become incapable of living performance, and will become the fragment of a Colossus, an Egyptian pyramid which everyone gazes at in amazement and no one understands" ("Shakespeare" 176). The Ossianic poems, which Herder accepted at face value as genuinely ancient documents, are for him precisely such fragments of a dismembered Colossus and are therefore no longer capable of "living" performance; that is, they cannot now generate the same energetic vitality that they did in their presumed original social contexts. Such poems have the power to bring back a hint of the living world out of which they sprang, but they cannot bring back that world itself.

There is thus a powerful elegiac tone to Herder's praise of the poets of old, an attitude toward a vanished nature that Schiller would later define as "sentimental" and that depends upon a consciousness (most visible in the ambivalent valorization of letters) that something might be irretrievably gone. This consciousness manifests itself as an intellectual and emotional fascination with the gloomy "Ossian" poems, a set of forgeries that Herder accepted as genuine relics of the distant past. They were connected with death not only because they allegedly had their origin in a world now dead and gone but also because their narratives dwell on dead and dying persons. The lugubrious contents of Macpherson's verses tend to repel readers today but were a great part of their attraction for Herder, Goethe, and their contemporaries. It was in fact this whiff of the grave that testified to their authenticity. Homer, who sings the praises of dead heroes, held a similar attraction. Herder's enthusiasm for "barbarous" poetry of all sorts is intimately connected to his fascination with mortality. His delight with the savage "Greenlander" who sings vivid tales of the seal hunt reaches its peak when the subject matter is death: "When he holds a graveside eulogy and sings a funeral dirge for his departed, he does not sing praise or lament, but paints, and the dead man's life [*das Leben des Verstorbenen selbst*], vividly portrayed with all the sudden leaps of the imagination, cannot but speak and cry" ("Correspondence" 160–61). This is nothing less than the raising of the dead, the revivification of the departed spirit. The paradoxical formulation "dead man's life" is calculated to put us in mind of magic and miracles, for it is nothing short of miraculous that the defunct heroes of Homer and Ossian should seem so vividly present to us when we read. The great emotional power that literature exercises over the Romantic imagination derives in no small measure from its ability to perform such miracles.

Paul's language of letter and spirit played a crucial role in the development of aesthetics in late eighteenth-century Europe because it offered an established, even culturally enshrined model for the interaction of life and death that philosophy and science had suggested was genuine, natural, and even universal. Hamann, Herder, Kant, Fichte, Coleridge, and others all made use of this language in their theoretical works, and writers of fiction over the course of nearly a century — from Goethe in 1775 to Gautier in 1865 — demonstrated its effects in their narratives. Paul's discourse focused on written texts and acts of reading, and Romantic writers followed his example — at times with a vengeance. In their fictions the written word serves as the paradigmatic metonymy for all signifying processes in which a meaning (understood as "living") is conveyed by material objects (understood as "dead"). Both reading and the aesthetic experience in general demonstrate the possibility of life emerging from dead matter, and the fictional depictions of acts of revivification therefore serve not only as figures for all artistic and even all symbolic activity but also for the emergence in nature of spirit out of organized material bodies.

Romantic literature thus participated in an important and still ongoing intellectual enterprise of the modern world: the attempt to locate and understand the boundary (if there is one) between living organisms and dead matter. It is both appropriate and convenient to call such an enterprise "the theory of life." The problem confronting poets, philosophers, and scientists engaged in developing a theory of life was not simply a stark choice between mechanism and vitalism, or between matter and spirit: it could and often did involve a more nuanced consideration of the relationship between material bodies and intellectual capability. Writers of the Romantic century found an effective means for exploring this relationship in fictions of the revivifying word.

My goal in this book is to demonstrate how one strand of philosophic thought about the relation between "living spirit" and "dead letter" permeated Romantic literature for nearly a century. I explore that philosophic strand in the next chapter. It was not philosophy alone, however, that engendered and fostered this strand of literary creativity. Clearly, the Christian religion played a key role in supplying important elements — the texts and some of the basic concepts — upon which philosophers built their aesthetic theory. It was contemporary science, though, that first provided the intellectual foundation upon which such a structure of ideas could be erected. Chapter 2 is devoted to that topic.

The principle evidence for the ubiquity and persistence of this intellectual constellation is a set of works of fiction composed in the Romantic century that display a fascination with the miraculous — and often dismaying — revivifying power of texts. Such fictions display two characteristic concerns, examined in detail in Parts II and III. They take up the problem of how the past, no matter how dead it may appear, can come back to life and affect the present (Part II); and they investigate the interaction of matter and spirit as a process of incarnation in which bodies take on the character of texts and texts the character of bodies (Part III). All these narratives explore the twilight zone in which language shuttles back and forth between life and death; they display characters who are the literary cousins of Pygmalion and his statue — characters like Shelley's Victor Frankenstein and the monster he assembles, Poe's Madeline Usher, Kleist's gypsy woman in "Michael Kohlhaas," and Gautier's Spirite. They and others like them have significant encounters with the revivifying word that deserve our close attention.[7]

Notes

[1] The scientific (natural-philosophical) context for such a view is discussed in Chapter 2.

[2] Abrams recognizes Hamann as an important figure in early Romantic thought, although he discusses him primarily as a precursor of Wordsworth (*Natural Supernaturalism* 399–408). Abrams does not discuss the *Aesthetica*.

[3] Cf. Abrams on Augustine and the Romantics, especially in *Natural Supernaturalism* 83–87.

[4] Cf. Ong on Ramism: "The unit of speech is considered as a mark on a surface, rather than as a phone (a speech sound). Thus, without even a second thought, Ramus will insist that all the elements of words and of all expression are not sound but such marks; that is, not syllables, but letters" (308).

[5] Michaelis was an important scholar of the Bible and of Semitic languages. He was a pioneer in approaching the study of the Old Testament as a document embedded in its ancient Near Eastern cultural context. For discussions of both Hamann and Michaelis and their relation to Enlightenment rationalism, see O'Flaherty. Hess, on the other hand, examines the orientalism of Michaelis in the context of the development of German anti-Semitism.

[6] Hamann alludes to the traditional story that Origen, a third-century Christian scholar, castrated himself in accordance with a literal reading of Matthew 19:12, supposedly to keep himself pure for his studies and his teaching. The passage in Matthew quotes Jesus as saying: "For there are some eunuchs by natural constitution; others have been made eunuchs by men; and others have made themselves eunuchs on account of the Kingdom of Heaven. He who is able to do this, let him do it."

[7] "Close attention" certainly implies "close reading." The argument for the continued usefulness of this mode of analysis need not be reiterated here, since it has been made quite eloquently elsewhere: see for example Perloff (xi–xxxi) and Rooney.

1: "The Sound Which Echoes in Our Soul": The Romantic Aesthetics of Matter and Spirit

THE MIRACLE OF THE REVIVIFYING WORD results from the paradoxical coexistence of death and life in a single phenomenon, and the principal theater for the performance of such magic is the scene of reading. The vocabulary of Paul in 2 Corinthians provides an essential concept for Romantic aesthetics: the dead letter and the living spirit exist together in the poetic text.[1] Hamann was perhaps the first of the German aestheticians to put Paul's vocabulary to work in the service of a theory of art, but he was by no means the last or even the most prominent. The same idea — and the same vocabulary — recurs in Kant's *Critique of Judgment* (*Kritik der Urteilskraft*, 1790). While it would be difficult or impossible to reconcile Hamann's antirationalist mysticism with Kant's critical philosophy on most issues, there is a remarkable agreement in this one area. For like Hamann, Kant understands the central question of aesthetics to be "How are we to raise the defunct language of Nature from the dead?" When Hamann claims that "Nature and Scripture are the materials of the beautiful, creating, imitating spirit" (147; translation modified for clarity), he is very close to the path that his friend and fellow Königsberger Kant would follow a few years later. Kant, of course, does not share Hamann's views on Scripture, but with that one revision Hamann's assertion could stand as an epigraph to the Third Critique: Nature is the material of the creating spirit.

Section 49 of the Third Critique, which takes up explicitly the notion of "spirit" (*Geist*), shows how close this philosopher of Enlightenment comes in his aesthetic theory to the counter-Enlightenment position of Hamann:

> *Spirit* in an aesthetical sense, signifies the animating principle [*das belebende Prinzip*] in the mind. But that whereby this principle animates [*belebt*] the soul — the material which it employs for that purpose — is that which sets the mental powers into swing that is final, i.e., into a play which is self-maintaining and which strengthens the powers for such activity. [. . .] this principle is nothing else than the faculty of presenting *aesthetic ideas*. But, by an aesthetic idea I mean that representation of the imagination which induces much thought, yet without the possibility of any definite thought whatever, i.e., *concept*, being adequate to it, and which language, consequently, can never get quite on level terms with or render completely intelligible. (60)

The imagination (as a productive faculty of cognition) is a powerful agent for creating, as it were, a second nature out of the material supplied to it by actual nature. Art thus works by "animating" (*beleben*, that is, "bringing life to") something. No process of animating would be necessary, of course, if the object of this process were already animate, already living. From the point of view of aesthetics, then (and perhaps from no other point of view in Kant's thinking), "actual nature" (as the material out of which the imagination creates a living "second nature") appears to be defunct. Kant's "aesthetic ideas" raise this defunct Nature from the dead by the very act of making "ideas" out of it. Ideas, as Kant defines them, transcend actual nature in that they "strain after something lying out beyond the confines of experience" (60). The creation of aesthetic ideas is an activity of the spirit (the "animating principle"), which enlivens the materials afforded by nature by "transgressing the limits of experience" (60), presenting not experiences themselves but *ideas* derived from them. Poets not only conceive of such ideas but "body them forth to sense with a completeness of which nature affords no parallel" (60).

Kant's language is very different from the enthusiastic and at times mystical prose of Hamann and Herder, but his professional philosopher's vocabulary aims to describe the same phenomenon: the power of poetry to seem more lively than reality itself. Even Kant must at times abandon his technical terminology and resort to the same powerful image Hamann and Herder had borrowed from Paul. He explains that the aesthetic idea, particularly as embodied in poetry, is able to use words to point toward "much that is indefinable in words" and thus "binds up the spirit with language, as a mere thing of the letter [*mit der Sprache, als bloßem Buchstaben, Geist verbindet*]" (61). Language "as a mere thing of the letter" must refer to nonpoetic language, which by implication is dead, devoid of animating spirit, until an aesthetic idea goes to work on it. The opposition between letter and spirit brings to the foreground the revivifying power of art, making clear that the stuff in which poetry embodies its ideas comes alive only in the presence of the spiritual power such ideas possess.

It seems likely that Kant means the "mere letter" of language to stand for all the materials with which the artist works: *both* the words out of which the poet fashions his songs and stories *and* also the experience of "actual nature," along with anything else that language can "get on level terms with." The great paradox of poetry is that it uses language to present something (an aesthetic idea) that Kant has defined as incapable of adequate expression in language. To be more blunt than Kant ever is or probably would care to be, poetry brings to language that which language cannot precisely define. When put thus, it is clear that Kant's understanding of the power of art is in its own way nearly as mystical as Hamann's or Herder's, and it is no wonder that he needs the theological terminology of Paul to express it. Kant's "spirit" is the capacity to "get an expression for what is indefinable in the mental state accompanying a particular representation and to make it universally communicable" (61). Such a spirit is a life-giving force. What it gives life to is the dead letter, not only of language itself but of everything that language can adequately define.

The Pauline vocabulary of "spirit" and "letter" brings us back to the question of reading, though Kant does not directly raise the question here. His language of "mere letters" cannot help but make us think of the use of letters we are most familiar with, letters arranged to make texts. Letters are meant to be read, and the act of reading will disclose whether they are "mere letters," that is, language that has not been animated by the spirit, or the vivified letters of genuine poetry. Kant does not provide in the Third Critique any description of such a scene of reading, but one can be found in the work of one of Kant's contemporaries, Johann Gottlieb Fichte. In 1794, only four years after the publication of the *Critique of Judgment,* Fichte set to work on a project that was doubtless inspired by Kant's (and perhaps also, though less directly, Hamann's) provocative use of Paul's vocabulary of spirit and letter, an exploration of the topic of the "spirit and letter in philosophy."[2]

Fichte's meditation *On the Spirit and the Letter in Philosophy* (*Über Geist und Buchstab in der Philosophie,* 1795) is cast in epistolary form, in apparent imitation of and answer to Schiller's *On the Aesthetic Education of Mankind.* Fichte's epistolary premise is that a fictional friend is uncomfortable with the distinction between letter and spirit "made by one or two modern writers," including Fichte himself. The letter writer, essentially the voice of Fichte, declares that he wishes to offer his correspondent sufficient grounds to set the friend's doubts to rest and that to do so he must "take you a longer way round" and begin by trying to explain what "spirit in general" is. This explanation begins with a scene of reading:

> You remember the complaints you made when you were reading a certain book [. . .]. You could not read yourself into it. You had it in front of you, and your eyes were firmly fixed on it, but you found that every time you began thinking about yourself you were miles away from the book. Each of your attempts to get to grips with the content and the action failed, and every time you thought you had neared grasping the unyielding spirit of the text, it slipped out of your hands. [. . .] Did the fault rest solely with you, with your lack of attention and your own inability to relate to the depth and profundity of that book? You don't appear to believe this. The mood you found yourself in when reading the works of other no less profound writers allowed you to form a more favourable opinion of yourself. You felt drawn to and captivated by them. (76)

Fichte goes on to relate the story of a French woman who was to attend a court ball but found herself engrossed in Rousseau's *La nouvelle Héloïse* when it came time to leave for the party. She kept putting off her departure until it was too late. She kept reading all through the evening and never got to the ball. Fichte draws his conclusion:

> Thus it is with books, and thus it is with other works of art, as with nature. One thing leaves us cold and disinterested, or even repels us; another attracts, invites us to linger awhile in contemplation and lose ourselves in it. [. . .] Therefore it certainly seems worthwhile — and it perhaps lies on our path — to investigate what it actually might be that on the one hand draws us so powerfully, whether to frivolities or to serious and important investigations, and on the other hand drives us uncontrollably in the opposite direction, however important or useful the subject matter in question might be. (76–77)

The difference between the first and the second sort of books, Fichte argues, depends on the presence or absence of a "vitalizing force" which he calls spirit.[3] The central question for aesthetics is thus, "How does a work created by man receive that vitalizing force [*belebende Kraft*] and where does the ingenious [*geistvolle*] artist learn the secret of breathing it into a work of art?" (77) What is it, in other words, that accounts for the two opposite experiences of reading?

Much of this argument is relatively clear and even to some extent conventional, but one element in Fichte's language calls attention to itself and stands out as problematic, perhaps even contradictory. While Fichte announces that his immediate concern is with works "created by man," his description of the experience of the presence and absence of spirit explicitly includes everything that is *not* made by man as well. His discourse moves rapidly from "books" to "other works of art" to "nature." If the experience of reading is to be taken as an example of experience in general, then all experience must be at least potentially graspable as an aesthetic phenomenon. The issues central to aesthetic theory must be those central to all philosophy. Works created by man are in fact not the primary focus of Fichte's attention; his real interest is in the "vitalizing force" that comes into play in all acts of contemplation (*Betrachtung*). When he says that one sort of object, whether man-made or natural, "invites us to linger awhile in contemplation" and another sort does not, he is pointing toward his actual area of interest. The interplay between spirit and letter, between inert material and a power that gives it life, is at work in all acts of contemplation that meet the conditions Fichte will shortly specify, not just in the contemplation of works of art.

Fichte begins his discussion with a scene of reading not only because it offers a concrete example with which to illustrate the problem of the presence or absence of spirit but also because it can serve as a paradigm for the sort of contemplative activity he is going to describe in more abstract terms.[4] When Fichte speaks of lingering in contemplation, he is talking about not only the effects of art but also its origins, though this will not become clear until much later, in the second letter. What slowly emerges as Fichte develops his argument is that spirit, the "vitalizing force," comes into being during moments of lingering in contemplation that are exactly like the examples of reading with which he opens the discussion. "We begin by letting our inner [i.e., "spiritual" — *geistig*] eye wander over objects and linger awhile [. . .]. During this peaceful and unmotivated contemplation of objects, when our mind [or "spirit" — *Geist*] is secure and not keeping a watch on itself, our aesthetic sense develops" (86). The object of such contemplation need not be a work of art into which an "ingenious artist" has "breathed" his spirit. In fact, the example Fichte offers of the developing aesthetic sense is his correspondent's contemplation of "the land to the west of your country dwelling" (87):

> If you could look at it with no particular goal in mind [. . .] then you would not just see the green grass [. . .] but your contemplative eye would linger with pleasure on the fresh green of the grass, would look further at the numerous blossoms of the clover, and would glide softly over the rippling waves of the corn towards the heights beyond. There ought, you would say, to be a little village at the top under some trees, or perhaps a wood. [. . .] It would have been just the same to you if, without your knowing it, someone had conjured up what you wished for by means of an optical illusion. How did this come about? (87)[5]

It comes about, Fichte argues, because the aesthetic sense is not content with what it actual sees, it is "offended that this view should cease so abruptly," and so it supplies with the help of the imagination the little village that would "round off the beautiful whole that had been begun" (87).[6]

The process of *Betrachtung* thus described is no passive reception of stimuli from outside the observer, though such stimuli do play an important role in the activity; it is rather a productive activity, a "free creative ability" to which Fichte attaches the term "spirit" in all its Pauline connotations. It is as if Fichte understood the term "Betrachtung" as a form of "trachten," that is, of "striving" toward something. The spirit strives toward life, and indeed it is no very great leap from Paul's assertion that the spirit gives life to Fichte's doctrine that the spirit "creates." It is evident in fact that, for Fichte, "creation" is the process of bringing life to a dead matter that may therefore — precisely because it is dead — be called, in Paul's terms, the "letter" (*Buchstabe*).

Fichte's explanation of how and why this transformation of dead matter into living art takes place is remarkable for its simplicity of presentation and complexity of implication. He draws an analogy between the spirit of a creative artist and a vibrating string, such as the string of a violin:

> Thus the fundamental principle of *sound* exists in the harmonious pulsations and vibrations of the string, which would produce and determine on another, fulfill their inner potential, and even form the note to just the same extent in a vacuum. But only in the surrounding air do they have an external medium for creating their effect. They impress themselves on it

and reproduce themselves again and again until they reach the ears of the delighted listener: and it is from this marriage alone that the sound which echoes in our soul is born. In the same way the inspired artist expresses the mood of his nature in a flexible physical form, and the motion, action and continuity of his forms is the expression of the inner vibrations of his soul. (90)

Here Fichte makes a point of fundamental importance to Romantic aesthetics: art comes into being when the living spirit of the artist passes through a dead medium to make contact once again with another living soul. Fichte's artist is not so much a creator *ex nihilo*, not so much a version of God the Father, as a figure of God the Son bringing life out of death, spirit out of flesh. The artist "lent his soul to dead matter so that it could communicate itself to us" (90).

Just as only divinity could bring the dead flesh of the crucified body back to life, so can only the vital "mood" (*Stimmung*) of the artistic genius bring to life the dead medium through which soul communicates with soul. No "mere technician" (90) can succeed in accomplishing what amounts to a miraculous passage across the chasm of death, because no technician has the requisite *Stimmung* to start with. If art is the communication of an inner mood, Fichte suggests, then no one lacking such a mood, no matter how good a communicator, can be a successful artist. The "inner mood of the artist is the spirit [*Geist*] of the work he creates, and the contingent forms in which he expresses it are the embodiment or the letter [*Buchstabe*] of it" (90).

The possibility of art — and indeed the necessity for it — arises not out of the expressive richness of language (or other artistic medium) but out of its poverty and failure. The artist makes art because he cannot use communicative language to describe the all-important inner mood of his soul:

> What goes on in the soul of the artist, the numerous twistings and turnings of his inner life and of his self-active force, cannot be described. No language has found the words for it, and if they were found then the pregnant fullness of its life would be lost in the description gradually drawn out to one simple thread. (89)

Poetic language thus understood derives its power from the vivifying spirit of the poet and not from any vital quality in the language itself. Language without such spirit is merely dead letters, an inanimate material indistinguishable in quality from the sculptor's marble or the painter's pigments. Fichte's poetic medium, like Plato's τρίτον τι, is useful only to the degree that it has no specific character of its own.

The notion of a poetic *medium* (that is, a "middle thing" that stands between two communicating entities) propounds the paradox that the animating force of poetry must necessarily pass across a chasm of death. Does the dead medium come fully to life in the process? Some of Fichte's language suggests very strongly that it does. He distinguishes, for example, between two sorts of artists. There are those who

> first seize the spirit and then search for the lump of clay into which they breathe the living soul. There are others in whom the spirit and the corporeal form are born simultaneously, and from whose souls the whole new living thing tears itself away at the same time. (92)

This imagery of birth appears to proclaim the work of art to be an independent organism possessing a life of its own apart from that of artist or audience. But Fichte's central metaphor of letter and spirit suggests that the independent life of the work of art may be partial or illusory. He asserts, for example, that a successful artist must "work upon objects [. . .] so that, in his hands, dead matter seems to have taken on a formative structure and organization of its own accord" (90).

The claim here, then, is not that dead matter actually comes to life but that it "seems" to do so. Fichte acknowledges furthermore that the presence of the living spirit is not obvious to every observer: "Certain higher moods [. . .] are not for common eyes, and cannot be communicated to them. And, with others who are open to such communication, it is certainly not apparent how it happens that the work soars up to them" (92). An even more vivid formulation of this same notion is Fichte's reformulation of the legend of Pygmalion, maker of the statue that came to life: "he ought [. . .] to have given her, as well as life, the secret advantage of being seen as living only by those full of spirit, remaining cold and dead for the common and dull" (92). Great works of art that are enlivened by the spirit of genius may seem dead to an unresponsive audience, and even a responsive audience may fail to recognize the source of the lively force that grips it.

It is evidently not enough that the artist pour his spirit into the work of art. The work must encounter a second source of vivifying spirit in the recipient. This second source of spiritual vitality is at least as important as the first, for it is capable of bringing dead letters to life. Fichte recommends that the "rules governing art which are to be found in the textbooks" — rules that he obviously does not think are the products of the creative spirit, since they are concerned "mostly with its mechanical side" — should be "interpreted in the spirit, and not according to the letter" (92–93). The act of reading must thus be understood as another creative process philosophically equivalent to the act of writing. Reading and writing, both of which are acts of bringing the spirit to the letter, cooperate to make full artistic communication. The artist does, as it were, only half the work:

> The inspired artist does not address himself at all to our freedom. So little does he do so that, on the contrary, his magic begins only when we have given it up. Through his art he momentarily raises us, through no agency of our own, to a higher sphere. We do not become any better for

it. But the unploughed fields of our minds are nevertheless opened up, and if for other reasons we one day decide in freedom to take possession of them, we find half the resistance removed and half the work done. (93)

Fichte evidently meant to stress the power of the artist's spirit in comparison to the relative weakness of an audience who is raised "to a higher sphere" solely by the efforts of the artist. And yet the concluding sentence reminds us that the mighty work of the artist is not sufficient to complete the job of cultivating the unploughed fields of our minds. We must finish that task ourselves.

The Pauline rhetoric of dead letter and living spirit invoked by Hamann, Herder, Kant, and Fichte to theorize the functioning of art sets up an indissoluble association between reading and revivification in the aesthetic moment. Every work of art, according to this view, participates in a paradoxical and potentially uncomfortable combination of dead letters (material) and living spirit (God, genius, or simply the "animating principle"), whether the "letters" in question be actual writing or some other artistic medium. This medium, like the medium at a séance, stands on the boundary between life and death and participates in both realms at the same time. Is Pygmalion's statue, in Fichte's version of the story, alive or dead? It must be both at once, for it is alive for those whose eyes are imbued with spirit ("von geistvollen Augen") but dead to everyone else. It is not just beauty, then, that is in the eye of the beholder: it is life itself. The artist is himself such a beholder, for the sculptor uses his spiritual eye to discover in the dead rock the living shape that his imagination (and his trained hand) will release. Both the creator and the recipient of such a work of art may be filled with joy and wonder at the miracle of life-in-death, but both will also necessarily suffer from considerable anxiety. What if this thing I love and suppose is alive turns out to be "really" dead? What if this thing that I think is safely dead and no longer a source of concern should turn out to be alive? What if indeed it is simply impossible to determine what is "really" dead or alive? That danger must be very real for those who believe in the possibility of raising the dead letter to life by means of the spirit.

Fichte expands somewhat on Paul's discourse by implying that "letter" and "spirit" may be read as figures that signify not just written texts and acts of reading, but any interaction involving matter imbued by some animating principle. But he always foregrounds the legible text as the paradigm for all signifying processes in which a meaning (understood as "living") is conveyed by material objects (understood as "dead"). Both reading and the aesthetic experience in general are forms of raising the dead, and the fictional depiction of revivification may serve as figures for all artistic and even all symbolic activity.

One can recognize, without taking anything away from the originality of Fichte and other Romantic writers, that their aesthetic theory has roots in a notion of the operation of reading that goes back at least to late antiquity. Coleridge offers a clue in chapter 9 of the *Biographia Literaria* (1817) as to the connection between Romantic notions of the interaction of letter and spirit and older concepts. In a discussion of what he calls, in another allusion to Paul, the "difference between the letter and the spirit of Kant's writings," he offers a defense of the "prudent" obscurity of some of Kant's writing:

> An idea, in the *highest* sense of that word, cannot be conveyed but by a *symbol*; and, except in geometry, all symbols involve an apparent contradiction. Φώνησε συνετοῖσιν ["He spoke to the wise"]: and for those who could not pierce through this symbolic husk his writings were not intended. (156–57; Coleridge's emphasis)

The quotation about speaking to the wise is from Pindar, but the passage as a whole surely alludes to the parables of the Bible and the tradition of reading Scripture associated with them. Jesus, in a parable explaining his use of parables, had likened his discourse to seeds scattered on the ground, some finding fertile soil in which to sprout, some landing on rocks and never germinating at all (Matt. 13).[7] The church fathers, most notably Augustine, developed this image of the seed into a familiar analogy:

> You know that barley is formed in such a way that it is very difficult to get at its kernel; for the kernel [*medulla*] is covered in a coating of husk [*tegmine paleae*], with the husk itself adhering tenaciously, so that it can be stripped off only with labor. Such is the letter of the Old Testament [*talis est littera Veteris Testamenti*], shut up in a covering of carnal sacraments: and yet, once we get at its kernel, it feeds and satisfies us. (*In Evangelium Ioannis*, Tractatus 24)

Coleridge proposes that the "letter" of Kant's prose, like Augustine's "letter of the Old Testament," is such a protective husk that preserves a vulnerable but valuable "spirit" within.

The image of the text as a double structure of husk-and-kernel was transferred from the divine to the secular realm when defenders of secular literature such as Giovanni Boccaccio argued that poetry ought to be read with the same care used in reading the Bible. Every fiction (*fabula* in Boccaccio's terminology) has the double structure of husk-and-kernel ascribed to the word of God, even, as Boccaccio was forced to admit, the babbling of "a maundering old woman, sitting with others late of a winter's night at the home fireside" (Osgood 54). Fabulae may appear unimportant, vulgar, silly, and even outrageously contrary to fact, but appearances are deceiving. The real value of a discourse does not lie in the exterior husk but in the kernel of meaning that lies within. The process of reading could thus be understood as an act of penetration on the part of the reader, who passes through the protective outer layer to discover the vulnerable but valuable intention hidden inside.

Students of Scripture could hardly fail to make the connection Coleridge makes between the external husk of a text and its dead letters, between the inner kernel and its living spirit. If sophisticated reading imposes the necessity of passing beyond the literal sense to an allegorical sense or set of senses, it also imposes the obligation of attending to the living spirit rather than the dead letter. But if the text is not only the container of a kernel but the habitation of the spirit, then it is perhaps at least as much like an animate person as it is like an externally inanimate nut or seed.[8] It has a body that is subject to death and a spirit that is not. Such a body may look dead (as the dry husk of a nut seems inert), and indeed as pure body it is dead. A body has life only insofar as it is animated by the living spirit. Attention to the literal husk of a text is warranted only to the extent that it helps us to pass through, to see beyond its dead letters to the living spirit that lies as its heart.

The language of letter and spirit so prominent in Romantic aesthetics reiterates our tradition's most fundamental textual metaphor — but with a significant shift of emphasis. The textual body of the Romantics is like a human body, and the spirit of a poem is like a human soul. The analogy is useful and reassuring in that it helps to explain the peculiar fact that texts are both physical objects and mental events; they may look like dead matter to those unable to read them but seem full of life to those with the necessary skill. To the degree that we know in some rudimentary sense what we ourselves are, we may also know what texts are. The analogy between poems (and other works of art) and the human organism supplants the trope of husk-and-kernel because it seems to have greater explanatory power: it fits the facts better. The analogy of the nut requires us to "open up" the text, to "remove" the surface, in order to get at the meaning; but in our encounters with texts, the exterior or literal level seems undamaged by the interaction. It's still there, still intact, when we're done opening it up. If a text is more like a living organism, it is easier to understand how we can interact with it, sense its spirit, as it were, without doing damage to its physical body. The material body may now be understood less as a barrier to be penetrated or removed and more as a mediator or carrier whose integrity is not a hindrance but an essential precondition for interaction with the inner, spiritual level.

The Romantic preference for the concept of an informing spirit over that of a concealed kernel of meaning is both illustrated and to some extent explained in the following paragraph from Schiller's essay "On Naïve and Sentimental Poetry":

> From the naïve mode of thought there necessarily follows naïve expression in word as well as gesture, and this is the most important element in gracefulness. By this naïve grace genius expresses its most sublime and profound thought; the utterances of a god in the mouth of a child. The understanding of the schools, always fearful of error, crucifies its words and its

concepts upon the cross of grammar and logic, and is severe and stiff to avoid uncertainty at all costs, employs many words to be quite sure of not saying too much, and deprives its thoughts of their strength and edge so that they may not cut the unwary. But genius delineates its own thoughts at a single felicitous stroke of the brush and with an eternally determined, firm, and yet absolutely free outline. If to the former the sign remains forever heterogeneous and alien to the thing signified, to the latter language springs as by some inner necessity out of thought, and is so at one with it that even beneath the corporeal frame the spirit appears as if laid bare [*selbst unter der körperlichen Hülle der Geist wie entblößet erscheint*]. It is precisely this mode of expression in which the sign disappears completely in the thing signified, and in which language, while giving expression to a thought, yet leaves it exposed [*noch gleichsam nackend läßt*] (whereas the other mode cannot represent it without simultaneously concealing it); and this it is we generally call a gifted style displaying genius. (187)

Schiller associates the notion of language as a protective cover (*Hülle*, very loosely translated above as "frame") with the schools and, by means of his selection of tropes, with religion. These associations are historically correct and not merely the product of Schiller's antipathy toward neoclassical regularity. Although he mixes the language of the husk-and-kernel metaphor with that of body-and-spirit, employing "husk [*Hülle*]" and "spirit [*Geist*]" in the same phrase, Schiller does not really want to squeeze the two ideas together. He does not believe that meaning should be covered over by a protective layer of language or that the signified should be hidden within the signifier. He prizes instead a discourse in which "the sign disappears completely in the thing signified" so that thought, the spirit of the language, actually shows through its linguistic covering as if it were quite "naked [*nackend*]."[9] Reading a text displaying naked thoughts would not require the labor (or violence) called for in Augustine's husk-and-kernel analogy, for it is not necessary to remove or penetrate the signifier to get at the signified. The signifier has already been effaced by the vital power of the informing spirit.

Schiller's desire for a transparent sign in which the signifier would disappear beneath the shining clarity of the signified reflects the Romantic desire for an "unmediated vision" that Geoffrey Hartman identified more than half a century ago as an important goal of the Romantic poetic enterprise. But Hartman also pointed out that the process of mediation could not be simply done away with; it could only be suppressed or evaded (156–73). Aestheticians of the late eighteenth century, including particularly Schiller, actually understood this very well, as is evident in the passage quoted here. Some "bodily covering [*körperliche Hülle*]" is necessary to convey the spirit from one mind to another. Necessary though it may be, however, that bodily element has no importance in itself and serves its purpose best, Schiller proposes, when it disappears. It has no vitality of its own; it is only a carrier or medium that would be quite lifeless without the spirit that informs it.

When we read a text according to the Romantic model, the dead letters seem to disappear, and we become aware only of a living voice that emerges from the page. When the "sign disappears completely in the thing signified," we are left with a purely spiritual text — a legible void like the pearly blank shell that Keats's hero Endymion is enjoined to read.[10] When reading goes well, something like this may seem to happen. But when reading does not go well, the dead letters reassert their uncomfortable presence.

Here the demonic underside of Romantic reading begins to show — an underside that is far less troublesome to the paradigm of husk-and-kernel. For Boccaccio as for Augustine, an unread or unreadable text was like an unopened nut, challenging but by no means frightening. For the Romantics, an unread or illegible text could be a terrifying corpse that frightens not only or even principally because it is dead but because it has the unrealized potential of coming to life. Romantic Europe knew both the exhilaration and the anxiety that accompany the prospect of reading a hitherto unread text; indeed one could say that Europe had collectively experienced these feelings while the mysterious Egyptian hieroglyphics were being studied and, at last in 1822, successfully deciphered. The dead contents of tombs could come to life as the previously illegible inscriptions on their walls were read, and one might well imagine that the mummies themselves might arise and walk again under the powerful influence of this revivifying reading. The apparently lifeless stones could speak after all, for they had been imprinted with a spirit that had not been obliterated by the intervening millennia. It was wonderful, but it was also terrifying.

Romantic aesthetic theory was less interested in exploring the terror of revivification than Romantic fiction would prove to be, but it recognized the illegible text as the locus of a powerful mystery. For Hamann and several other German Romantics, the image of the hieroglyph served to express a kind of ultimate symbolic potency. Hamann particularizes his central image of the world as God's book by referring to elements of the creation as graphic signs. Adam is not simply the first man, he is the "hieroglyphic Adam" who embodies "the history of the entire race" (142). That Adam is a hieroglyph means both that he contains an enormous amount of information and that the information is unavailable to us. Friedrich Schlegel, in his defense of obscurity in the essay "On Incomprehensibility," recalls how he had "with the thoughtlessness of youth" attempted to portray "nakedly and naively" the great mystery of "a real language" when he "made [his novel] *Lucinde* reveal the nature of love in an eternal hieroglyph" (33). Certainly many of Schlegel's readers would agree that *Lucinde* is as incomprehensible as a hieroglyph to the average layman, but Schlegel is proposing that the novel's illegibility — indeed the alleged incomprehensibility of much of his writing — should be taken as a positive value. Schegel's essay is admittedly ironic, but his notion of irony does not preclude a large dose of sympathy for the positions he appears to attack with his irony. Schlegel may be joking when he calls his novel a hieroglyph, but it is a serious joke. Like Hamann, he sees great worth in that which cannot be easily comprehended. He is also entranced with the idea that a single sign, whether a hieroglyph or a work of fiction, could encompass a vast field of meaning.

Jean Paul Richter goes so far as to compare the human imagination to a set of hieroglyphs: "If wit is the playful *anagram* of nature, the imagination is its *hieroglyphic alphabet*, which expresses all nature in a few images" (162; Jean Paul's italics). He wrote the first draft of this text in 1804, nearly two decades before Champollion's first decipherment of ancient Egyptian revealed the true phonetic nature of hieroglyphics. Jean Paul obviously assumed, as had Schlegel and Hamann, that the signs were ideograms, each of which might convey very large amounts of information. The images produced by the imagination would be comparable to such ideographs because they express much in a little compass. But they also tease us with a plenitude of significance that lies just outside our limited abilities to read them. In this way they are, as Hamann suggested, an emblem of nature as a whole.

Although late eighteenth-century writers embraced this view of nature-as-hieroglyph, Champollion and the Egyptologists radically devalued hieroglyphics as a magical semantic cornucopia capable of expressing "all nature in a few images" when they revealed that they were just fairly ordinary signs in a fairly ordinary writing system. As soon as they became legible, hieroglyphics became somewhat less attractive as figures of the borderland between dead letters and living spirit. Still, the very idea of bringing a lost civilization back to life, as the archaeologists were doing, converged with the hopes and fears of a culture uncertain about the boundary between life and death. The later Romantics would be able to witness the drama of revivification through reading that took place as the science of Egyptology began to raise the defunct language of one small part of the world from the dead. Romantic scenes of the revivifying word seemed appropriately connected to the process of unearthing the Egyptian past, as Victor Hugo's extensive use of the figure of the hieroglyph in *Notre-Dame de Paris* clearly demonstrates.[11] Even a century and more later, an American movie house would very naturally show *Frankenstein* and *The Mummy* as a double feature, and audiences would readily understand the two films as alternate versions of the same engagingly scary drama of revivification. Elegant Romantic fiction and pseudo-Egyptological fantasy merged together in the pop culture melting pot — and not without considerable historical justice. Mary Shelley herself had invited just this merger when she let Victor Frankenstein compare his monster to a "mummy again endued with animation" (SF 53).

Both Mary Shelley and her husband Percy were interested in the implications of a revivified Egypt. One of Percy's most famous sonnets, the Egyptological meditation "Ozymandias," displays in lyric form the same interest in the possibility of life emerging out of dead matter through acts of reading that we find in Romantic fiction. In "Ozymandias" a dramatic scene of death and decay is unexpectedly and ironically revivified:

> I met a traveler from an antique land
> Who said — "Two vast and trunkless legs of stone
> Stand in the desert. Near them, on the sand,
> Half, sunk, a shattered visage lies, whose frown,
> And wrinkled lips, and sneer of cold command,
> Tell that its sculptor well those passions read
> Which yet survive, stamped on these lifeless things,
> The hand that mocked them and the heart that fed;
> And on the pedestal these words appear:
> 'My name is Ozymandias, King of Kings:
> Look on my Works, ye Mighty, and despair!'
> Nothing beside remains. Round the decay
> Of that colossal Wreck, boundless and bare
> The lone and level sands stretch far away." (1–14)

The king's command to look at his works and despair is obviously relevant to the circumstances of a modern visitor surrounded by ruins, though of course not in the way we suppose the actual Ozymandias (Egyptian pharaoh Rameses II) would have envisioned. The sonnet recontextualizes the pharaoh's (fictional) boasting inscription in such a way as to make it take on a new life that is perhaps even more meaningful to us moderns than it would have been to its supposed ancient readers. The king's works may be utterly destroyed, but this one text survives in such a way as to make vividly significant the very absence of those works. Both works and text were once the products of living persons (Ozymandias and his many agents), but only the text has the chance at re-production that reading offers. The statues, palaces, gardens, and so on, are either completely gone or decayed to such an extent that they cannot be reconstructed. The legible text, however, can be read anew. Legible "passions" can be "stamped" upon "lifeless" material, the poem claims, first by appreciating the talent of the sculptor who "read" and then "mocked" (both "imitated" and "made fun of") the king's imperious demeanor, and then by demonstrating how the dead inscription can bring a living affect back to a scene of emptiness and ruin.

"Ozymandias" is not unique among Percy Shelley's poems in its urgent concern with the possibility of revivification through reading. We find precisely that same urgency in the final stanza of the "Ode to the West Wind," which stages at its conclusion a dramatic reemergence of life out of death:

> Make me thy lyre, even as the forest is:
>   What if my leaves are falling like its own?
> The tumult of thy mighty harmonies
>   Will take from both a deep autumnal tone,
> Sweet though in sadness. Be thou, Spirit fierce,
>   My spirit! Be thou me, impetuous one!
> Drive my dead thoughts over the universe,
>   Like wither'd leaves, to quicken a new birth;
> And, by the incantation of this verse,
>   Scatter, as from an unextinguish'd hearth
> Ashes and sparks, my words among mankind!
>   Be through my lips to unawaken'd earth
> The trumpet of a prophecy! O Wind,
>   If Winter comes, can Spring be far behind? (57–70)

The poet envisions a time in which his thoughts, as presumably he himself, will be as dead as the vegetation about to be struck down by the oncoming winter. But with the help of a conventional but nonetheless effective wordplay, the vegetable leaves are transformed into the leaves of a book, a set of apparently dead letters subject to reawakening at the touch of the living spirit. An act of reading, "the incantation of this verse," restores the poet's "dead thoughts" to life.

Works of fiction from Percy and Mary Shelley's generation — and the one before, and the one after — explored the exciting realms of the revivified dead conjured up by visions similar to Mary's reanimated mummies and Percy's legible statue of a long-dead pharaoh. These writers did so in part because, like the Shelleys and their circle, they were fascinated with contemporary speculation on the relation between inanimate and animate matter that arose in the context of new scientific discoveries. Egyptology was one of the sciences contributing to such speculation, but in fact nearly all the sciences dealing with life fostered thinking along these lines. The context of "natural philosophy" requires some further consideration; the next chapter therefore examines the theory of life in the first decades of the Romantic century.

Notes

[1] The theme of letter and spirit has received the attention of many scholars. Of particular importance for the period under discussion here are Weissberg, who undertakes a thorough examination of the topic as it relates to the interaction between philosophy and literature in the late eighteenth century; and Librett, who is particularly interested in the implications of the equation of "letter" with "Jewish" and "spirit" with "Christian" (especially "protestant") intellectual concerns (see esp. 103–75).

[2] Fichte worked on the "spirit and letter" material over a relatively long period of time and in several different forms. The discussion here concens the three epistolary essays Fichte prepared for publication. Weissberg, one of the most prominent commentators on these essays, calls them Fichte's "erste ausführliche Skizze einer ästhetischen Theorie" (205).

[3] Weissberg points to other differences between the two examples Fichte offers: "Das mahnende Gewissen und die wartende Kutsche, die zum Hofball führen soll, bilden bei Fichte unterschiedliche Begleiter, die an Belehrung und Vergnügen mahnen. [. . .] Die verschiedenen Lektüreweisen scheinen Bücher zu betreffen, deren unterschiedliche Bestimmung in Fichtes Lehre gleichzeitig zurückgenommen wird" (208).

[4] Weissberg understands Fichte's scene of reading as a metaphor for the process whereby the self is constituted in a paradoxal "Selbstfindung als Selbstvergessen" (211).

[5] I have altered the translation slightly. The Simpson edition translates "ohne alle Absicht" as "completely disinterestedly" rather than as "with no particular goal in mind," thus unintentionally suggesting a reference to Kant's aesthetic theory that does not exist in Fichte's German.

[6] Fichte's idea of aesthetic completion is very close to William Gilpin's late eighteenth-century notion of the picturesque. Indeed, Gilpin forthrightly recommended that travelers, when making keepsake drawings of memorable scenery, make appropriate additions to fulfill the aesthetic potential where nature had come up short. See J.H. Koelb, 101–11.

[7] Plato had also used the metaphor of seeds, in a slightly different way, in the *Phaedrus* (276B–277A), recommending the figurative planting of the seeds of wisdom inside the soul of the learner. For subtle discussion of the metaphor of the garden in Plato, see Sayre.

[8] Seeds are often presented as dead in the NT: John 12:24 and 1 Corinthians 15:36–37 are important examples. See Müller-Sievers (79) for a discussion of the figure of the seed in relation to the theory of epigenetic generation.

[9] Schiller's trope was apparently too daring for the translator, who felt it necessary to tame the unblushing German "nackend" into a more decorous English "exposed."

[10] Keats's *Endymion* is discussed in detail in chapter 4.

[11] See Chaitin, as well as chapter 5.

2: "Spirit Thinks Only Through the Body": Materialist Spiritualism in Romantic Europe

> What is *not* Life that really *is?*
> — Coleridge, *Theory of Life*

"I KNOW OF NO MOMENT IN THE HISTORY of modern European culture in which science and literature were more intrinsically interrelated" than in the Romantic age, wrote G. S. Rousseau in 1969 (131).[1] The pursuit of science and the practice of poetry certainly worked comfortably together during the late eighteenth and early nineteenth centuries, sometimes even combined in the same person: Goethe was a particularly notable example. It would be equally true to claim that at no moment in European history were science and philosophy so closely interrelated, since what we call "science" was generally still called "natural philosophy," and since major trends in the scientific thinking of the time actually emerged from contemporaneous developments in philosophy. Literature, science, and philosophy were therefore so closely bound together that they may be regarded as a single cultural phenomenon.

It would be impractical — and certainly far beyond my competence — to attempt here any thorough account of the scientific thinking of the Enlightenment and early Romanticism;[2] instead I outline one particularly relevant conception of nature that runs through much of the eighteenth century and into the early nineteenth. Though there is no single origin for this line of thought, a reasonable start can be made with the *Monadology* (1714) of Gottfried Wilhelm Leibniz. In the following famous passage, Leibniz presents one of his core ideas in language that is as much poetry as philosophy:

> Each bit of matter can be imagined as a garden full of plants and as a pond full of fish. But every branch of a plant, every limb of an animal's body, every drop of the liquids they contain is in its turn another such garden or pond. And although the earth and the air interposed between the plants in the garden, or the water interposed between the fishes in the pond, is not itself a plant or a fish, yet they contain still more of them, only mostly too small to be visible.
>
> Thus there is nothing uncultivated, sterile or dead in the universe [*Ainsi il n'y a rien d'inculte, de stérile, de mort dans l'univers*], no chaos or confusion, except in appearance; rather the way a pond appears from a

distance, in which you can see a confused motion and milling around, so to speak, of the fishes in the pond, but without being able to make out the individual fishes themselves. (Secs. 67–69)

Leibniz could not have put it more directly: nothing in the world is dead.[3] But if everything is always alive, what is happening when organisms "die"? One can hardly deny that a major event has taken place. How are we to understand this decisive moment of transition?[4]

The answer for Leibniz seems to be that the death of an organic being should not be understood as the departure of the living essence, which in fact resides — always — in the core of every particle of matter. Instead, Leibniz suggests, the death of creatures is the rupture of a complex formal organization. George McDonald Ross offers a succinct summation of Leibniz's view:

> What makes an organism an organic whole is the way in which its parts are interconnected. For Leibniz, this was not simply a question of co-ordinated activity and mutual responsiveness, since these could also be found in sophisticated machinery. In his view, the defining characteristic of an organism was that each part depended for its very identity on its relation to that particular whole.[5]

What is lost when organisms die is not the spark of life but rather the powerful set of connections linking all the (living) monads together into an organic whole. Leibniz, trying to resolve the opposition between a purely mechanistic, materialist view of the world and a purely vitalist, spiritual view, was proposing a unified account of nature in which the spark of life was not some extra added element found only in some privileged parts of the natural world (or something apart from material nature altogether) but a necessary property of all matter. What the human mind apprehends as "living spirit," then, is not so much the presence of life as, rather, the presence of a very high level of organization.

The unified conception of nature advanced by Leibniz clearly had implications for natural science, and scientists did not fail to see them. Indeed, one of the most influential scientific thinkers of the late eighteenth century, Jean Baptiste René Robinet, presented in his encyclopedic *De la nature* (1761) a complete theory of the natural world firmly based on the foundation built by Leibniz.[6] Robinet's great work presents a systematic and scientific account of everything from rocks and stars to abstract human thought based on the firm assumption that life permeates all the matter in the universe.

Robinet's essential agreement with Leibniz's assertion of the ubiquity of life is especially clear in his discussion of minerals:

> Look at a globular or oval pyrite in its whole state: just by looking at it you will suspect it to be the product of a developed organic germ: break it in the direction of the rays which spread from its axis to its circumference,

and you will find your first conjecture confirmed. Under the magnifying glass the lines that form the rays will appear to you joined together by other filaments: you will see further the tubular adhesions that unify the two filamentous layers that you have separated: the microscope will cause you to discover glandular points and vascular grains.

If you compare any section at all of this mineral with the trunk of a young tree cut horizontally, you will not be able to distinguish the organization of the one from that of the other. (269–70)

The organization of the pyrite, indistinguishable from that of a plant, is the result of the mineral's character as a living substance. It also shares with other forms of life the ability to reproduce: "stones engender stones, metals produce metals, just as animals engender others like them, just as plants engender plants, by means of sperm, seeds, or eggs — for all these words are synonyms" (265). Hegel comments in his *Lectures on the History of Philosophy* that in Robinet's account of nature

> nothing is isolated, everything is combined and connected and in harmony. Robinet here goes through the plants, the animals, and also the metals, the elements air, fire, water &c.; and seeks from them to demonstrate the existence of the germ in whatever has life, and also how metals are organized in themselves. (Part 3, Sec. 2, Chap. 2.C.2.b)

Life is everywhere, Robinet argues, but "spirit [*esprit*]" manifests itself primarily in those living beings that have an especially high level of organization. He emphasizes that "*the manifestation of the faculties of the spirit follows the progress of bodily organization*" (Robinet's italics), and adds that "spirit thinks only through the body" (369). Robinet is thus a spiritual idealist, in that he believes in an immaterial essence (called "soul [*âme*]" in human beings) that engages in thinking; but his spiritualism is founded on a thoroughly materialist basis.[7] It is the existence of a highly organized body that makes possible a thinking spirit.[8]

Robinet's argument forbids any simple equation of "life" with "spirit." We cannot make distinctions between the amount of life in, say, an oyster as opposed to a monkey, but we can distinguish the amount of spirit:

> it is always true to say that a monkey has more spirit than an oyster; and that the spirit of the monkey is such an important characteristic of that species of creature that, if it did not possess it, it would not be a real monkey, but some other creature that looked like a monkey. (346)[9]

The reason for the difference between the monkey and the oyster is surely not that one is more alive than the other but rather that one is more highly organized than the other. It is for this reason that a monkey can perform acts that seem to be the result of "thinking," though the oyster cannot. "The necessary condition in the body that enables the spirit to think is its organization. This condition is filled successively. The spirit thus arrives successively at the perfection of its faculties" (369).

Robinet's account of nature pays careful attention to differing levels of organization but does not make much of the boundary between life and death. Indeed, one could properly say that he "denied the distinction between living and dead nature" (Reill 182). Life and death are so mixed together in Robinet's view of the world that distinguishing between the two becomes impossible:

> It is quite true to say that creatures live and die at the same instant. They die all the time in that, at every moment, they are losing the existence that they had the instant before. They live nonetheless, because the momentary existence that they lose at any particular point in time is instantaneously replaced by a new existence of the same order. Thus creatures lose at each and every moment as much existence as they receive. (48)

Robinet was well aware that such paradoxical claims about life and death commingling in such an intimate fashion might strike some of his readers as unscientific, as more poetry than philosophy. He was unapologetic:

> One will say that these ideas are more poetic than philosophical; but what difference does it make whether it is poets or philosophers who discover the truth, so long as the truth becomes known? These ideas reestablish for all orders of being the legitimate rights which we have seized from them so despotically [*rétablissent tous les Etres dans leurs droits légitimes dont nous les avons dépouillés si despotiquement*. . . .] These ideas re-animate Nature [*Ces idées raniment la Nature*], which we have caused to languish. They spread gaiety, life, and interest all around us.[10]

Robinet's language makes clear that he understood philosophy (that is, what we would call "science") as having robbed nature of the right to life; a better sort of science, therefore, could "re-animate" her by restoring that right.

We should take note of Robinet's brief against his fellow philosopher-scientists, appearing as it does many years before we hear a similar complaint coming from Romantic poets. Keats's famous worry about the effects of Newtonian science ("cold philosophy") in *Lamia* (1819) came more than two generations after the publication of Robinet's treatise:

> Do not all charms fly
> At the mere touch of cold philosophy?
> There was an awful rainbow once in heaven:
> We know her woof, her texture; she is given
> In the dull catalogue of common things.
> Philosophy will clip an Angel's wings,
> Conquer all mysteries by rule and line,
> Empty the haunted air, and gnomed mine —
> Unweave a rainbow, as it erewhile made
> The tender-person'd Lamia melt into a shade. (2.229–38)

Though Keats's formulation is particularly memorable and is often cited, the issue was far from new in his time. It was current among European intellectuals such as Robinet not only long before Keats and earlier British Romantic poets, but also long before the French Revolution and the Napoleonic era. Remarkable as it may seem, this strain of intellectual history antedates the political upheavals of the turn of the century.

If indeed Newton and other proponents of mechanistic science had unweaved the rainbow, Robinet clearly thought that his philosophic-poetical approach had weaved it back together again and restored the animate quality to nature. Keats, too, believed — at least at times — that the right sort of philosophy had the power to bring nature back to life. The deadly (though perfectly accurate) power of observation ascribed to Apollonius in *Lamia* may profitably be contrasted with the case of Glaucus in *Endymion*. Chapter 4 discusses how Glaucus is enjoined by the book he finds to explore "all forms and substances / Straight homeward to their symbol-essences" (699–700). Should he be successful in this endeavor — which cannot be understood as anything other than some version of Neoplatonic philosophy — the book promises that "he shall not die" (701). Apparently he meets the book's demands, for not only is he rejuvenated but also with Endymion's help he brings back to life his dead beloved and an untold number of drowned lovers. With Glaucus in mind, one must suspect that the deadly consequences of Apollonius's "sophist's eye, / Like a sharp spear" (*Lamia* 299–300) are so destructively negative precisely because the philosopher has in fact failed to perceive Lamia deeply enough, that he has not penetrated to her "symbol-essence." Yes, in one sense she is a serpent, and her womanly form is a mere appearance; but her love for Lycius is so entirely genuine that her underlying humanity might well be acknowledged as more "essential" than her serpentine character. It would be a defective, cold sort of philosophy, then, that would penetrate only part way into the mystery of nature, unweave the rainbow, and cause Lamia to melt into a shade.

Robinet was just as dissatisfied as Keats with philosophy as practiced by the likes of Apollonius and his brethren. He was convinced that, like Glaucus and Endymion, he could re-animate that part of the world that others had unjustifiably depicted as dead. But the biological science that developed out of Robinet's ideas attempted at times to reassert a strict division between living things and dead ones, though without definitive success. One of Robinet's intellectual heirs was the famous physiologist Xavier Bichat, who in his *Recherches physiologiques sur la vie et la mort* (1800) helped to establish the distinction between organic and inorganic nature. There is no doubt that Bichat shared the view of Robinet and Leibniz that organization is a fundamental characteristic of life. He refers to living things as "organized beings [*êtres organisés*]" (for example, 8) and points out that a creature's organization is the only thing about it that does not constantly vary: "what it [a living being] was at one time, it ceases to be at another; its organization remains ever the same, though its elements vary continually" (11). But he clearly differs from Robinet in insisting that living "organic" beings can be readily and appropriately distinguished from and indeed opposed to "inorganic" dead ones. Bichat's famous definition of life as "the sum of functions which resist death" (2) clearly draws a firm boundary between the two realms. Of course a living being needs to be organized in order to have such "functions," as Bichat's later elaborations on the topic make clear, but the sort of organization one finds in an oval pyrite would not rise to the level of a death-resisting function.

Bichat's line of reasoning reappears in a relatively clear and concise form in the early work of one of his more prominent disciples, the British physiologist Sir William Lawrence. When Lawrence asserts in 1816 that "life is the assemblage of all the functions, and the general result of their exercise" (Introduction 121), we seem to be hearing a condensed English version of this definition offered by Bichat: "I call organic life the combination of functions of the first class, because all organized beings, whether vegetable or animal, participate in it to one degree or another, and because organic texture is the sole condition necessary for its exercise [*J'appelle vie organique l'ensemble des fonctions de la première classe, parce que tous les êtres organisés, végétaux ou animaux, en jouissent à un degré plus ou moins marqué, et que la texture organique est la seule condition nécessaire à son exercice*]" (8–9). Parts of Lawrence's *Lectures on Physiology* (1819) also display a clear debt to Bichat (and, through him, to Robinet and Leibniz), as when the physician explains to the College of Surgeons:

> Living bodies exhibit a constant internal motion, in which we observe an uninterrupted admission and assimilation of new, and a corresponding separation and expulsion of old particles. The form remains the same, the component parts are continually changing. While this motion lasts, the body is said to be alive. (Lectures 93)

But Lawrence makes a far more explicit argument than his predecessor in favor of the position that organization is the principal hallmark of life:

> Organization means the peculiar composition, which distinguishes living bodies; in this point of view they are contrasted with inorganic, inert, or dead bodies. [. . .] Thus organization, vital properties, functions, and life are expressions related to each other; in which organization is the instrument, vital properties the acting power, function the mode of action, life the result. (Introduction 120–21)

Bichat had never said exactly that, though one could certainly derive such a position from the implications of the argument presented in the *Recherches physiologiques.*

There was certainly considerable justification for the charge made by Lawrence's opponents, among them his renowned senior colleague John Abernethy, that Lawrence was deeply indebted to French thought in general, and Bichat's *Recherches* in particular, for his claim that organization was the principal distinguishing feature of life. There was even good reason to charge that Lawrence had essentially cribbed some of his argument directly from Bichat.[11] But there was really very little justification for the charge that the position taken by Bichat and Lawrence was purely and simply "materialist." It had a materialist aspect, to be sure, in that it insisted (as Robinet had insisted) on the reliance of living spirit on physical embodiment; but it readily acknowledged the presence of a spiritual quality in sentient life. Bichat frequently referred to the perceiving subject as a "soul [*âme*]" (29, 35, 59, 61, 65, and so on). His insistence on leaving spiritual factors out of his account of physiological processes was therefore not based on any outright rejection of their presence. He argued that the vital principle could be "appreciated only through its phenomena" because its "fundamental nature [is] unknown [*inconnu dans sa nature*]" (2). Bichat's insistence on studying life solely through its visible, phenomenal properties and actions was therefore no assertion of pure materialism but rather a kind of necessary epistemological strategy. Sharon Ruston and others have pointed out that Lawrence never denied the existence of the soul and that by resorting to explanatory notions like "vital properties" he clearly displayed a vitalist line of thinking that was "neither mechanical nor materialist" (Ruston 13).[12] Indeed, Lawrence participated in a well-established intellectual position that was both materialist and vitalist at the same time. He and Bichat were by no means denying the existence of a living spirit; they were simply following the principle laid down by Robinet that "the spirit thinks only through the body."

In spite of Lawrence's vehement and evidently quite genuine protestations, the accusations of Abernethy and his party that Lawrence was a dangerous materialist who denied the existence of the soul were devastatingly effective. The stakes, as Abernethy set them out in 1821, were nothing less than the moral health of society. Moral order depended, he claimed, on "the belief of the distinct and independent nature of mind," without which there would be no reason for citizens to "practice and extol whatever is virtuous, excellent and honorable" and to "shun and condemn whatever is vicious and base" (50). The group who rallied to Abernethy's battle trumpet was large and distinguished.[13] It included even so august a personage as S. T. Coleridge, acting in this case as an aspiring scientist rather than as a poet. During the 1820s or early 1830s Coleridge worked on his own, ultimately unfinished theory of life, published posthumously in 1848 as *Hints Towards the Formation of a More Comprehensive Theory of Life*.[14] In the course of setting forth his theory, Coleridge claims to reject utterly "the assertion and even the supposition that the functions are the offspring of the structure, and 'Life the result of organization,' connecting with it as effect with cause" (34). Lest the reader miss the reference, Coleridge adds a note: "Vide Lawrence's Lecture." Elsewhere in the

Hints, he speaks in praise of Abernethy, who has "the presentiment of a great truth. [. . .] If the opinions here supported are the same with those of Mr. Abernethy, I rejoice in his authority" (65).

Coleridge's rejection of Lawrence and solidarity with Abernethy rests primarily on Coleridge's stated conviction that he has "a rational and responsible soul" (33) and on his erroneous assumption, carefully nurtured by Abernethy and his allies, that Lawrence had denied the soul's existence. Other factors were involved as well — they are cataloged at length in the middle of the essay (59–65) — but they were certainly secondary to the matter of the soul. When one examines the substance of Coleridge's theory, however, it turns out he actually had far more in common with Lawrence than he cared to admit.

In the first place, Coleridge's claim that he opposed Lawrence's view as to the basis of life in organization is put into question by statements that suggest quite the opposite:

> The living power will be most intense in that individual which, as a whole, has the greatest number of integral parts presupposed in it; when, moreover, these integral parts, together with a proportional increase of their independence, as *parts*, have themselves the character of wholes in the sphere occupied by them. (44–45)

This integral relation of part to whole in which each part also has the character of a (smaller) whole would ordinarily be called "organization." That Coleridge avoided calling it by this name shows how much he wished to avoid the taint of the word, poisoned as it was in the wake of the Abernethy-Lawrence debate. But he obviously did not want to avoid taking an intellectual position very much in keeping with the tradition that flowed from Leibniz and Robinet to Bichat and Lawrence.

Just how much he shared with that tradition can be readily observed in the way Coleridge treats "inorganic" substances. Here is his surprisingly Robinet-like discussion of gold:

> If I were asked [. . .] whether the ingot of gold expressed *life*, I should answer without hesitation, as the *ingot* of gold assuredly not [. . .]. But as *gold*, as that special union of absolute and relative gravity, ductility, and hardness, which, wherever they are found, constitute *gold*, I should answer no less fearlessly, in the affirmative. (47)

The individual lump of gold may be lifeless, but the element in its specific individuality possesses "the simplest form of unity, namely, the unity of powers and properties" (*Hints* 46), and therefore a spark of vitality.

Ultimately, Coleridge cannot deny that spark to anything that unifies several things into a single thing, since his definition of life (couched in learned Latin as if to underline its importance) ultimately boils down to precisely that: "*vis ab intra, cujus proprium est coadunare plura in rem unicam, quantum est res unica* [*an internal capacity, the particular property of which is to join many things in a single unified thing, to the extent that it remains a single unified thing*]" (44; Coleridge's italics). "What is Life?" he asks. "Were such a question proposed, we should be tempted to answer, what is *not* Life that really *is*?" (38). Neither Robinet nor Leibniz would have found anything objectionable in such a rhetorical question. Advocates of the notion that the crucial characteristic of life is organization could only rejoice at a definition of life such as Coleridge proposed. Anyone not bending over backwards to avoid a taboo word would normally call the property of joining many things in one single unified thing "organization."

The vitalists of Abernethy's party would have found only very partial support for their position in Coleridge's theory of life, had they known of it. Like Lawrence and others in the tradition of Robinet, Coleridge actually rejected the notion of a vital substance that could exist apart from matter. He was very clear about it: "Life itself is not a *thing* — a self-subsistent *hypostasis* — but an *act* and a *process*" (94). Such a definition of life would have held little attraction for Abernethy, but it would have been entirely congenial to other Romantic writers, including the friend of Coleridge's youth, William Wordsworth. In Book VIII of *The Prelude*, Wordsworth explains that the crucial characteristic of "the spirit of things" that distinguishes it from the "dead letter" is that the "truth" of spirit is "a motion or a shape / Instinct with vital functions" (432–34). The association of spirit with motion and vitality that emerges (as discussed earlier) from the wellspring of discourse inaugurated by Paul in 2 Corinthians 3 thus flows quite comfortably into one of the main streams of early nineteenth-century poetry and natural philosophy.

Coleridge's notion of life as process is, as Owen Barfield suggests, hardly distinguishable from the notion of *natura naturans* ("nature in action") set forth elsewhere in Coleridge's writings. "There seems no need to regard *life* and *natura naturans* as other than virtual synonyms" (58), Barfield claims:

> *Natura naturans* is supersensuous, but not supernatural. It has nothing to do with those "occult qualities" [Coleridge's phrase], whose final expulsion (or intended expulsion) from the domain of science was one of the major achievements of the scientific revolution. We shall see that, so far from reintroducing occult qualities, he considered his concept of spirit, as the antithesis or correlative to "nature," to be the only possible means of *eliminating* those occult qualities. [. . .] An "occult quality" is anything that is deemed to possess an exclusively objective existence, in spite of being imperceptible. (25; Barfield's emphasis)

Coleridge could therefore never embrace a vitalism that took as its fundamental assumption the existence of an objective, yet imperceptible something that caused organisms to be alive. Nor could he accept a pure materialism that would deny the role of spirit in the living world, especially that of human beings, in spite of his evident belief in the crucial importance of material bodies.[15]

Life — for Coleridge and for many others sharing his intellectual heritage — could best be understood as a *vis ab intra*, an internal capability of many material bodies, not excluding such things as gold. It is no "occult quality" any more than the human capacity to eat or walk or sneeze; and, like those capabilities, it manifests itself as an act or process. We find nothing even remotely supernatural about these processes, nor should we imagine that the process of life is at bottom any more supernatural. But that it is natural does not mean that it cannot also be spiritual. Coleridge was deeply committed to the idea of spirit, and that idea takes a central place in his account of the human world. Like life (as Coleridge defines it) and like nature itself, the "spirit in man [. . .] shows its own state in and by its acts alone" (*Aids to Reflection*, quoted in Barfield 15). But spirit, though it is natural, is not found in all living things. In the *Biographia Literaria*, he admits to using the terms "spirit, self, and self-consciousness" indiscriminately as synonyms (272–73). It does not appear that Coleridge would argue that gold, which he affirms to have life, would also possess spirit to any meaningful extent, for there is no reason to think that gold has self-consciousness.

Once again, there is little in Coleridge's view of spirit that would have surprised or troubled continental philosophers of the eighteenth century. Robinet never claimed that an oval pyrite possessed spirit, and he proposed only that a monkey had far more of it than an oyster — which was certainly not much. Not one among these thinkers went so far as to claim that the highest forms of life, those possessing the most complex organization, were soulless machines. That sort of unalloyed materialism was quite rare in the mainstream intellectual tradition of the time. Even prominent Romantic radicals like Percy Shelley, an unabashed atheist with a strong materialist leaning, never embraced a materialism so absolute that it could do away completely with the notion of spirit.[16] In the following remarkable passage from a letter to Elizabeth Hitchener, Shelley sets forth a position that mixes materialism and spiritualism in a manner quite consistent with the tradition of Robinet and Lawrence:

> When we speak of the soul of man, we speak of that unknown cause which produces the observable effect evinced by his intelligence & bodily animation which are in their nature conjoined, and as we suppose, as we observe, inseparable. The word God, then, in the sense which you take it analogises with the *universe*, as the soul of man to his body, the vegetative power to vegetables, the stony power to stones. Yet were each of these adjuncts taken away what would be the remainded — what is man without his soul? he is not man. (11 June 1811; Shelley's emphasis)

While this passage does offer evidence that, for Shelley, "there is no inert body to which animation is attached as an appendage: animation itself is material" (Ruston 86), it also offers evidence that Shelley's materialism was considerably diluted by an admixture of spiritualism. Shelley was entirely comfortable with calling the essential human component in humanity a "soul" and even went so far as to allow, just a bit later in the letter, that he could "acknowledge a God" of the universe in the same sense that he acknowledged a soul in human beings.

If we find in the Shelley of 1811 a materialist with more than a touch of spiritual idealism, we may not be especially surprised to find the Shelley of 1819 proclaiming himself a spiritual idealist, no longer committed to materialism at all:

> The shocking absurdities of the popular philosophy of mind and matter, and its fatal consequences in morals, their violent dogmatism concerning the source of all things, had early conducted me to materialism. [. . .] But I was discontented with such a view of things as it afforded; man is a being of high aspirations [. . .], disclaiming alliance with transience and decay, incapable of imagining to himself annihilation, existing but in the future and the past, being not what he is, but what he has been, and shall be. Whatever may be his true and final destination, there is a spirit within him at enmity with nothingness and dissolution, change and extinction. This is the character of all life and being. ("On Life" 634)

In spite of the forcefulness of this language, there is reason to believe that Shelley's divorce from materialism was no more complete than his earlier marriage to it had been. There is no evidence in Shelley's later writings that he ever abandoned his sense of the necessary embodiment of spirit, even though he may have given up belief in the primacy of matter.[17] Quite the contrary: "As music and splendour / Survive not the lamp and the lute, / The heart's echoes render / No song when the spirit is mute," he wrote only months before his death ("When the Lamp is Shattered" 9–12). These lines allow no decision as to whether the material body (the lute) or the spirit is more important to the production of music. When either is lacking, there can be no song.

Romantic philosophers and poets found themselves faced with the task of negotiating a difficult twilight landscape in which they could not readily separate matter from spirit, or life from death. It was a task set them in part by the theory of life, developed during the eighteenth century, that proposed the emergence of spirit out of matter. If "the necessary condition in the body that enables the spirit to think is its organization," as Robinet had proposed, it would follow that all highly organized material bodies might be repositories of spirit, even if such bodies gave every appearance of being dead. The language of Paul in 2 Corinthians 3 suggested a way both to understand and to experience this notion by way of our interaction with texts: in the act of reading, an apparently dead but highly organized material body can be brought back to life, provided only that one has the requisite skill to unlock the dormant spirit within it.

The Romantic theory of art arose in this intellectual-historical context. It answered Johann Georg Hamann's question, "But how are we to raise the defunct language of Nature from the dead?" in terms that not only Christian theologians but also Leibniz and Robinet could approve. Art of all kinds, but literary art especially, became the means by which the (apparently) dead matter found in nature could be re-animated by the living spirit. If, as René Wellek once argued, Romanticism broadly conceived was an effort to "overcome the split between subject and object, the self and the world, the conscious and the unconscious" (220), it was also an even more ambitious attempt to overcome and perhaps to erase the gap between the living and the dead. Romantic interest in antiquity, the Middle Ages, the "primitive," and "Gothic" supernaturalism had its roots in a desire to bring the present into contact with the absent, to bring the living spirit to the dead letter.

Notes

[1] Rousseau based his claim on the work of such mid-century scholars as Marjorie Hope Nicolson, who had helped to establish the close relationship between developments in the science of geology in the eighteenth century and the Romantic literary landscape, as well as that between Newtonian optics and Romantic poetic imagery. Similar opinions recur in more recent scholarship, as for example the contention of Edward Profitt that "the romantic and the scientific grow up together and share the same angle of vision" (56). For a classic study of the relation between science and Romanticism, see Eichner, "Rise of Modern Science."

[2] For a detailed history of one relevant strain of natural philosophy in this period, see Reill.

[3] One is perplexed by Ruston's comment: "By the year 1800 a new concept of life had emerged, likening animals to human and even plant life. For the first time, life was considered a universal state" (3). But life had been considered a universal state by some thinkers since at least the early eighteenth century, and among them were some very prominent figures, such as Leibniz. So the idea could hardly have seemed new in 1800.

[4] Reill devotes a section of his book to "Death, Dying, and Resurrection" (171-82). He points out that "Enlightenment Vitalism" (by which he means the whole constellation of anti-mechanist theories of life in the eighteenth century) led to "anxieties and fears about what death was, how it could be infallibly determined, whether it was possible to bring the dead back to life or even to generate life where there had been none" (172).

[5] Chapter 5, "Phenomenalists versus realists." The web text is not divided into pages.

[6] Robinet was one among several influential thinkers of the period who took a similar position. Robinet's friend Charles Bonnet could also be cited as an advocate of the universality of life and the importance of organization. See Reill 136–37, 182.

[7] I assume it is clear that I use the term "spiritualism" to mean "the tendency towards, or advocacy of, a spiritual view or estimate of things, especially as a leading principle in philosophy" (OED, sense 2). I certainly do not mean "the belief that the spirits of the dead can hold communication with the living" (OED, sense 3).

[8] Reill presents Robinet as a pure vitalist, following the broad understanding of "vitalism" that underlies Reill's entire argument; and indeed there can be no doubt about Robinet's commitment to the ominipresence of life in nature. But Robinet did not share the view of certain other vitalists who believed in a vital essence separable from the material body. It is clear that Robinet's version of vitalism was based on a very materialist assumption: life is a basic and universal property of all matter. Living spirit, however, is a different thing altogether, since in Robinet's view it emerges only as material bodies become highly organized.

[9] Robinet's oyster continues to make key appearances up to the present day. Cf. Ruston's characterization of the central question of Romantic biology: "how could life exist in so many bodies organized so completely differently, from oyster to man?" (3–4).

[10] The passage is quoted in N. Vuillemin's essay published on the web. There are no page numbers.

[11] Thomas Rennell (64) argued that Lawrence had essentially plagiarized parts of the *Lectures* from Bichat.

[12] While Ruston (13) acknowledges a strain in Lawrence that is not consonant with materialism, she seems to be thoroughly convinced that the charges of materialism leveled at Bichat were justified.

[13] For a sympathetic contemporary account of Abernethy's position, see Barclay.

[14] Seth Watson, a prominent physician and the editor of Coleridge's text, published the unfinished essay as part of the "Works on Medicine and Science" series under the imprint of John Churchill of London. The series included such titles as *A Manual of Physiology* and *On Diseases of the Liver*. This context is important, since it indicates that Coleridge's essay was being taken seriously by the scientific community of the mid-nineteenth century.

[15] For discussions of vitalism, its history and its opponents, see Reill; Driesch; Theodore Brown.

[16] Hoagwood faults Ruston for "confus[ing] 'materialism' with 'scepticism,' using those terms as if they were synonymous whereas in fact they designate contradictory positions" and asserts that the "equation of scepticism with materialism *is* a mistake" (251; Hoagwood's emphasis). Perhaps such an equation would be a mistake on a philosophy exam, but the historical situation is really more complicated. Hoagwood refers to a "philosophical scepticism," that "avoids all claims of knowledge about the external (mind-independent) world," but what is really at issue in the case of Shelley is a religious scepticism that tends to avoid claims of knowledge about God. Ruston is not mistaken in her contention that Shelley was both a materialist (mostly) and a religious skeptic (of a sort). I am proposing that Shelley's

materialism, like that of Lawrence, Robinet, and other scientists of the time, was compatible with a belief in the reality of the soul that neither embraced nor excluded monotheistic theology. Shelley's materialism was infused with spiritualism, but it never ceased being skeptical about many of the claims of institutional Christianity.

[17] Cf. Ruston: "For all his subsequent denial of the 'false' and 'pernicious' philosophy of the materialists, Shelley throughout his poetry and prose shows a preoccupation with the bodily, the physical and the material" (152).

Part II

The Dead and Living Past

3: "The Heavenly Revelation of Her Spirit": Goethe's *The Sorrows of Young Werther*

ALTHOUGH GOETHE'S NOVEL *The Sorrows of Young Werther* (*Die Leiden des jungen Werther*, 1774) is one of the most famous and most highly praised works in all of German literature, one of its principal climactic scenes almost always bores or mystifies modern readers almost to the point of ruining their pleasure in the story. It is a scene of reading. Werther arrives at Lotte's house unexpectedly, after the two had an agreement that they would have to keep apart from each other. It is to be their last meeting together, for Werther will commit suicide the next night by shooting himself in the head "above the right eye, driving his brains out" (GS 127; GW 124). Only the reader, but not Lotte nor anyone else, knows that Werther has resolved to die, but everyone concerned knows that the two young people will not see each other again. At this peak of emotional intensity, the lover and his beloved do not do anything like we would expect: they do not profess love to each other, they do not lament their fate, they certainly do not make love, and in fact actually speak very little to one another. Instead they read together a lengthy passage from Werther's translation of "Ossian," the heroic Irish poet so popular in Goethe's youth who turned out later to be a hoax perpetrated by the bard's alleged "translator," James MacPherson.[1]

Goethe does not simply tell us that this reading took place. He cites page after dreary page of Werther's "Ossian," giving us every single word that the wretched young man read to Lotte. Instead of hearing about how Werther and Lotte feel or learning what they think, the reader is treated to the melancholy adventures of people named Arindal, Daura, and Armar, who otherwise make no appearance whatsoever in the novel. One has to wonder: what possessed Goethe to divert our attention from the characters for whom he has worked so diligently to kindle our interest to these literary ghosts translated from a translation?

One answer is relatively easy. Goethe, even in his early twenties, was astute enough as a writer of fiction to realize that the emotional tension of the moment he sought to depict far surpassed the possibility of direct description available to the eighteenth-century novel. What was he to do with the surplus of feeling that would inevitably elude his best efforts at representation? His solution was to avoid trying to represent it at all, to transfer instead the emotional burden to another text whose unavoidable shortcomings could be inscribed within the narrative. He also strikes a note of psychological realism, for Lotte and Werther understandably prefer to divert the power of their feelings toward this safe object rather than risk hurting themselves and each other further. Arindal and Daura become stand-ins for Werther and Lotte, as the narrator takes pains to point out:

> A flood of tears streamed from Lotte's eyes, relieving her oppressed heart and preventing Werther from continuing. He threw the papers aside, took her hand, and wept bitterly. Lotte rested her head on her other hand and covered her eyes with her handkerchief. What both felt at that moment was agonizing. They experienced their own misery in the fate of these noble people, they felt it together [*fühlten es zusammen*], and their tears flowed as one [*vereinigten sich*]. (GS 118; GW 114)

The tears that flow in unison when the lovers read together merge their bodies in a union that both hints at and replaces a forbidden sexual union. Their experience is a sensual one in spite of its painful nature, for though what they feel is misery, they nonetheless "felt it together." Werther prolongs this moment of shared feeling by returning to his reading and finds in the text a confirmation of the erotic basis of all these tears. "Why dost thou awaken me, O zephyr of spring?" he reads. "Thou dost speak of love [*du buhlst*], saying, 'I spread the dew with drops from heaven' [*Tropfen des Himmels*]" (GS 118–19; GW 114). The drops from heaven that bedew the world in the translated poem seem to acknowledge the presence of the other drops that so liberally fall on the physical pages of the manuscript. The text also acknowledges the possibility of illicit sexuality by using the verb "buhlen," which might mean no more than "to speak of love" but often in fact refers to having illicit intercourse.

Werther's "Ossian" translation is awash in these sensual tears. The crying does not begin, we should notice, only after the reading is done but before it begins. When Werther "took them [the translated poems Lotte had just fetched] in his hands, he shivered, and as he looked at them, his eyes filled with tears [*die Augen standen ihm voll Tränen*]. He sat down and read" (GS 113; GW 108). Every word that Werther utters makes its way from the page to his lips through the medium of his tears, which did not simply pass temporarily but remained (*standen*) for an extended period. While one might normally expect that such a circumstance would make the reading difficult or impossible, there is evidence that quite the opposite may be the case, that this text's capacity to elicit tears is precisely the thing that makes it legible. How else are we to explain the peculiar circumstance that Werther, having just arrived with a number of books ("He put down several books he had brought with him"), answers Lotte's question "Haven't you brought anything to read? [*Haben Sie nichts zu lesen?*]" in the negative (GS 112–13; GW 107)? Why is it that the books he has just put down do not count — for him or for Lotte — as something to read, whereas the Ossian translation does? What is the difference between those texts and this one? Certainly an important difference is that the manuscript belongs more intimately to Werther and Lotte because he made it and has given it to her. It already marks out an area of shared feelings, the clearest sign of which is its ability to bring forth their tears. The books Werther has brought with him are apparently nothing worth weeping over, and so they are properly considered "nichts zu lesen." The complex and powerful set of meanings attached to this climactic act of reading suggests that the story of Werther and Lotte has been a story of reading all along, and it could properly conclude in no other way.[2] The relationship from the first was mediated by reading and determined in large measure by the interaction between literature and lived experience. When the unhappy couple turns to Ossian as the mirror in which they will see the reflected image of their own misery, they do nothing different from what they have always done in their relations with each other. For, much as they profess to prize lived experience, they are in fact able to experience fully only through the mediation of reading.

Werther is, above all, a passionate reader.[3] His sensitivity to books is so acute that his rhetoric treats them as if they were dangerous drugs that have an immediate and powerful effect on his physical being:

> You ask whether you should send me books. Dear friend, I beg of you — don't [*laß sie mir vom Halse*]. I have no wish to be influenced, encouraged, or inspired any more. My heart surges wildly enough without any outside influence. What I need is a lullaby, and I have found an abundance of them in my beloved Homer. How often I have to calm my rebellious blood! (GS 25–26; GW 10)

Books may be either stimulants or sedatives, but they are never without effect. Of course one wonders — and is meant to wonder — whether in fact Homer serves the sedative function Werther ascribes to him. The text suggests forcefully that in fact the opposite may be true, for when Werther subsequently mentions his regular visits to a favorite country inn, he describes himself as sitting at a table in the open air "drinking coffee and reading Homer [*und lese meinen Homer*]" (GS 29; GW 15). It is as if the two activities naturally belong together, one serving as physical, the other as spiritual stimulation. Werther's relation to "his" Homer (*meinen Homer*) is almost certainly just as emotionally intense as it is with Ossian and will be with Lotte.[4] When he first conceives his passion for Lotte, he can indeed express its power no more forcefully than by comparing it to his literary love:

> You should see what an idiot I am when she is mentioned in public. And when someone asks how I like her! *Like* her? I can't abide the word. [*Gefällt! Das Wort hasse ich auf den Tod.*] What kind of person could possibly "like" Lotte? What kind of person could possibly not be completely

fulfilled [*ausfüllt*] by her? Like her! The other day someone asked me if I like Ossian. (GS 49; GW 37)

Homer, Ossian, and Lotte all belong together in the same class of entities that are so electrifyingly stimulating that a person can be "completely fulfilled" by them. Expressing mere "liking" for such creatures engenders Werther's hatred "to death [*auf den Tod*]." Indeed it will come to that.

There is evidence early in the novel that Werther's mind is already replete with the atmosphere of his favorite poets. They fill him up so completely that they condition the way in which he sees the world. One of the most telling of the opening letters (the one immediately preceding the one in which Werther tells Wilhelm to send him no more books) offers a characteristically literary interpretation of everyday occurrence:

> Just outside town there is a spring to which I feel mysteriously drawn, like Melusina and her sisters. [. . .] Not a day passes without my spending an hour there. Young girls come from town to fetch water, a simple and very necessary business — in days of old [*ehemals*] the daughters of kings used to do it — and as I sit there, a patriarchal atmosphere comes to life all around me [*so lebt die patriarchalische Idee so lebhaft um mich*]. I can see our forefathers [*die Altväter*] meeting and courting at wells like this, and how good spirits hovered over all such places. Whoever can't feel with me has never refreshed himself at a cold spring after a long excursion on a hot summer's day. (GS 25; GW 9–10)

Werther's closing rhetorical flourish appeals to common human experience, but the reader recognizes that those most likely to feel the same as Werther are not those who have been thirsty on a hot day but those who have read stories from "days of old." The power of this spring does not derive so much from its ability to refresh the traveler as from Werther's projection on it of his readings of Homer, Ossian, and even the Old Testament. The reference to the daughters of kings fetching water recalls scenes in the *Odyssey*, and Werther's vision of "our forefathers meeting and courting at wells like this" is surely an echo of the Old Testament story of Rachel and Jacob, who do indeed meet and court at a well (*Genesis* 29:1–20). The revivified life (the words *lebt* and *lebhaft* crowd together in the same sentence) that Werther feels around the spring therefore comes from acts of reading — his readings of old books, to be sure, but then more directly his reading of this actual place as a literary place, a topos that belongs figuratively in the same world with the springs and wells of literature.

Werther does not readily separate literary from lived experience. That is part of his charm and one of the ways in which he shows himself to be in tune with the new aesthetic about to sweep through Europe. For Werther, as for the Romantics who will follow him, intensity of feeling is inherently poetic, so that a deeply felt experience seems to belong to the realm of literature even before it can be verbalized. He writes a letter in which he describes the "lively participation" produced in him by a peasant boy's account of his affection for a widow he served, prefacing it with an observation that would seem more at home in an essay on criticism: "What I said the other day about painting is also true of poetry. It is simply that one should recognize and try to express only what is excellent [*daß man das Vortreffliche erkenne und es auszusprechen wage*], and that is saying a great deal, in a few words" (GS 32; GW 17). This is surely a notion many could assent to without difficulty, but it is not clear what relevance it has to Werther's situation until he explains that he had experienced something that, "simply told, could be a beautiful idyll" (GS 32; GW 17). We expect, then, that we are going to hear this idyll. But before we get it, he immediately goes on to wonder, "what is poetry, episode, and idyll? Must it always be patchwork [*gebosselt sein*] when we participate in a revelation of nature?" (GS 32; GW 18). The rhetorical question hangs in the air as Werther moves on to recount the story of his meeting with the peasant boy, noting as he begins that he will "tell the tale badly, as usual" (GS 32; GW 18).

Since Werther does not claim to be a poet, or even a good writer, it is curious that the question of "what is poetry" should stand at the head of his offering of material he confesses is not "very lofty" or "highly refined." Why is Werther thinking about poetry when he is not producing any and when he is not, for once, telling us about Homer and Ossian? Clearly, he believes that his experience has a quality that is poetic and believes further that the textual form in which he puts that experience has little to do with that poetic quality. "I would have to be a great poet [*müßte die Gabe des größten Dichters besitzen*]," he says, to reproduce the details of the boy's speech and appearance "as spiritedly as I experienced them" (GS 33; GW 18). But he is not such a poet and therefore does not even attempt such a reproduction. In any case, no text could ever be adequate: "there are no words for the tenderness expressed by the man as a whole. Anything I might say would be clumsy in comparison" (GS 33; GW 18). But if this experience is "poetry," and if there are not words that could possibly describe it, then Werther means by "poetry" something quite apart from the texts. Werther has noticed the intensity of his feelings in reaction to the peasant boy, confessing: "I catch fire myself [*mir die innerste Seele glüht*] when I recall his innocence and honesty" (GS 33; GW 19). One can only conclude that he has drawn a silent analogy between his experience of the boy and his experience of reading Homer and Ossian. In both cases he has a sense of participating in a "revelation of nature [*Naturerscheinung*]" at bottom indistinguishable from the epiphanic, mysterious sensation he has at the spring (GS 32; GW 18).

Werther's description of his conversation with the peasant boy is a curious mixture of respect and skepticism for poetry. There is the implication that poetic texts may always be an inadequate "patchwork" when compared to lived experience and that words in general necessarily fall far short of fully reproducing such experience. This adds up to a distrust of the verbal medium itself, a conviction that structures of language can never completely convey the fullness of sensation or the richness of meaning available from events. On the other hand, Werther is bent on understanding his "lively participation" in the peasant boy's account of himself as somehow basically poetic precisely because it offers such a surplus beyond the capacities of language. His experience is one of those moments that prompts one to "recognize and try to express" the excellence that may well surpass expression, and the recognition is evidently at least as important as the (inevitably inadequate) attempt at expression. The poetic moment is therefore one in which one confronts experience as if it were a great poem requiring and rewarding vigorous reading. Poetry in this view has little to do with the formal qualities of texts and much to do with the way in which persons interpret experience, savor it, and try to touch the plenitude of its meaning. Poetic moments, whether they occur at the instigation of a literary text or of some nonliterary event, call for the "lively participation" of reading.

Such a notion of poetry helps to explain why Werther does not make any important distinction between the events and the texts that move him. Reading Homer or Ossian belongs to the same order of activity as conversing with the extraordinary peasant boy or watching the girls fetch water from the spring. It also helps to explain how and why Werther falls in love with Lotte. Werther describes his first sight of Lotte with all the artistic skill he claims to lack when speaking of the peasant lad, and once again it is the case of an epiphanic moment in which the poetic quality dominates. It is also one of the best-known and best-loved passages in German literature:

> I walked across the courtyard toward the attractive house, and when I had gone up the steps and through a doorway, I came upon the most charming sight imaginable. Six children, from about eleven to two, were swarming around a very pretty girl [*ein Mädchen von schöner Gestalt*] of medium height. She had on a simple white dress with pale pink bows on the sleeves and at her breast, and she was holding a loaf of black bread and cutting a slice for every one of her little ones [*und schnitt ihren Kleinen rings herum jedem sein Stück*], according to their ages and appetites. She gave each his share with the most enchanting graciousness, and the children cried out "thank you's" to her absolutely at their ease, stretching out the little hands for their slice before she even had a chance to cut it. Then they jumped off happily with their supper or, each according to his nature, walked away quietly in the direction of the courtyard to see the strange persons and the carriage in which their Lotte would soon drive away. (GS 35; GW 21)

The apparent simplicity of the scene and of the language describing it discloses on close inspection a carefully orchestrated cultural complexity. As soon as we read the words "Mädchen von schöner Gestalt" (translated as "very pretty girl") we suspect that this is the Charlotte S. about whom Werther has been warned. "You are about to meet a very pretty girl [*ein schönes Frauenzimmer*]," he is told. "Watch out that you don't fall in love with her" (GS 34; GW 20). She is not an appropriate object for love, Werther learns, because she is already engaged to another man. Before Werther even sees her, then, he knows her to be both an appropriate and an inappropriate object of desire. His first sight of her confirms this double message with mythic force. On the one hand, she wears the white dress of a maiden, the pale pink bows to which Werther will form a strong sentimental attachment hinting only slightly at the red blood of sexuality (menses, defloration). On the other, this maiden is already acting in the role of a mother of six, whom she cares for and who behave as her children (*ihre Kleinen*).

Her role as virgin-mother is given a specific mythical character in this scene in that Lotte plays the role of Ceres/Demeter, the maternal grain goddess who provides the nourishing fruits of the earth to her children. Like Demeter (whose name contains the Greek word for "mother"), Lotte's principal role in this little idyll is to give bread, but like the goddess, she retains mysteriously a maidenly innocence and sexual attraction. Demeter possessed "a younger double of herself, the 'Virgin' (*Kore*), who is regularly (not quite invariably) worshipped with her, and seems to be essentially the power which is in the corn itself and appears and disappears with it" (*OCD* 324). Werther is therefore able to see in this otherwise unprepossessing young woman a divine figure somehow transported out of the world of his beloved Homer into eighteenth-century Germany. She is in this respect only a more extreme example of the process outlined earlier in the letter concerning the girls at the spring.

Though the reader, aided by the touch of ironic distance inscribed in the text, knows that this is an ordinary girl, Werther never ceases to see her in the transforming light of literary myth. Later in the novel, at the close of Book 1, such a transforming light actually performs its magic in front of Werther's eyes. After a conversation in which Lotte speaks about the death of her mother and of feeling close to the departed soul "when I sit with her children . . . my children [*unter ihren Kindern, unter meinen Kindern*]" (GS 67; GW 57), Lotte and Albert walk out into the garden in the moonlight. "Below, in the shadows of the tall linden trees, I could see her white dress shimmering as the two moved toward the gate" (GS 69; GW 59). The white dress — either the same dress as on the day of their first meeting or its metaphorical double — now glows in the moonlight as if Lotte were herself the moon, as if she were transformed into the goddess of the moon, Diana/Artemis, the maiden who presides over childbirth. Werther focuses all his attention on the dress, which becomes the immediate object of his longing. "I stretched out my arms . . . and it vanished" (GS 69; GW 59).

The dress is magical, capable of glowing in the night and of suddenly disappearing. Lotte in the moonlight is a figure from a mythic world that is — characteristically enough — half Homer and half Ossian. The theme of the beloved in the moonlight reappears in the novel as part of the translation from Ossian that Werther reads to Lotte at their final meeting: "See . . . the moon appears, the river gleams in the valley [. . .]. But who lies down there on the heath? My beloved?" (GS 114; GW 109). It is in fact the corpse of the beloved, the beloved gone forever, who appears in the moonlight. The real Lotte is no more attainable than that fictional dead lover or than the moon itself, and that is part of her attraction.

Falling in love with a virgin-mother-goddess may be very exciting, but it is also perilous. "To be the consort of a mother-goddess is very dangerous" (*OCD*), as is demonstrated in the case of both Demeter and Artemis, whose male admirers often enough come to violent ends. Demeter, though she is a life-giving bringer of bread, is also a goddess of the dead, mother-in-law of Pluto, whose daughter (or alternative aspect) dwells half the year in the underworld. The mythic aura that surrounds Lotte also contains this darker aspect. Like the maiden Kore/Persephone she has been bestowed on one who will remove her from availability ("Sie ist schon vergeben" [GW 20]). It is dangerous to fall in love with such a creature, and Werther is duly warned not to do so. He pays no attention to this warning, not only because he does not know Lotte yet when he hears it but also because Werther, for all his sensitivity, reads the poetic texts he discovers all around him with greater enthusiasm than thoroughness. When he first sees Lotte and projects her into the literary world of Homer and Ossian, he wants to know only about the attractive and happy aspects of the text in which he inscribes her. Later, at the time of their last meeting, he will read her quite differently, as part of the world of fallen heroes and dying lovers. Then he will focus only upon what he had earlier suppressed, this time suppressing instead the vision of the benevolent maiden-mother that had earlier possessed him utterly.

When Werther actually gets to speak with Lotte, she confirms her participation in his literary world and thereby also confirms her erotic power over him. The first topic of conversation is, perhaps not unexpectedly, books. It is not Werther who initiates this topic of conversation — it is Lotte's cousin — but he quickly seizes upon it as evidence in support of his initial understanding of her:

> The cousin asked whether Lotte had read the book she had sent her recently. "No," Lotte said, "I don't like. You may have it back. I didn't like the one you sent me before that, either." When I asked her what the books were, and she told me, I was astonished. Altogether, I found that everything she said displayed a resolute character, and with every word she spoke I could see some new attraction in her and a fresh radiance in her face, which soon seemed free of all constraint, because she saw that I

understood her [*ich sah mit jedem Wort neue Reize, neue Strahlen des Geistes aus ihren Gesichtszügen hervorbrechen, die sich nach und nach zu entfalten schienen, weil sie an mir fühlte, daß ich sie verstand*]. (GS 36; GW 22–23)

This conversation speaks volumes. A powerful metonymy apparently at work in Werther's mind transforms the person talking about books into a book of marvelous legibility. Werther may be listening to her speech, but he describes himself not as hearing but seeing some new grace with each word she speaks. Her face becomes a page that "seems to unfold [*zu entfalten schienen*]" before his eyes and upon which he can read the "Strahlen des Geistes" that are impressed upon her features. This unfolding of her physiognomy occurs in response to Werther's sympathetic reading. She lets herself be read because he reads so well, and she can feel that he understands her.

Lotte goes on to describe her taste in books, and it is this shared set of literary values that forms the basis of the mutual attraction between her and Werther. Beyond this attraction through common interests, however, is the fact that Lotte appears to confirm Werther's opinion that literature and life are the same sort of thing. "I like those writers best who help me find my world again," she tells the company in the carriage, and in whose stories "the sort of things happen that happen all around me, and the story is as interesting and sympathetic as my own life at home [*als mein eigen häuslich Leben*]" (GS 37; GW 23). Literature and life should come together; each should mirror the other. That is what Werther believes also, though one doubts that Lotte would find her "life at home [*häuslich Leben*]" revealed in Homer and Ossian to quite the same degree that Werther does his own. Still, Lotte and Werther are united from the first moments of their acquaintance by the high value they place on literature in which they can find their own world reproduced.

Goethe hopes also to involve the novel's readers in this little society of shared literary values and mutual attraction. His efforts become particularly clear when one considers the "editor's" notes he appended to this passage in the novel.[5] A note affixed to the sentence "When I asked her what the books were, and she told me, I was astonished" gives the following explanation: "We have found it necessary to suppress this part of the letter in order to give no cause for complaint, although actually no author could care very much about the opinion of one girl and a young, unstable man" (GS 36; GW 22). A little later, when Lotte speaks "casually and very candidly about *The Vicar of Wakefield* and about _____," a note offers a justification for the blank: "Here, too, the names of some authors have been omitted. Those of whom Lotte approved will surely know it in their hearts, if they have read this far, and the rest need not know anything about it" (GS 36–37; GW 23). The "editor's" tactful suppression of names is ostensibly motivated by a desire to avoid giving offense to those authors the couple did not care for, but a more important motivation is surely Goethe's wish to allow his readers free rein to fill in these blanks with their own titles. We are free when we read of Lotte's literary likes and dislikes to match them up with our own and consequently to admire her for her outstanding good judgment. Just as we know that she is "pretty" but remain free within broad limits to imagine her as pretty in whatever way we choose, so do we know that she is judicious in her choice of books but retain our option of deciding for ourselves what those books were. The author has selected only a very few for us.

One of those he selects makes its appearance in yet another of the famous scenes with which this novel is filled: the thunderstorm and its aftermath, the description of which closes the letter of June 16th. During the storm, the young people attending the dance play a game of numbers that Lotte arranges as a distraction. Werther feels that Lotte singles him out for special attention during the game: "I was boxed on the ears twice, and with secret delight felt that she had boxed my ears harder than any of the others" (GS 40; GW 27). Perhaps this is only wishful thinking, but after the storm and the game are over, the two do share a special moment of intimacy mediated not by blows but by poetry:

> We walked over to the window. It was still thundering in the distance, the blessed rain was falling on the land, an almost refreshing scent rose up to us with a rush of warm air [*der herrliche Regen säuselte auf das Land, und der erquickendste Wohlgeruch stief in aller Fülle einer warmen Luft zu uns auf*]. She stood there, leaning on her elbows, her gaze penetrating the countryside; she looked up at the sky, at me, and I could see the tears in her eyes. She laid her hand on mine and said, "Klopstock." I knew at once what she was thinking — his magnificent ode — and was lost in the emotions that this one word aroused in me [*und versank in dem Strome von Empfindungen, den sie in dieser Losung über mich ausgoß*]. I bent down and kissed her hand, and now there were tears in my eyes too as I looked into hers again. Oh, noble poet, if you could have seen the adoration in those eyes [*Edler! Hättest du deine Vergötterung in diesem Blicke gesehen*]! I hope I never have to hear your name, so oft profaned, spoken again by any other lips! (GS 41; GW 27)

This is an experience of profound meaning for Werther, and perhaps for Lotte as well, an experience that brings the two together in a spiritual embrace as emotionally powerful as any physical embrace could be. Though the two never touch, they become united in a moment of understanding in which lived experience merges with literature.

Lotte shows that she reads the world the way Werther does, through the lens of poetry. The thunderstorm just passed is not only a particular meteorological event, it is a mythic re-enactment of a universal rite of revivification, the "Rites of Spring [*Frühlingsfeier*]" celebrated in Klopstock's poem. Lotte's reaction suggests that she understands the thunderstorm in "Die Frühlingsfeier" not as the textualized residue of a particular moment in Klopstock's life but rather as a mythic paradigm according to which all thunderstorms may be given meaning. Of course Werther reacts to this way of thinking with extravagant sympathy, because it is precisely his way of thinking, as we already know from the scene at the spring and the description of Lotte/Demeter distributing the fruits of the earth. We might guess, furthermore, that his view of the storm was shaped by Klopstock's poem before Lotte mentions it, because in fact elements of that poem are embedded in Werther's report of the storm's aftermath. When he says "der herrliche Regen säuselte auf das Land, und der erquickendste Wohlgeruch stief in aller Fülle einer warmen Luft zu uns auf [the blessed rain was falling on the land, an almost refreshing scent rose up to us with a rush of warm air]," he uses a vocabulary strikingly congruent with that of the "Frühlingsfeier's" closing verses: "Nun ist, wie dürstet sie! die Erd' erquickt, / Und der Himmel der Segensfüll' entlasstet! / [...] / Im stillen, sanfte Säuseln / Kommt Jehova [Now the earth — how thirsty she is! — is slaked, / and heaven is unburdened of its blessed bounty! / ... In the soft, quiet murmur comes Jehovah]." The terms *säuseln, erquicken,* and *Fülle* (*murmur, slake, bounty*), featured so prominently in Klopstock's final lines, reappear in Werther's letter without any apparent consciousness of literary indebtedness, because these terms are for him the only right and proper ones to use in describing the passing of a thunderstorm. As this text arranges matters, then, Klopstock's poem has already determined the (textual) nature of this thunderstorm for both Werther and his reader. Lotte's exclamation comes then only as a confirmation of a relationship which the text's rhetoric has firmly established.

When Werther says that he remembered "at once" the poem Lotte refers to when she mentions the poet's name, he is telling only part of the story. As he reports events, the poem was certainly in his mind — even if not his consciousness — all along, and he was not really in need of being reminded of it. The great torrent of feelings that overwhelms him in response to her utterance of "Klopstock," this word of power (*Losung*: "watchword"), results not from his sudden understanding of her literary allusion but from the revelation that she had been thinking in exactly the same way he was thinking, reading the landscape through the lens of the poetic text. Lotte's "gaze" ("Blick") is a powerful, penetrating faculty that orders the natural world in accordance with Klopstock's terms. Werther's language suggests that Lotte's gaze, which "penetrates the countryside" in its fervor, belongs in part to Klopstock. Werther's apostrophe to the poet, "Edler! hättest du deine Vergötterung in diesem Blicke gesehn," can be read as ambiguous, as suggesting not only that Lotte's eyes shone with adoration of the poet but also that the poet's act of worship in this poem is recreated in Lotte's perception of the countryside. The possessive adjective in the phrase "deine Vergötterung" might be a genuine possessive rather than the "objective genitive" it is regularly interpreted to be, and Lotte's eyes may contain "worship belonging to" Klopstock rather than "worship directed toward" him.

Lotte's eyes contain pieces of Klopstock's poem even as Werther's text does. Not only are they full of Klopstock's "Vergötterung [worship, deification]," but they are full too of the wonderful, fructifying drops that appear in the poem as rain and in her eyes as tears. These drops (which quickly spread to Werther's eyes as well) have the same positive value in the novel as the raindrops do in the poem. Indeed, Lotte's tears are for Werther the locus of "Segensfülle," a plenitude of blessing, just as the rain in "Die Frühlingsfeier." Werther's language in fact makes Lotte figuratively equivalent to the thunderstorm in that she "pours forth a stream" of emotions over Werther by uttering the name of the poet ("in dem Strome . . . , den sie . . . über mich ausgoß," translated as "in the emotions . . . aroused in me"). Evidently, then, there is a reciprocal action of penetration at work here, for as Lotte's gaze penetrates this (already poeticized) landscape, she in turn is penetrated by the text she alludes to. It fills her up and makes her part of its discourse, while at the same time Werther makes the poem part of his own discourse about her. It becomes impossible to tell where "Klopstock" leaves off and "Lotte" begins.

The emotional saturation of the moment Werther experiences in Lotte's citation of Klopstock is so intense that he can hardly bear it. He says in fact that he could not bear it ("Ich ertrug's nicht," for some reason omitted from the translation; GW 27). Later on, he exclaims that he has lost all contact with his surroundings that night with Lotte: "The world around me has vanished." Of course this is a hyperbole, the kind of rhetorical extremism typical of Werther even in his more subdued moments, but the events of the story make it seem in retrospect alarmingly close to the truth. So do they, too, in the case of his exclamation of joy that his favorite spot for contemplation and reading, Wahlheim, is only half-an-hour's walk from Lotte's house: "Who would have thought, when I chose Wahlheim as a goal for my walks, that it lay so close to heaven?" (GS 42; GW 28). Werther wants "heaven" to be a figure of pure joy, indeed "the purest joy life can hold" (GS 42; GW 28), which he claims to be experiencing in the days immediately following his magic moment of intimacy with Lotte. But the language slips out of his control, as indeed events slip out of his control as the story progresses, and "heaven" comes to seem less the place of life's pure happiness and more the abode of death.

Werther is slowly but surely reading himself into a tale that ends in death, though he steadfastly avoids attending to the signs that would tell him so. In the same letter in which he describes Wahlheim as being close to heaven, he gives an account of yet another scene of reading:

> When I ride out to Wahlheim in the morning with the rising sun and pick some sweet young peas in the garden behind the inn and string them and read a little Homer as I do so; when I then go into the small kitchen and get a pan and melt some butter and put the pan on the fire to cook them and cover them and sit down beside them to toss them a little every now and then — I can feel so vividly how Penelope's high-spirited suitors [*übermütigen Freier*] slaughtered oxen and swine and carved them up and roasted them. Nothing can fill me with such true, serene emotions as any features of ancient, primitive life [*die Züge des patriarchalischen Lebens*] like this. Thank God I know how to fit them into my life without conceit [*ohne Affektation*]. (GS 42–43; GW 29)

Werther confesses his pride in his ability to weave together "without affectation" his own everyday experiences and the stories he reads in his beloved literary texts, and he is certainly justified. Nearly every letter displays some form of merger between life and literature that Werther takes to be part of the natural order of things. He does not congratulate himself on possessing some special talent for integrating traits of "patriarchal life" into his own but instead accepts that ability with thanks. There is only a little irony, then, in Werther's claim of avoiding affectation. There is considerable irony, though, in the choice he has made of a text to weave into his life just now. On the one hand, the comparison seems strained: Werther cooking his peas in the little kitchen in Wahlheim does not really seem comparable to the epic proportions of the suitors' mealtimes. These few, modest peas are next to nothing compared to the huge quantities of livestock slaughtered, butchered, roasted, and consumed by suitors who are "high-spirited," but perhaps also "arrogant" ("übermutig" can mean both). On the other hand, his comparison is entirely appropriate; it's just that Werther chooses not to draw attention to its most strikingly apposite features.

Werther surely is like the suitors in the *Odyssey,* though not really much like them when it comes to cooking and eating. The most immediately relevant point of comparison is that Werther, too, is now a suitor in pursuit of a woman who is already officially bonded to another. The man to whom she is bonded is, furthermore, a "worthy man who is away just now on business," just as Odysseus is away on the business of the Trojan War. It is striking that Werther carefully avoids mentioning this obvious parallel while he draws out in detail another comparison that does not seem particularly apt at all. He does not want to think of himself as engaging in the same inappropriate behavior as the suitors in Homer's poem — and yet he does identify with them. Because he cannot admit the important but painful similarity he distracts himself with another, the trivial matter of the food.[6]

It is easy to understand why Werther does not want to linger too long over the possibility of his figurative participation in the suitors' courting of Penelope. The outcome of that story involved the death of the suitors at the hands of the righteously angry Odysseus, and Werther does not care to think very much about that. He does not want to attend to a powerful warning that his own reading of Homer has offered him, though he cannot help but acknowledge the power of the reading. He knows he belongs in the story, but he refuses to read the text fully to its end. Like Dante's Paolo and Francesca, he is willing to use reading as the means of establishing intimacy with the forbidden partner, but he is unwilling to let himself see that a more careful reading would warn him off, would remind him that his "heaven" might be more a figure of death than one of erotic joy. There may not be any "affectation" in his mode of reading, as he says, but there is certainly a great deal of self-deception.

The text Werther cites as evidence of the extremity of his happiness would reveal, if read at all conscientiously, the deadly fate in store for him. He claims that his reading fills him with "true, serene emotions," but the story he reads can only produce serenity by being partially ignored. The characters in Homer's poem with whom he identifies and whom he cites as the standard by which he measures how full of life ("lebhaft") he feels function in the poem as agents and objects of death. They slaughter the livestock, squander the wealth of Odysseus's household, and finally get slaughtered themselves when the hero comes home and takes his vengeance. If one were to go looking for figures of liveliness in the *Odyssey*, one could hardly do worse than to settle on the suitors.

And yet, Werther's reading is still in its way appropriate and even correct. It is correct not only because the suitors are indeed the proper analogs of the man who sees himself now as Lotte's suitor but also because their attempt to fill the space left by the missing Odysseus is an attempt, though a mistaken and ultimately fatal one, on the part of the living to fill the gap left by one presumed dead. The suitors do live high while they live. But Werther's classical image may be inappropriate in a more profound and subtle way precisely because it puts into play precisely that which Werther would prefer to exclude. The citation of the suitors represents an uncanny moment of reading in which the repressed element of fatality returns, though still repressed, to infect a moment of "serene" happiness. Werther really does know his Homer, and he really does understand the negative aspects of his own situation, though he would prefer to keep some of that understanding out of sight. By comparing himself to Penelope's suitors he shows what he knows while at the same time denying that he knows it.

In addition to knowing that the Homer he loves for being full of life is full of death, Werther seems to know, or at least to suspect, that the process of reading, so essential to his experience of "the purest joy life can hold," inevitably brings with it a participation in death. He is therefore understandably ambivalent about reading, finding in it, on the one hand, intimations of heavenly bliss, but on the other, a repulsive whiff of the tomb. He falls in love with Lotte by way of texts and enjoys his closest contact with her when the two of them dissolve together as it were in the solvent of Klopstock's raindrops, but he also wants to keep her from being contaminated by dead letters. In a later letter to Wilhelm in which he reproduces — apparently word for word — Lotte's remarks about the death of her mother and her responsibilities toward her brothers and sisters, Werther complains: "That is what she said. But William, who can possibly repeat what she said? How can cold, dead letters express the heavenly revelation of her spirit? [*Wie kann der kalte, tote Buchstabe diese himmlische Blüte des Geistes darstellen*]" (GS 68; GW 58). The figurative transformation of Lotte into text (a figure out of myth, or a character from Homer, or the voice of Klopstock's ode) may be wonderful, but the actual transformation of Lotte's voice into the text of Werther's letter is distressing. But even in this moment of suspicion, in which he recognizes textuality as complicit with death and as destructive of genuine experience, Werther cannot help engaging in another characteristic act of self-textualization. The reader (whether Wilhelm or us) can be expected to recognize that the distinction Werther draws between deadly letter and the heavenly spirit derives not from Werther's experience of the moment but from reading the apostle Paul's famous dictum, "the letter kills, but the spirit gives life [*denn der Buchstabe tötet, der Geist aber macht lebendig*]."

Werther must both affirm and deny the possibility that a person can be a text. He must affirm it because the readability of a text is a quality that, when applied to persons, enriches, complicates, and deepens experience. It makes the living more alive. He must deny it because the fixity of a text is a deadly quality that, when applied to persons, becomes a form of rigor mortis. He wants Lotte and himself to possess the "good" qualities of texts, but he wants also to keep away the "bad" ones. His ambivalence is such that often, as in the passages just cited, he tries to do both at once, to ward off a deadly textuality while at the same time making use of a text's life-giving virtues. He just cannot be certain whether being like a book is a wonderful or a terrible thing, whether reading brings people into closer contact or drives them apart. He complains to Wilhelm about the Prince with whom he socializes while trying to stay away from Lotte:

> The Prince sees to it that I am well cared for, as well as could possibly be, but still I do not feel at home. (Basically we have nothing in common [*nichts gemein*] with each other.) He is a man of intellect, yet there is nothing extraordinary about his mind [*aber von ganz gemeinem Verstande*]; being with him is no more entertaining than reading a good book. (GS 83; GW 74)

At other times, as we know, Werther describes reading a good book in passionate and positive terms. In fact, the worst thing he can think of to say about Albert is that he does not respond to books with passion: "his heart does not respond to certain passages in a book over which Lotte's and mine would meet" (GS 84; GW 75). Reading with depth of feeling is the marker of sensitivity and depth, in this view. When Lotte is most like a book, as she is on the evening when Werther first meets her, she is most desirable. The Prince, however, is legible in the "dead" rather than the lively way, and reading him like a book is not thrilling but deadly dull. It is not that the Prince is a bad book and Lotte is a good one — but rather that Werther reads him as "letters" instead of "spirit." Deadly letters evidently infect Werther's understanding of him, as Werther's description moves from the assertion that the two of them have nothing in common ("nichts gemein") to an equally definite assertion that the Prince's intelligence is perfectly ordinary ("ganz gemein"). What was at first cited as a complete absence becomes almost instantly plenitude, as if the Prince had been suddenly turned into a pure text in which the citation of the term "gemein," even in a denial, makes "Gemeinheit" its most salient characteristic. When speaking with Lotte, Werther avoids saying that he and she share "etwas gemein," that is, both "something in common" and "something common." He prefers to speak of "Sympathie" and thereby (he hopes) spare her contamination with these deadly letters.

Scenes of reading are so important and so frequent in Goethe's novel because the uncertain valorization of legibility is precisely the point of greatest interest — and greatest danger — about Werther's personality. The dead letters of the word "gemein" may infect the Prince with their negativity, but other letters offer the possibility of joy. Werther is prepared to find in an unfinished note Lotte wrote to Albert the occasion for casting himself in the role of Lotte's beloved:

> She wrote a little note to her husband, who is away on business. It started off with the words, "My best, my dearest one. Come home as soon as you can. I live in joyous anticipation of your return [*ich erwarte dich mit tausend Freuden*]." Just then a friend came in [. . .]. The little note was forgotten, and in the course of the evening I came across it. I read it and smiled, and she asked me why I was smiling. "What a divine gift our imagination [*Einbildungskraft*] is!" I said. "For a moment I imagined [*ich konnte mir einen Augeblick vorspiegeln*] it was written for me." She said nothing, but she seemed displeased by my behavior, and I was silenced. (GS 87; GW 79)

The fragmentary letter leaves a gap to be filled in by the unintended reader. Its very fragmentariness makes it even more open to reading than it would normally be. Not only is the addressee uncertain but so too is the nature of the contents. The opening words may be (as the translation suggests) entirely conventional, indicating no more than that Lotte understands the tone she is to adopt in speaking to her fiancé. They may be construed, on the other hand, as an unconventional and explicit promise of erotic attention. The phrase "ich erwarte dich mit tausend Freuden" shuttles back and forth in the ambiguity surrounding the possessor of the "thousand joys." Is the writer merely saying that the thought of her beloved's return gives her great joy, or is she telling him that she has ready a thousand joys for him when he gets back? The former is a proper message, appropriate for a young lady to send to her honored fiancé; the latter is an improper message, appropriate only in an erotically charged situation.

In order to read it in the second way one must ignore its context, and that is what Werther does. He allows himself to imagine that the words he reads represent the opening of a passionate love letter directed to himself. This act of imagination is also, however, an act of self-delusion, as Werther's language seems to recognize. When he exclaims that "imagination" is a "divine gift," he uses the word "Einbildungskraft," a term that has a potential for negative valorization far greater than the English "imagination." It suggests both the power of mental construction and the possibility of hallucination. This same uncertainty is even more prominent in the verb "vorspiegeln" that Werther uses in the next sentence, once again translated as "imagine." This word can mean both "to present (something) clearly" and "to deceive." Werther may be either "presenting to himself" the perfectly reasonable possibility that Lotte would write him a love letter or he may be "deluding himself" with wild fantasy. Werther's rhetoric thus withholds a decision as to whether his reading of the note is reasonable and proper, though mistaken, or hopelessly delusional.

Lotte is clearly troubled by this unsettled rhetoric. She cannot be sure what Werther is telling her, whether he means to make a joke about the outrageousness of his reading or to suggest that it might after all have been the correct one. If it is a joke it is perhaps harmless, though still clearly out of bounds under the circumstances; if it is a serious suggestion, it calls for denial. Her displeasure demonstrates her knowledge that she ought somehow to put a stop to Werther's improper acts of reading, but her subsequent silence shows that she cannot bring herself to do it. Sensing this, Werther falls silent, ostensibly terminating this act of reading. It becomes evident soon enough, however, that he has not given up on it at all, that on the contrary he preserves and cherishes his impertinent construction. In the letter after the one immediately following this episode, Werther says that he greeted Lotte after a short absence by kissing her hand "mit tausend Freuden" (loosely translated as "my heart overflowing with joy"). By appropriating to himself the phrase from Lotte's letter he confirms the interpretation in which it is the lover, none other than Werther himself, who is to experience the thousand joys Lotte had mentioned. He does indeed experience them, and he does so by kissing her. She therefore fulfills, unwittingly, the unintended erotic promise of the fragmentary note and confirms the correctness of Werther's improper reading.

Werther's employment of an aggressive, "oblivious" form of reading on Lotte's letter, a reading that deliberately ignores the text's intention, is part of his attempt to make the texts he reads conform as closely as possible to the structure of his internal, emotional world.[7] Although it is clear enough that, on one level at any rate, Werther knows that his interpretation of the note-fragment is both incorrect and improper, it is also evident that he hopes to take advantage of the opportunity offered by his ostensible mistake to flush out a word or gesture of reassurance from Lotte, to get her to say in effect, "No, you're not completely wrong. Even though the letter was not meant for you, its sentiments were." Since her embarrassed silence is readable as precisely this assurance, Werther can imagine to himself that his strategy has been successful and that by purloining this letter intended for another he has in fact taken it to its appropriate, though unnamed, addressee. His imaginative reading of the letter has actually changed its nature, transformed it into what he wanted it to be.

The close relation between the books Werther reads and the state of Werther's soul shapes not only the meaning of the material read but also the way in which the reader perceives Werther. We read him through his reading. Goethe depends heavily on Werther's descriptions of his interactions with books as an extremely effective way of signaling what is happening to Werther's feelings, perhaps even before Werther himself becomes aware of them. When he exclaims that "Ossian has replaced Homer in my heart" (GS 90; GW 82), it is a trumpet-clear announcement that depression is replacing the manic excitement he had felt on first falling in love with Lotte. His description of what most attracts him to Ossian expresses his changed mood:

> What a world it is into which this divine poet leads me! Oh, to wander across the heath in a blustering wind storm, by the light of a waning moon, as it conjures up the ghosts of our ancestors in clouds of mist! Oh, to hear, above the rushing of a forest stream, the half-fading groans of spectres issuing from caves in the hillside, and the keening maiden weeping herself into the grave beside the four moss-clad grass-o'ergrown stones of her noble fallen hero — her beloved. When I see him — the roving, hoary bard — seeking the footsteps of his forefathers on the wide moor only to find their gravestones; [. . .] when I can read the profound sorrow on his brow and see this last, forsaken, magnificent one reel exhausted to his grave [. . .] Ah my friend, then, like a noble armiger, I would like to draw my sword and in a trice free my liege lord from the agonizing torment of a life that is a gradual death and send my soul after the liberated demigod! (GS 90–91; GW 82)

The world of Werther's Ossian is dominated by graves (the word "Grab" appears again and again in the passage) and with the imagery of decline. "Life" in such a world cannot be distinguished from "a gradual death." It is a world one would prefer to leave quickly, which is precisely why Werther wants to linger in the text that presents it.

Werther loves the liveliness of this death.[8] The dead of poetry are a very active group, and this scene of death is in fact full of sound and movement. Ghosts make noise enough to be heard over the roar of the forest stream, and the dying maiden and the dying bard make their deaths action-filled events. The winds blow, the mists roll in, figures cross the moor in the moonlight, the tall grasses wave. Ossian's characters do not just lay themselves down and die but rather enact vivid dramas of spiritual liberation. The dying that takes place in the text therefore appears more full of life, and indeed more attractive, than the drab existence Werther leads when separated from Lotte. The legible sorrow of all this death, read both on the page and on the brow of the bard conjured up by the words on the page, seems preferable to a life rendered illegible by the unavailability of the beloved. "A friend came to see Lotte, I went into the next room to find a book — and couldn't read" (GS 91; GW 83). The text that he is in fact unable to read is the conversation between Lotte and her friend concerning some mortally ill people about whom they clearly do not care at all. Werther feels himself rejected by this conversation, rejected metaphorically too from Lotte's household and from her heart, whereas the morbid text of Ossian had welcomed him in.

As the novel progresses, Werther reads himself further and further into the dead world of letters. The lively spirit he finds in books is no longer the joyful liveliness of sympathy and desire; it is instead the spirit of suffering and of death. Books are still the mirror of Werther's soul, but the quality of the soul has changed: "Sometimes I tell myself my fate is unique. Consider all men fortunate, I tell myself; no one has ever suffered like you. Then I read a poet of ancient times, and it is as though I were looking deep into my own heart" (GS 95; GW 88). Where formerly Werther could see only the joy in ancient texts, as when he carefully ignored the deadly implications of comparing himself to Penelope's suitors, now he finds only immense sorrow. He is still sure, however, that his true home is in these texts, and he is no less eager than before to inscribe himself in these ancient tomes. When he finally makes his decision to commit suicide, he imagines the consequence of his death to be a world straight out of Ossian. Here are some lines from the letter to Wilhelm about the wonderful world of Ossian:

> When I see him [. . .], still finding a melancholy yet glowing joy in the powerless presence of the shades of his departed ones, and can hear him cry as he looks down upon the cold earth and the tall waving grasses, "The wanderer will come, will come who knew me in my glory and will ask, 'Where is the bard, oh, where is Fingal's admirable son?' His footsteps cross my grave and he asks in vain for me on earth!" (GS 90–91; GW 82)

And here are some lines from Werther's last letter to Lotte, containing his vision of her life after his death:

> When you climb the hilltop on a beautiful summer's evening, think of me. Think of how I used to come walking up the valley, then glance at the churchyard and look at my grave, see how the wind causes the tall

grass to wave in the light of the setting sun. I was so calm when I began to write this, and now — now I am crying like a child because I can see it all so vividly [*da alles so lebhaft um mich wird*]. (GS 110; GW 104–5)

We know very well why he can see it so vividly (*lebhaft*): he has seen it all before, including even the tall grass waving in the wind, in "Ossian." He finds this scene so attractive that he finds another version of it to translate into German and to read to Lotte at their final meeting: "And in the morn the wanderer will come, the wanderer will come who saw me in my glory. His eye will seek me in the field but he will not find me" (GS 119; GW 114). Since he cannot be Lotte's actual lover and become a constant presence in her life, he seeks instead to fill her mind with his absence, made permanent as a legible trace. His life-after-death will be as a textualized remainder that holds forever open the space that he no longer occupies.

But to hold the space open in the way he wants, he has to try to make sure that his death has the character of a noble sacrifice, that it is not seen simply as the despairing gesture of a man unable to cope with the kinds of adversities others learn to live with. His attempt in this direction is to stage another scene of reading, one in which he can no longer participate because it takes place after his death. He leaves a copy of Lessing's *Emilia Galotti* open on his lectern. By reading this particular text, and by leaving it for others to read when he is gone, Werther signals his desire to have his suicide understood in the context of Emilia's death in the play. Emilia is threatened with dishonor at the hands of a lecherous and tyrannical prince. When it becomes clear what the prince has in mind for Emilia, her father, like an ancient Roman paterfamilias, stabs her to death to keep her from a fate he at any rate considers worse than death. Werther's choice of this as his final reading material suggests that he saw himself, and hoped others would see him, as saving Lotte from a similar dishonor by removing temptation permanently from her path. Werther's death might even be considered more noble than Emilia's, since it is not his own but a loved one's honor that is saved by it.

This attempt to read himself into the noble plot of *Emilia Galotti* depends, of course, on a willingness on the part of the reader (whoever that reader may be) to accept the implied analogy between Werther and Emilia. But here again, just as in the case of his citation of Penelope's suitors, a negative reading *in malo* refuses to be suppressed. The comparison between the plot of *Werther* and the plot of Lessing's play is in fact most obvious in terms of the love-triangles. In each there is a desirable woman who is loved by two men, an appropriate and an inappropriate lover. The inappropriate lover attempts to seduce the woman away from the appropriate one. In this analogy, Werther is not like the noble Emilia at all, but more like the villainous Prince of Guastalla. This distressing reading is rendered all the more pertinent by the fact that Lotte has made it quite clear, at the close of the reading from Werther's translation of Ossian, that she is in no danger of being tempted to sin. She firmly thrusts Werther away from her and locks herself in another room.

Werther's attempts to read himself into Homer, Ossian, and even *Emilia Galotti* are in a way all too successful. The sensitive young man makes himself so completely into a text that he becomes, like a true text, unable to control the acts of reading performed upon him. He becomes a set of dead letters in need of a spirit, friendly or unfriendly, to guide him and give him life. He hopes for the best, but the novel's closing sentence suggests the worst. Though his lifeless body is now more than ever in need of *Geist*, the narrator reports that "Kein Geistlicher hat ihn begleitet" — "No pastor [spiritual person] accompanied him" (GW 150).

Notes

[1] For a discussion of the relation between Goethe's version of Ossian and the "Gaelic" poet, see Ó Dochartaigh. An examination of various scenes of translation in Goethe's works can be found in Asman.

[2] On the relation between Werther's "sorrows" and his experience of literature, see Pütz.

[3] The topic of Werther as a reader has been examined from other perspectives, notably by Waniek and by Duncan. Dotzler examines the novel from the perspective of reception theory, basing his interpretation primarily on a notion of reading derived from Iser's concept of the *Leerstelle*. Dotzler's focus is not so much on Werther the reader as on the problem of how to read *Werther*.

[4] For a canny assessment of Werther's relation to Homer, see Tobol and Washington. The topic has been addressed in a comparative context by Tisch.

[5] On the role and identity of the "editor," see Schweitzer. For a different view of the editorial intervention at the end of the novel, see Bennett.

[6] Tobol and Washington comment on this passage: "A comparison of Werther's circumstances with those in the Homeric passage suggests that the situation has already developed an ominous turn. While superficially both show the preparation of a meal, in the *Odyssey* this is the last meal of the suitors" (598).

[7] For a discussion of "oblivious" reading and its cultural context, see Koelb, *Incredulous Reader* 143–44.

[8] Goethe and his creation Werther were hardly alone in experiencing a paradoxical liveliness in the lugubrious "Ossian" poems. A short poem by the Russian Romantic Mikhail Lermontov called "Ossian's Grave" captures precisely this same mood: "Under a covering of fog, / On a moor under a stormy heaven, / Lies the grave of Ossian, / In Scottish hills I call my own. // And there my slumbering spirit flies / To breathe the air that he inhaled / And from this now forgotten grave / To come alive again myself! . . ." (Ferber 440). The dead past is redolent with the breath of life in a fashion comparable to Shelley's "Ode on the West Wind."

4: "O Read for Pity's Sake!": Keats's *Endymion*

JOHN KEATS'S *ENDYMION: A POETIC ROMANCE* begins with a famous assertion of immortality: "A thing of beauty is a joy for ever" (1.1). Chief among the poet's examples of deathless loveliness is the tale he is about to tell of Endymion, for it depicts "the grandeur of the dooms / We have imagined for the mighty dead." It belongs among the "lovely tales that we have heard or read" issuing from "an endless fountain of immortal drink" whose source is the realms of heaven (1.20–24).

Why would Keats expect himself or his audience to gain access to the immortality of beauty by reading about the doings of the dead?

I am proposing that the answer to this question runs as follows: Romantic poetics often associate undying aesthetic power with reading about the "mighty dead," and therefore a Romantic narrative wishing to invoke the power of the aesthetic moment will very often make a gesture equivalent to Keats's rhyme of "dead" and "read." Such a narrative is quite likely to depict as part of its story the revivification of apparently lifeless matter in a scene of reading.

Endymion offers just such a scene in Book 3, which recounts the hero's dream-adventures under the sea. Endymion, wandering through the ocean "with nothing save that hollow vast, that foam'd, / Above, around, and at his feet; save things / More dead than Morpheus' imaginings" (3.120–22), comes at last upon a figure that at least appears to be alive, an old man:

> Upon a weeded rock this old man sat,
> And his white hair was awful, and a mat
> Of weeds were cold beneath his cold thin feet;
> And, ample as the largest winding-sheet,
> A cloak of blue wrapp'd up his aged bones,
> O'er wrought with symbols by the deepest groans
> Of ambitious magic: every ocean-form
> Was woven in with black distinctness; storm
> And calm, and whispering, and hideous roar,
> Quicksand and whirlpool, and deserted shore
> Were emblem'd in the woof (3.193–203)

This old man is in the sea both literally and figuratively, for the cloak he wears is a kind of text of the sea, its blue folds imprinted with representations of "every shape / That swims, or dives, or sleeps, 'twixt cape and cape" (3.203–4). The vast ocean that engulfs him is mastered and made legible by this picture book of a cloak. Upon it even the sprightly sea nymphs in Neptune's court "look up and wait" in eternal attendance upon their lord. Like the figures on the Grecian urn Keats would later describe, the inhabitants of the sea have all been immortalized in a kind of living death, inscribed in perfect legibility upon the garment of a dead man, a "winding-sheet."

The old man has in addition to the text he wears another, which he reads:

> Beside this old man lay a pearly wand,
> And in his lap a book, the which he conn'd
> So steadfastly, that the new denizen
> Had time to keep him in amazed ken,
> To mark these shadowings, and stand in awe. (3.213–17)

While the old man, who we learn subsequently is called Glaucus,[1] sits engrossed in reading a traditional book, the young man Endymion has time to decipher the markings on the remarkable text-cloak. Eventually, however, the old man becomes aware of his visitor, and immediately upon taking note of him exclaims, "O Jove! I shall be young again, be young! / O shell-borne Neptune, I am pierc'd and stung, / With new-born life!" (3.237–39). There is a connection, though at this point it is only implicit in the juxtaposition, between the reading going on and the "new life" Glaucus feels surging within himself. The exact nature of that connection is not made clear: all Keats's reader knows for sure is that the old man, the reader of the book, believes that the young man, the reader of the cloak, will bring him back from the brink of death.

As Glaucus tells his story, we learn that he has in fact been expecting Endymion to come and rejuvenate him. Long ago Glaucus had read the story of Endymion's coming in a book that he acquired mysteriously — the very book Endymion has found him reading. Glaucus had witnessed a shipwreck in which all hands were lost:

> The crew had gone,
> By one and one, to pale oblivion;
> And I was gazing on the surges prone,
> With many a scalding tear and many a groan,
> When at my feet emerg'd an old man's hand,
> Grasping this scroll, and this same slender wand.
> I knelt with pain — reach'd out my hand — had grasp'd
> These treasures [. . .] I was athirst
> To search the book, and in the warming air
> Parted its dripping leaves with eager care. (3.665–78)

Glaucus thus receives the book almost from the hand of death itself, but this potentially daunting circumstance does not diminish his interest. On the contrary, his desire to read is so powerful that it is indistinguishable from a physical appetite. The book becomes in the old man's trope a liquid that can be consumed to slake his spiritual thirst. "Strange matters did it treat of, and drew on / My soul page after page, till well nigh won / Into forgetfulness" (3.679–81). But suddenly Glaucus comes upon a passage that seems to bear directly on his situation. It describes a "forlorn wretch" (3.689) living in the sea, condemned to die after spending a thousand years as a feeble old man. But the text offers a ray of hope for this old man: if he spends his life in study, exploring "all forms and substances / Straight homeward to their symbol-essences" (3.699–700), and if he carefully gathers all the bodies of lovers lost at sea, then one day a young man will come and perform a special act that will set him free.

Glaucus does not quote enough of the text of his mysterious book for us to know what this act might be, nor does Endymion know; but the young hero nonetheless declares himself ready to perform it. As it turns out, it involves more interactions with the mysterious texts in Glaucus's possession:

> "Let us commence,"
> Whisper'd the guide, stuttering with joy, "even now."
> He spake, and, trembling like an aspen-bough,
> Began to tear his scroll in pieces small,
> Uttering the whole time mumblings funeral.
> He tore it into pieces small as snow
> That drifts unfeather'd when bleak northerns blow;
> And having done it, took his dark blue cloak
> And bound it round Endymion. (3.744–52)

After waving his wand in the air, he tells Endymion to undo a thread (perhaps from the blue cloak — we are not told) and tie the end to a "clue" (ball of thread). Although no specific information is given, it may be that Endymion is meant to unravel the mystical garment that Glaucus has placed upon him. The young man accomplishes the task, whatever it is, with stunning swiftness; then he is given another: "Here is a shell; 'tis pearly blank to me, / Nor mark'd with any sign or charactery — / Canst thou read aught? O read for pity's sake!" (3.761–63). Although the shell is devoid of markings, the fact that its blankness is "pearly" indicates that its apparent emptiness may conceal something of very high value. In the New Testament Jesus explicitly analogizes the Kingdom of Heaven itself to "a pearl of great price" (Matt. 13:45–46).

The idea of "reading" a blank shell must have been associated in Keats's mind with the familiar game of holding a shell to the ear and "hearing" the ocean. That this association was readily available to him is attested by a poem he wrote in the summer of 1815, just under two years before beginning work on *Endymion*. In the seventh and eighth stanzas of "On

Receiving a Curious Shell from the Same Ladies," he imagines the shell he has received from the Mathew sisters as a fairy tent, a "canopy" under which the fairy king Oberon played sad songs on his lute in anguished longing for the absent Titiania. The ninth stanza, anticipating one of the central themes of the "Ode on a Grecian Urn," proclaims the immortality of this fairy music:

> In this little dome, all those melodies strange,
> Soft, plaintive, and melting, for ever will sigh;
> Nor e'er will the notes from their tenderness change;
> Nor e'er will the music of Oberon die. (33–36)

Keats was evidently, even at the very beginning of his poetic career, deeply interested in the mysterious capability of the imagination to find something both deathless and endlessly significant in an empty space.

The shell embodies a further paradox, clearly fascinating to the young poet, of immensity — the ocean itself — residing inside the most intimately tiny places.[2] That a seashell could be a microcosm enfolding within itself the macrocosmic universe was a notion Keats could have found — and probably did find — in one of his favorite poems, Wordsworth's *Excursion* (1814):[3]

> I have seen
> A curious Child, who dwelt upon a tract
> Of inland ground, applying to his ear
> The convolutions of a smooth-lipped Shell;
> To which, in silence hushed, his very soul
> Listened intensely; and his countenance soon
> Brightened with joy; for murmurings from within
> Were heard, — sonorous cadences! whereby,
> To his belief, the Monitor expressed
> Mysterious union with its native Sea.
> Even such a Shell the Universe itself
> Is to the ear of Faith. (*Excursion* 191–92)[4]

The shell passage in *Endymion* certainly alludes to this paradox of enormous significance inhabiting a small, empty space, but it does so in a truly bizarre fashion. Having introduced the topic at a moment of high drama, the poem suddenly veers away. The text says nothing more about the shell; it does not even tell us whether or not Endymion attempted to read it, or whether or not he was successful. The reader can only guess that the hero does somehow decipher the pearly blank space, for Glaucus immediately exclaims, "Olympus! we are safe!" It seems unlikely that he would have uttered such a cry if, having implored the youth to read, Endymion had failed to do so. The poem, however, is as blank on this matter as the shell itself, and the injunction to "read for pity's sake" carries over from events depicted in the poem to the interaction between the poem and its audience. The poem actually requires its readers to follow the example of its protagonist by imaginatively supplying much missing information. Keats's audience is obliged to imagine where the mysterious thread comes from, what happens when its end is tied, and what Endymion finds to read in the precious unmarked spaces of the shell.

Even when the poem seems filled with specific information, the reader is often left with the perplexing task of filling that information with meaning. After telling Endymion to read the shell, for example, Glaucus instructs him to break the wand against a lyre. We are told directly that " 'twas done" and are given a description of the results of the action: "and straight with sudden swell and fall / Sweet music breath'd her soul away, and sigh'd / A lullaby to silence" (3.766–68). The language is highly ambiguous, almost as much in need of filling in as the shell. What are we to suppose happens when the music "breath'd her soul away"? Does this mean that the music started, or that it stopped? We are not brought any greater clarity when we hear that whatever happened could be described as "a lullaby to silence." Would such a lullaby be a noise that ushers silence away, or one that ushers it in? We will have to decide for ourselves whether something is beginning or ending here, whether the language is describing a void or a plenitude. A few lines later, to be sure, the text unmistakably announces the presence of music from "flutes and viols," but it is by no means certain that this is the "lullaby to silence" mentioned before. One would not expect a lute to produce the sounds of flutes and viols, but this is a magical scene, after all, and who's to say what magical lyres sound like?

The magical music, or equally magical silence, that follows upon the breaking of the wand accompanies the next of Endymion's tasks: he is to scatter the torn-up pieces of the scroll on Glaucus and the corpses of dead lovers he had assembled according to the instructions in his book. As soon as he is touched by the fragments, Glaucus transforms into a young man, and his beloved Scylla arises from the dead. Endymion then goes about the business of reanimating all the drowned corpses, "showering those powerful fragments on the dead" (3.784). The shower of textual remnants is as potent as the rays of the sun:

> And, as he passed, each [corpse] lifted up its head,
> As doth a flower at Apollo's touch,
> Death felt it to his inwards: 'twas too much:
> Death fell a weeping in his charnel-house. (3.785–88)

This sweeping and successful campaign against the kingdom of death takes place in a context of books and reading. The reanimation of the dead lovers results directly from their contact with a text, as if indeed the vital force had entered the lifeless bodies from the fragments themselves.

The book containing the power to bring the dead back to life is itself destroyed in the process of reanimation, or at any rate its physical manifestation is obliterated. Whatever is left of the book now inhabits the revivified bodies, and we cannot be more precise about the nature of the residue than to identify it as the vital force, life itself. The book disperses its little fragments of life like a shower of sunlight, but in so doing it makes itself incorporeal, no longer "mark'd with any sign of charactery." The magical scroll is now like the shell that Endymion was to read — an illegible but nonetheless powerful force.

The poem keeps its readers' attention principally focused on the joyous scene of revivification, the reunion of the lovers, and the discomfiture of Death, but we cannot ignore the fact that this happy revivification is accomplished by means of multiple acts of destruction. Glaucus tears up the scroll, Endymion breaks the wand, and the great blue cloak/winding-sheet possibly gets unraveled. It would be easy to suppose that all of these undoings represent no more than the magician's abjuration of the tools of magic, something like Prospero's breaking his staff and drowning his book in *The Tempest* (5.1). Indeed, Keats probably did have Shakespeare in mind when he composed the passage, but he radically changed the situation. The magician is not casting away tools he no longer needs; rather, by destroying these objects he makes the magic happen. The music swells, or falls, or both, only after the wand is broken upon the lyre, and the corpses come to life only in response to the touch of the dismembered book.

The cloak's unraveling (if that is what happens) suggests one metaphorical explanation for these uncanny actions. As weaving cloth is a classical figure for accomplishing the fate of the living, so is unraveling the "winding-sheet" a figure for undoing the work of death. Destroying the book may be a similar act of undoing history. Although this seems a promising line of interpretation, it fails to explain why the dead do not arise as soon as the book is torn up. Why do they need to feel the actual touch of the fragments? And why, in the midst of this tale of destruction and reanimation, must Endymion read the blank space of the shell?

Evidently reading is crucially important to the process, no less important in fact than the acts of undoing that accompany it. Strangely enough, Endymion's reading of the shell is recounted among the various moments of destruction, as if tearing up the book, unraveling the cloak, breaking the wand, and reading the shell were all equivalent in some mystic way. It would be easy to assent to this equivalence if we could conceive of what is happening as a process of creation or re-creation, for we readily suppose that reading is such a re-creative process. But we tend to withhold assent when we consider that the book, among other things, is destroyed. Reading is not supposed to destroy books but rather to make them, and their readers, come to life.

It is possible to get an idea of how Keats might imagine a reading process that could both destroy the text and reanimate its readers, its characters, and its fictional world by looking at another passage in *Endymion* from much earlier in the poem. It describes the hero himself, who has fallen into a deep swoon:

> But in the self-same fixed trance he kept,
> Like one that on the earth had never slept.
> Aye, even as dead still as a marble man,
> Frozen in that old tale Arabian. (1.403–6)

Endymion is not really dead, as the drowned lovers are supposed to be, but only figuratively "dead still." In a tale such as this, however, in which death may be only a temporary state and life takes on every appearance of death, the difference between literal and figurative death counts for very little. The "dead" Endymion, then, participates in an additional figure that places him in a book. The phrase "frozen in that old tale Arabian" surely refers to the "actual" action of a person being immobilized, as is indeed related in the "Tale of the Ensorceled Prince" (and other stories) in the *Thousand and One Nights*. But it might also refer to the figurative "freezing" of a person considered as a depiction in a work of art rather than as a living being, like the "marble men" Keats speaks of in the "Grecian Urn" (42). The marble man may thus become unfrozen in two ways: either by the reversal of the magic act recounted in the story (as when the spell on the Prince is reversed, or when "the frozen God" Saturn is aroused by Thea in *Hyperion* [1.87–90]); or by reversing the process that figuratively embedded the person in the artwork in the first place. In the case of a written tale, that embedding was the writing; and so to "thaw out" the frozen text and release the living person within, one would have to "undo" the writing. One would read.

The interplay between life and death through reading that makes up much of the subject matter of Book 3 appears to be based on a paradoxical notion that a text may be both the source of life and a locus of death and destruction. One might wonder why Keats could expect his readers to accept this paradox without a word of explanation, but the explanation lay relatively close at hand. Keats could count on assent and even understanding because his figures are based on terms set forth in the familiar biblical topos of letter and spirit from 2 Corinthians. Paul's figure deploys a set of concepts that allow for exactly the sort of fictional narrative we find in *Endymion* and for just such a scene as the revivification of the drowned corpses in Book 3. One logical extension of Paul's proposition is that texts in general must be some kind of mixture of dead matter (letters) and vivifying spirit. A purely spiritual text would have no letters at all — and Keats has placed such a text right in the middle of his scene of revivification in the form of the shell Glaucus asks Endymion to read "for pity's sake." True to the logic of such a text, Keats refrains from attempting to ensnare it in letters of his own, leaving us to fill in the blank with imagination.

In Keats's view the imagination is capable of just such remarkable feats of revivification. In Book 1 of *Endymion* there is a discourse on the power of music, part of a passage that Keats described in a letter as "a regular stepping of the Imagination towards a Truth," and as "perhaps [. . .] the greatest Service to me of any thing I ever did" (*Letters* 59). In the music passage we find another vivid scene of raising the dead:

> hist, when the airy stress
> Of music's kiss impregnates the free winds,
> And with a sympathetic touch unbinds
> Eolian magic from their lucid wombs;
> Then old songs waken from enclouded tombs;
> Old ditties sigh above their father's grave;
> Ghosts of melodious prophecyings rave
> Round every spot where trod Apollo's foot;
> Bronze clarions awake, and faintly bruit,
> Where long ago a giant battle was. (1.783–92)

The "Eolian magic" in this passage may refer simply to the action whereby music is carried from its origin to the listener through the air; or it may pick up on the image made famous by Coleridge in his "Eolian Harp" poem, first published in 1796 but revised and republished in 1817, almost exactly while Keats was at work on the first draft of *Endymion*. Coleridge's figure of the wind-harp, hung in the window of his cottage in Somerset, expands on the idea of the wind animating the harp-strings to propose that the whole living natural world is brought to life by a universal spirit:

> And what if all of animated nature
> Be but organic Harps diversely fram'd,
> That tremble into thought, as o'er them sweeps,
> Plastic and vast, one intellectual breeze,
> At once the Soul of each, and God of all? (44–48)

Although we cannot be certain that Keats had in mind Coleridge's Eolian harp while he wrote *Endymion*, it is clear enough that he was thinking along similar lines about the animating power of the spirit.[5] Both Keats and Coleridge call upon the tradition that equates moving air (the breathing of animals, the winds, the *ruach* of the Lord in the opening of *Genesis*) with the divine, life-giving spirit, just as Paul does in 2 Corinthians. What is most strikingly different about Keats's treatment of the topic is that, while Coleridge leaves open the possibility that "animated nature" might be at least partially alive *before* the "intellectual breeze" works upon it, Keats appears to insist that the material is dead to begin with. The repetition of burial places, first "tombs" and then a "grave," assures that the reader cannot miss the point: the revivifying power of the spirit works upon matter that we ordinarily assume to be completely dead. Given this sort of power, the imagination might easily produce a purely spiritual text out of the emptiness of an unwritten blank, as is called for by Glaucus's command that Endymion read a lifeless shell.

Glaucus's command invites comparison with that of the beholder of the Grecian urn: "therefore, ye soft pipes, play on / Not to the sensual ear, but more endear'd, / Pipe to the spirit ditties of no tone" (12–14). This spiritual music has the same power that animates the purely spiritual text: it has a life that passes through and beyond death. The actual function of such a funerary urn as the one Keats describes is to contain the ashes of the dead, and for that reason the inside of the vessel necessarily represents the habitation of a dead soul. But such a soul can also be understood as a dormant spirit awaiting rebirth. The intellectual charm of the urn is the possibility of such a renewal.

Even the concept of a vessel fosters such a notion, for it defines an emptiness that may be refilled endlessly. The "happy melodist" is able to produce "songs for ever new" (23–24) because only imaginary songs provided by the viewer can ever emerge from his pipes. Keats portrays the urn as a paradigmatic work of art, not for what it offers (which may be nothing at all, or only ashes), but for what we must bring to it. It tells no story itself but instead offers only hints that can become occasions for the viewer to read a story into it. Its ability to express "a flowery tale more sweetly than our rhyme" (4) lies in the set of questions it elicits:

> What leaf-fring'd legend haunts about thy shape
>   Of deities or mortals, or of both,
>   In Tempe or the dales of Arcady?
> What men or gods are these? What maidens loth?
> What mad pursuit? What struggle to escape?
>   What pipes and timbrels? What wild ecstasy? (5–10)

The urn offers no answers to these rhetorical questions. Its discourse is mostly a blank, at best a few sketchy lines that one may readily read between.

The power of the urn, then, lies in the way it interacts with the beholder. The urn-as-figure, transformed by the imagination of the beholder/poet, is a living thing, a "foster-child of silence" (2); but the urn-as-object is an inert piece of matter with no voice, a "silent form" that does not think for itself but rather can "tease *us* out of thought" (44; emphasis added) without recourse to words of its own. The "bold lover" (17) can love forever because his love is eternally renewed by those who interpret the shapes fused into the pottery surface. The loving couple on the urn, then, is much like the couples in *Endymion* who are revived by the touch of a fragmented text. The "marble men" (42) depicted on the urn, the "marble man" (*Endymion* 1:405) in the Arabian tale, and the corpses Glaucus has gathered are all frozen in a story in which we may intervene. We may, like Endymion, read for pity's sake and thaw them out, reanimate them, by offering our living spirit to their dead letters.

It may be true that Keats, a little older, could present in the "Ode on a Grecian Urn" a more successful and more concise expression of how a modern imagination interacts with what he called, in his little preface to *Endymion*, "the beautiful mythology of Greece" (*Complete Poems* 64),[6] but *Endymion* gives in some respects a more complete picture of how Keats wrestled with the implications of the aesthetic values he espoused. The "dooms we have imagined for the dead" are the subject of both poems, and both treat the unsettling relation between death, emptiness, and matter on the one hand, and life, plenitude, and spirit on the other. What emerges more clearly in *Endymion*, however, is that from early in his career Keats recognized as a core myth of his poetic enterprise the revivification of the dead through reading. He may not have recognized, however, as we now do, that this myth was a central element not only of his work but of the entire Romantic phenomenon.

Notes

[1] The Latin word *glaucus* means "blue-gray" and was ordinarily used to indicate the color of the sea. Various sea-divinities bore the name "Glaucus" in classical mythology, including in particular a mortal fisherman who was transformed into a god of the sea (see *Oxford Latin Dictionary*, "glaucus").

[2] Bachelard, who devotes an entire chapter to shells, reports the assertion of a priest that "the shells of shell-fish, after being ground to a powder, come to life again and start reproducing, if this powder is sprinkled with salt water" (115).

[3] In a letter to the painter B. R. Haydon (10 Jan. 1818), Keats wrote, "I am convinced that there are three things to rejoice at in this Age — The Excursion[,] Your Pictures, and Hazlitt's depth of Taste" (*Letters* 48). It is noteworthy that Keats puts Wordsworth's poem first in this list, even before the work of the letter's recipient.

[4] References to Wordsworth's *Excursion* are to page numbers instead of line numbers, as there are no line numbers in the 1814 edition.

[5] Though Keats was certainly familiar with Coleridge's work, his thinking about the way in which nature is made animate by the spirit may have been just as profoundly influenced by Wordsworth's *Excursion*. For more on the impact of the *Excursion* on the second generation of Romantic poets, see Piper 154–64.

[6] It seems likely that Keats got much of his sense of the importance of Greek mythology from Book 4 of Wordsworth's *Excursion*, as Piper explains (154–64).

5: "Graecum Est, Non Legitur": Hugo's *Notre-Dame de Paris*

THE FIRST SCENE OF READING THAT ONE ENCOUNTERS in Victor Hugo's *Notre-Dame de Paris* (1831) does not belong to the story proper but to the paratextual apparatus that the author placed before it. A prefatory note dated March, 1831, explains that Hugo had visited the great cathedral a few years before writing his novel and had found inscribed on a wall "in a dark recess of one of the towers" the Greek word for fate, ἀνάγκη:

> The Greek capitals, black with age and cut quite deep into the stone, the forms and attitudes of their calligraphy, which had something peculiarly gothic about it [*je ne sais quels signes propres à la calligraphie gothique empreints dans leurs formes et dans leurs attitudes*], as if to show that the hand which had inscribed them there were a medieval one, and above all their grim and fatal import [*le sens lugubre et fatal*], made a keen impression on the author [*frappèrent vivement l'auteur*].
>
> He wondered, and tried to guess who the tormented soul [*l'âme en peine*] might have been who had not wanted to depart this world without leaving behind, on the brow of the old church [*au front de la vieille église*], this stigma of crime or misfortune. (HE 25; HF 3)

The author reads in the most profound sense, for he does not simply decipher the Greek letters — something of an accomplishment in itself for one who was not trained as a paleographer — but he reconstructs and interprets the message imbedded in their inscription. He reads in the actual shapes of the letters, their "forms and attitudes," evidence of their medieval origins. Remarkably enough, he is able to do this even though he does not really know just what there is about the letters that enables him to make the identification. "Je ne sais quels signes propres à la calligraphie gothique" alert him. They reveal the era of the inscription's origin so unmistakably that the author finds no need for additional evidence. This knowing-without-knowing suggests a certain intimacy between the message and the author who reads it. He is able to recognize the subtle signs of gothic calligraphy without having to identify them, just as one is able to recognize a familiar face without consciously noting any of the features that make the identification possible. The man who can do this must be on very close terms indeed with the Middle Ages.

In this moment of intimacy the dead letters come to life. Paradoxically, it is precisely that which is deadly about them that comes to life, for it is their "grim and fatal import" that strikes the author vividly ("frappèrent vivement l'auteur"). The intimacy between the message and the author becomes even more intense, for now it is no longer only the church wall that has received the lively impression of the writing implement; now it is the author himself. The dead letters may remain on the stone, but their ominous meaning is inscribed on Hugo himself. That the message is particularly deadly is evident not only or even primarily from the meaning of the Greek word ("fate" or "necessity") but also from the biblical metaphor with which Hugo surrounds it. It is a "stigma or crime or misfortune," and it is affixed to the "brow" of the church. The word "brow" (that is, "forehead," French "front") is striking, since the author has just finished telling us that the inscription was in an obscure corner. What is involved is evidently not a spatial but a moral figure: "front" is not so much a physical space as a mythic forehead upon which has been set the mark of Cain. Surely it was the inscriber and not the church that was guilty of the supposed "crime," but the brow of the church is, from the author's point of view, the proper place for it. The purpose of the mark, after all, was not to identify Cain's crime but to "prevent anyone who chanced upon him from hurting him" (Genesis 4:15). As becomes clear just a bit later on, the author would dearly wish to have such a protection for his beloved cathedral.

The deadliness of the mark borne on the brow of the church becomes more intense in Hugo's construction of its meaning. He says that it carries a "grim and fatal import," though this is perhaps more an artifact of the French translation Hugo provides later in the novel than of the Greek word itself. Aristotle and other ancient writers used ἀνάγκη quite regularly simply to mean "necessity," with no implication of grimness. Hugo, however, lets his character Jehan Frollo translate the term as "fatalité" and thereby stresses the lugubrious possibilities inherent in the concept. The dead letters may be read as the trace of a living spirit (*âme*), but that spirit is presented as already on the way to death, as "tormented [*en peine*]" and driven by misfortune or guilt. It is overcome by a sense of "fatality" that is not simply exigency but looming mortality. The word is the sign of the pressing danger of death.

The danger can perhaps only be imagined in the case of the original writer of the inscription, but it can be seen with stark clarity in the case of the inscription itself and the building upon which it stands:

> Since then [that is, the time when the author first saw the inscription], the wall has either been distempered or scraped (I forget which) and the inscription has gone. For such is the treatment accorded to the marvelous churches of the Middle Ages for close on two hundred years. Mutilation has come on them from all sides, from both within and without. The priest distempers them, the architect scrapes them, then along comes the populace and demolishes them. (HE 25; HF 3)

The letters discovered once by the author mean "fatality" in terms of their own history. The text that was once so clearly legible that Hugo could read its calligraphy without even knowing how is gone, and the great book in which it was inscribed is threatened as well. But is it a book, or a building, or an object — or is it a person? The author has already given it a brow, and now he speaks of its continuous mutilation as if it were a living body suffering deadly torture. Hugo's reader is moved to wonder whether the issue at stake here is really the "tormented soul" imagined by the author, writer of the ancient word, or the great book of which that world is a part, the cathedral that stands under the threat of extinction.

The author and his novel stand as the last barrier between the word (along with everything associated with it) and oblivion:

> Thus, apart from the fragile memento here dedicated to it by the author of this book, there is today nothing left of that mysterious word engraved in the gloom of the tower of Notre-Dame, nothing left of the unknown destiny of which it was so cheerless a summary. The man who wrote that word on that wall was erased from the midst of the generations several centuries ago, the word in its turn has been erased from the wall of the church, and soon perhaps the church itself will be erased from the earth.
>
> This book was written about that word [*C'est sur ce mot qu'on a fait ce livre*]. (HE 25; HF 3–4)

As the Greek word was engraved on the church, so is Hugo's book alleged to be written "upon" ("sur") the word. No wonder he refers to it as a "fragile memento," inscribed as it is on a base that has already suffered permanent effacement. The unexpressed hope that lingers behind all of these erasures is that, while the writing may disappear, the act of reading remains alive. The full version of that reading is the novel hereby introduced. Even if the cathedral called Notre-Dame de Paris should perish along with the already perished word, the book called *Notre-Dame de Paris* will live on and thereby secure if not its substance at least its memory. The novel is presented as the latest in a series of erasings pointing back to the intersection between a building and a person represented by the fateful letters. Its function is to preserve the legibility of this intersection from the absolute effacement that seems to threaten so pressingly.[1]

The book called *Notre-Dame* stands on the boundary between life and death, keeping alive as it were the deadliness of a grim and fatal sign. The story told in the book patrols this boundary, offering a cast of characters almost all of whom have one foot in the grave. Quasimodo looks like a creature belonging to the realm of the dead. The king's prothonotary, seeing the child abandoned in the cathedral, offers the opinion that it was "found by the look of it on the parapet of the river Phlegethon!" (HE 157; HF 141) — that is, on the banks of a mythic river in the classical realm of the dead — and shares the popular sentiment that it should be destroyed forthwith. Claude Frollo saves little Quasimodo from this fate, though he acknowledges by the name with which he christens the child "just how incomplete and half finished the poor little creature was" (HE 163; HF

147). The impulse to save Quasimodo is the result in turn of Frollo's commitment to saving his brother Jehan, the only member of his family to escape the outbreak of plague in 1466. Frollo is overcome by a "monstrous fancy" that "were he [Quasimodo] to die, his dear little Jehan too might be miserably cast away on the foundlings' wooden plank" (HE 162; HF 147). The fragility of Jehan's existence serves to change Frollo's relation to the world. Threatened by the closeness of death, "he was beginning to live in life" (HE 160; HF 145).

Like Quasimodo and Jehan Frollo, Pierre Gringoire seems to live under sentence of execution. As Frollo saves his brother and the hunchback, so does Esmeralda save Gringoire when he is sentenced to hang by the beggar-king Clopin. Gringoire, like Claude and Jehan Frollo, and like Esmeralda herself, is an orphan who barely clings to life in a world of violent death. "My father was hanged by the Burgundians and my mother disemboweled by the Picards" (HE 120; HF 103), and were it not for the gypsy-girl's kindness he would have met a similar fate. Esmeralda, of course, eventually comes under a sentence of death under which she is able to survive for a time in the sanctuary of Notre-Dame. Her beloved Phoebus, apparently murdered, miraculously survives the blows of Frollo's dagger, though that survival does nothing to prevent Esmeralda's conviction for his murder. And then there is Esmeralda's mother, the miserable inhabitant of the Rat-Hole, "a living person cut off from the community of men and to be numbered henceforth among the dead," whose existence is readily described as "the remnants of a life flickering in a grave" (HE 215; HF 201–2).

All of these figures brought to life in Hugo's story are living traces of death, dying traces of life. They are readings of the effaced letters on the brow of the cathedral, and their lives are dedicated to the memorialization of "fatality." All of them seem to be in one way or another only remnants of life barely flickering in a grave. They are no less lively in the face of so much death; indeed, their vitality shines forth all the more clearly against the somber background of mortality on which Hugo has inscribed them. But their meaning seems to shuttle back and forth along the boundary between hope and despair. Phoebus's miraculous revivification offers a hope for Esmeralda that is never fulfilled: he never intervenes to save her, though he has the opportunity to do so. His survival ultimately serves to destroy her last chance of escape, because she reveals herself to her pursuers, instead of remaining hidden in the Rat-Hole, by crying out when she sees him. One of the grimmest ironies in this grim novel is that Esmeralda would have been saved if her beloved Phoebus had died.

How are we to evaluate Phoebus' recovery? How should we judge poor Gudule, whose love for her daughter contributes materially to her daughter's death? The undecidable status of these questions rests on the irony of reversible readings. The lively, deadly inscription upon which the novel is based offers a model of such reading that is then doubled within the story by the inscription placed upon the cell in which Gudule passes her bitter days:

> As there was no door to the walled-up cell of the Tour-Roland, the two words TU, ORA had been engraved in large Romanesque characters above the window.
>
> As a result of which the populace, whose common sense ignores fine distinctions and happily translates *Ludovico Magno* as Porte Saint-Denis, has given this black, damp and dismal cavity the name of Trou-aux-rats (Rat-hole). A less sublime explanation, perhaps, than the other, but a more picturesque one. (HE 216; HF 203)

The purpose of the Latin legend, the narrator tells us, was to inform "the literate passer-by of the devout purpose of the cell" (HE 216; HF 203). But the reading *in bono* of the Latin inscription, the injunction to pray, is transformed by paronomasia into French[2] and simultaneously into a reading *in malo*. The same object (the cell) is being interpreted in both cases, and the same or almost the same sounds are employed in both readings, but the valorizations are utterly different. In fact, when we consider the matter more carefully, we realize that the Latin words are already ambiguous. Are they directed toward the inhabitant of the cell or to the passers-by? We cannot say for sure, but we can say that they are properly placed in a liminal position, next to the only means of communication between the inhabitant and the outside world. They function as a textual Janus, pointing toward the inside and the outside, both toward the heaven to which prayers are addressed and the hell suggested by "Rat-hole."

The cell becomes, with the help of the Latin legend, an interpretable sign. Like Notre-Dame itself, the cell is a set of legible stones. "In those days, in fact, every building was an idea" (HE 216; HF 203). And buildings are books, too. The story proposes that long before Hugo got the notion of transforming the cathedral of Notre-Dame into the novel *Notre-Dame*, the medieval mind had already made the analogy. A pair of visitors ask Claude Frollo about his work, and the archdeacon gives an elaborate reply based on the notion of reading architecture:[3]

> "But especially shall I make you read one by one the marble letters of the alphabet, the granite pages of the book. [. . .] I shall make you read the hieroglyphics covering the four great andirons in the portal of the Hôpital Saint-Gervais and in the Rue de la Ferronnerie. And together we shall spell out the facades of Saint-Côme, Saint-Geneviève-des-Ardents, Saint-Martin and Saint-Jacques-de-la-Boucherie . . ."
>
> For all the intelligence in his eyes, the Tourangeau did not seem to have understood Dom Claude for quite some while. He broke in.
>
> "*Pasque-Dieu*, what *are* your books?"
>
> "Here is one of them," said the archdeacon.
>
> And opening the window of the cell, he pointed to the immense church of Notre-Dame [. . .]. (HE 187; HF 172–73)

Frollo then points to the church with one hand and a printed book lying on his desk with the other, proclaiming sadly, "this will kill that. [. . .] Alas and alack, small things overcome great ones! [. . .] the book will kill the building" (HE 187–88; HF 173).

The importance of the archdeacon's prediction lies more in its relevance to the central project of Hugo's novel than in its evident and explicitly elaborated relation to Hugo's conception of cultural history. Hugo, as the narrator of *Notre-Dame*, voices his agreement with Frollo's opinion in the famous chapter "This Will Kill That" (deleted from the first edition but restored, with a certain fanfare, in the form of a new prefatory note, in 1832). But Hugo as the originator of the idea of writing *Notre-Dame*, the "author" alluded to in the prefatory note of 1831 about the ἀνάγκη inscription, declares himself to believe just the opposite, that his book will save at least the memory of the building by serving as a "fragile memento." The reading of "the book" as a cultural phenomenon is thus powerfully ambivalent throughout the novel, now promising to restore life, now threatening to bring death.

Whether the book destroys or preserves the building (which is also a book) is a less pressing issue than legibility itself, the feature that makes both books and buildings interesting. Readability is a kind of alchemy, a power that enables all sorts of transformations to take place. The two men who visit Frollo's cell, one of whom turns out to be King Louis XI, are particularly interested in the scholar's alchemical researches and most especially in the possibility of transmuting base materials into gold. Frollo has not yet become so adept as a reader as to achieve that goal, but he has hopes:

> "I catch glimpses, I do not contemplate! I do not read, I spell out!"
> "And when you can read," asked the compere [King Louis], "will you make gold?"
> "Who can doubt it?" said the archdeacon.
> "In that case, Notre-Dame knows I have great need of money, and I would like very much to learn to read from your books." (HE 185–86; HF 171)

Frollo is quite willing to teach what he knows about this sort of reading, but it turns out to be something quite different from what the King expects. The relevant books turn out to be buildings. It is instructive to observe just how Frollo makes the transition from the topic of alchemy to that of legible architecture:

> I will show you the particles of gold left in the bottom of Nicholas Flamel's crucible, and you shall compare them with the gold of William of Paris. I will teach you the secret powers of the Greek word *peristera*. But especially shall I make you read one by one the marble letters of the alphabet, the granite pages of the book. (HE 186–87; HF 172)

The crux on which Frollo's logic turns is the double meaning of a particular Greek word, περιστερά, which ordinarily indicates an animal, a dove, but can also be understood in a more esoteric usage as a plant, verbena. The possibility of metamorphosis suggested by this otherwise unimportant word links the procedures and goals of alchemy with those of architecture and of books. There is not a question in Frollo's mind, as there is none in Hugo's, that a productive transformation by way of reading is possible. The question that bothers both is what the moral quality of such a transformation might be. Is it wonderful and vital, or is it terrible and deadly?

This is the supreme Romantic question, since Romanticism is characterized by a steady concern with the possibilities of human acts of transformation. The secularization of Christian culture, which M. H. Abrams has shown to be one of the basic elements of the Romantic project (*Natural Supernaturalism* 65–70), did not eliminate the perceived spiritual need for renewal, regeneration, in short the mythic cycle of death and resurrection; it simply transferred the arena of action from the heavenly to the earthly sphere. Reading offered a paradigmatic method for engaging in productive acts of transformation that were all the more attractive for having facilitated the very process of secularization that made new methods necessary. It is the (at least partially) secularized rereading of Christian material, after all, visible in a huge range of works from *Faust* to *Frankenstein*, that stocks the storehouse of Romantic mythology.[4] But what is the moral status of these new myths made from old, these living bodies formed from the remains of dead ones? Hugo has to regard his regeneration of Notre-Dame into *Notre-Dame* with the same mixture of triumphant satisfaction and deadly fear with which Dr. Frankenstein regards his new Adam. There is no way to completely suppress the suspicion that the latter is not so much the regeneration of the former as its replacement, that ultimately "this will kill that." Hugo, like many Romantics, depicts a scene of reading whereupon are enacted the rituals of slaughter that give life to new cultural forms.

This altogether typical Romantic ambivalence saturates the restored second chapter of Book V, "This Will Kill That." Hugo wants nothing more than to preserve the great stone books of the past, but he knows perfectly well that he belongs to the culture of printing that has dealt a deathblow to this sort of architecture. The demise of architecture and the rise of the printed book go hand in hand, according to the theory of cultural history set forth in Hugo's argument, because both are embodiments of language and are therefore natural competitors for a single cultural function, the recording of ideas:

> Architecture began like any other form of writing. It was first of all an alphabet. [. . .] Later on they formed words. [. . .] Finally, they wrote books. [. . .] They combined and amalgamated [. . .] until, at the dictate

of the general idea of an epoch, they had written those marvelous books which were also marvelous buildings: the pagoda of Eklinga, the Ramesseum of Egypt, the Temple of Solomon.

The idea that engendered them, the word, was not only the foundation of all these buildings, it was also in their form. The Temple of Solomon, for instance, was not merely the binding of the sacred book, it was the sacred book itself. From each of its concentric ring-walls, the priests could read the word translated and made manifest to the eye, and could thus follow its transformations from sanctuary to sanctuary until, in its ultimate tabernacle, they could grasp it in its most concrete yet still architectural form: the ark [of the covenant]. Thus the word was enclosed in the building, but its image was on the envelope like the human figure on the coffin of a mummy. (HE 189–91; HF 175–76)

The most surprising thing about this extraordinary passage is that the Temple of Solomon, the Notre-Dame of its day, the embodiment of the central principle of architecture, is troped as a container of death, a coffin.[5] One might well have expected that Hugo would have wished to present ancient architecture as the domicile of a *living* word: it is, after all, supposed to be a "bible of stone" (HE 200; HF 187) and the supreme achievement of the people who created it. It is, in Hugo's own version of history, capable of being "killed" by printing.

But Hugo has constructed his story in such a way as to limit the guilt that might otherwise infect those (like himself) implicated in the overthrow of architecture. The narrator forthrightly calls his historical narrative "This Will Kill That," but he arranges the story in such a way as to suggest that "that" was already dead. The ark of the covenant and the building that surrounds it do not appear in Hugo's imagery as houses inhabited by a living presence but rather as tombs encasing a mummy. Printed books, on the other hand, bring life to a language that was not previously alive:

> In its printed form, thought is more imperishable than ever; it is volatile, elusive, indestructible. It mingles with the air. In the days of architecture, thought had turned into a mountain and taken powerful hold of a century and of a place. Now it turned into a flock of birds and was scattered on the four winds, occupying every point of air and space simultaneously.
>
> We repeat: who cannot see that in this guise it is far more indelible? Before it was solid, now it is alive [*De solide qu'elle était elle devient vivace*]. (HE 196; HF 182)

The process that Frollo and the chapter title announce as a murder emerges in the rhetoric of the argument as a passage from death to life, from the immobile mountain to the ubiquitous flock of birds. Hope and fear struggle to pull the text in two opposite directions, as the narrator desperately fears that he is taking part in the destruction of legibility while at the same time he hopes that he is instead insuring its continued existence. His text finds a way to accommodate both impulses.

For all its ambivalence the chapter makes abundantly clear that architecture is absolutely dead without hope of recovery: "Let there be no mistake, architecture is dead, dead beyond recall, killed by the printed book, killed because it is less enduring, killed because it is more expensive" (HE 199; HF 186). When Hugo refers to "architecture" here, he does not mean exactly "the art of making buildings," since it is obvious that that art is not dead. "The great accident of an architect of genius might occur in the twentieth century" (HE 200; HF 186), just as there were great writers before the ascendancy of printing. Indeed, the art of building might have further moments of glory sometime in the future, but such moments would not bring back to life the thing whose loss the narrator is lamenting (or celebrating) here. Architecture will never again be the "essential expression of society" (HE 197; HF 183), even if it should "accidentally revive" one day. It is dead insofar as it can no longer be the "master" (HE 200; HF 187 — the French actually says "mistress," in keeping with the grammatical gender of the noun "architecture"), the chief form in which culture recorded and indeed constructed itself.

It is this death of architecture as the principal vehicle of culture that makes its old monuments so valuable. Their legibility remains vital, even if the mastery that created them has passed away. The narrator urgently calls for us, the children of the age of printing, to "study" the masonry book, the Old Testament written in stone. "We must re-read the past from these marble pages" (HE 201; HF 187). And we must do so precisely because no new marble pages are to be written and because those were the most important pages the past ever wrote. The image of mummification seems altogether appropriate, for it is the fact of death that compels the effort of preservation. Hugo does not exhort us or himself to care for literature, because literature is alive and capable of taking care of itself. It is the dead body of architecture that calls for our most strenuous efforts.

We must, then, read the book represented by old buildings, and we can read it, because it is finished. The great edifice of literature, on the other hand, still alive, still under construction, seems less and less intelligible the more thoroughly Hugo describes it. He pursues the symmetry of his equation of building and book by closing the chapter "This Will Kill That" with an extended image of literary history as a huge building under construction. By the time he completes the last flourish of his literary conceit, the question of intelligibility has become a complex and troubled one:

> For the rest, this prodigious edifice remains perpetually unfinished. The printing press, that giant machine, tirelessly pumping the whole intellectual sap of society, is constantly spewing out fresh materials for its erection. The entire human race is on the scaffolding. Each mind is a mason. [. . .] This is indeed a construction which grows and mounts in spirals without end; here is a confusion of tongues, ceaseless activity, indefatigable labour,

fierce rivalry between all of mankind, the intellect's promised refuge against a second deluge, against submersion by the barbarians. This is the human race's second Tower of Babel. (HE 201–2; HF 188)

The book of architecture is a completed volume whose marble pages we may study at leisure and whose overall shape can be grasped. Not so with the edifice of literature, which has so much growth yet ahead of it that we can have no idea what its ultimate form will be. Further more, the prognosis for the future is not reassuring, if we take seriously the biblical imagery offered at the end. We must take it seriously, of course, since we have already been told that literary history is the "bible of paper," one of the "two testaments" of cultural history (HE 200; HF 187). The bible of paper, turned to stone by Hugo's rhetoric, discloses itself as a second Tower of Babel characterized by the confusion of tongues that the account in Genesis tells us prevented the first from becoming completed. Unintelligibility causes the project to be abandoned.

The dead art of architecture is a readable book, but the living art of literature seems on the way to becoming an unreadable building. The legibility of architecture is threatened by effacement, the destruction or desecration of buildings like Notre-Dame that can never be replaced. But the legibility of literature appears to be equally threatened, now endangered not by the effects of death but the process of life. The "giant machine," the printing press (HE 201; HF 188), produces such a quantity of stuff to be incorporated into the building that completion is out of the question. The narrator declares in the midst of his description of the mighty literary edifice that its "harmony comes from the whole" (HE 201; HF 188). But there is not and cannot be a whole as long as the machine keeps pumping out material, as long as the organism stays alive. The harmony that seems to be asserted in the center of the image disappears in the rhetoric of incompletion that dominates its close.

Death may not be so bad nor life so good for reading as one might have thought at first. Homer, Shakespeare, and other monumental writers of the past are easier to comprehend when they are presented as versions of "dead" buildings than as parts of the "living" Tower of writing. If the *Iliad* is a literary version of the Parthenon, or if Shakespeare is "the last Gothic cathedral" (HE 200; HF 187), then we may at least understand them as discrete objects belonging to a graspable context. But if Homer is instead a "white marble bas-relief" that hangs "on the left of the entrance" to a building still long from finished (HE 201; HF 188), how are we to decide what his cultural meaning is? We will be able to make only the most tentative of readings. The word becomes most readily legible when it is enclosed in a finished monument that impresses its image "on the envelope like the human figure on the coffin of a mummy." The lively edifice produced by the printing press is no such monument.

Hugo's complex rhetoric of reading returns with startling regularity to ambivalent images such as these to embody his equally complex attitude toward the project of cultural renewal in which he was engaged. One nexus around which such images gather is "Egypt," as in the image of the mummy's coffin. Indeed, at times it almost seems as if the distant antiquity of "Egypt" is more important to Hugo's historical novel than the Middle Ages, in which it is set. For if the narrator-author seems preoccupied with the threat of effacement confronting the monuments of medieval culture, he clearly also has in the back of his mind the recent extraordinary drama of revivification that had followed on the discovery in 1799 of the Rosetta Stone by members of Napoleon's expeditionary force in Egypt. When Hugo was writing *Notre-Dame* in 1830 the scholarly world was still reacting to the publication of Champollion's *Précis du système hiéroglyphique* in 1824. The issue of the legibility of antiquity was one of urgent current interest, since the hieroglyphics that had turned back would-be readers with their bewildering incomprehensibility now invited reading. When Frollo tells his guests that he will make them "read the hieroglyphs" of architecture, he is promising something that had just become possible for Hugo's contemporaries. The dead letters were coming back to life.[6]

The term "hieroglyphics" appears a number of times, always to refer to difficult but nonetheless legible writing. Egypt thus enters the discussion as the cultural archetype of the liminal position of reading and writing, arts that dwell on the threshold of life and death, of oblivion and rediscovery. "Egypt" also stands for the realm of magic, as when the narrator attempts to explain Claude Frollo's complex attitude toward "the sciences of Egypt, necromancy and magic" (HE 175; HF 161). The archdeacon is in public the enemy, in private the practitioner of the alchemical arts regularly assumed to be magical or even diabolical in nature. His love-hate relation with these "sciences of Egypt" parallels the more violent ambivalence he feels toward Esmeralda, who is presented as another representative of "Egypt." She is regularly referred to in the narrative as "l'égyptienne" (correctly but not entirely satisfactorily translated as "gypsy"), and her name is assumed by Gringoire at the close of Book I to be "Egyptiac" (HE 75; HF 56).[7]

It is altogether likely, in fact, that Hugo focuses so much attention on Esmeralda principally because her (adoptive) social group is referred to in French as "Egyptians." She is the representative of something mysterious, something not quite respectable, something attractive that nonetheless remains forbidden, something that has traffic with the underworld. She is an Egyptian who is also not an Egyptian, a metaphorical "Egyptian" who in fact turns out not even to be a true gypsy but rather the lost daughter of the woman who lives under the legend "TU ORA / Trou-aux-rats." She is a hieroglyphic that seems at first wholly illegible: "*La Esmeralda*, what does it mean?" wonders Gringoire, who exclaims later, "But the devil take me if I understand what they mean with their Esmeralda!" (HE 74–75; HF 55–56). In this regard she stands for all of her fellow "Egyptians," and ultimately for all the things connected with Egypt by the novel's complex rhetoric:

> "*La buona mancia, signor! La Buona mancia!*"
> "Devil take you, and me with you," said Gringoire, "if I know what you mean!"
> And he pressed on. [. . .] "*Señor caballero, para comprar un pedaso de pan!*"
> "This one seems to talk too," said Gringoire, "but an uncouth language and anyone who understands it is a luckier man than I."
> Then a sudden association of ideas make him strike his brow: "Come to think of it, what on earth did they mean this morning with their *Esmeralda*?" [. . .] "*La buona mancia!*" sang the legless man.
> And the lame man provided the counterpoint, repeating "*Un pedaso de pan!*"
> Gringoire blocked his ears. "What a Tower of Babel [*Ó tour de Babel*]!" he exclaimed. (HE 98–99; HF 80–81)

Esmeralda thus belongs to the family of images associated with the issues of life and death, legibility and illegibility, books of letters and books of stones, discussed at length in "This Will Kill That." The underworld to which Esmeralda belongs shares with the bright and lively edifice of literature the character of being a Tower of Babel. Both are repositories of meaning that cannot be entirely grasped, and one cannot be sure whether their import, once understood, would be vital or deadly. Gringoire's accidental penetration into the gypsy underworld, the "Court of Miracles," leads to an immediate though inexplicable threat of death by hanging. He is saved, equally inexplicably, by Esmeralda's offer to marry him. The whole business is thoroughly "Egyptian" because it seems so magical in its sudden movement from life to death and back again:

> There was an element of magic about the adventure. He was beginning seriously to see himself as a character in a fairy-tale; from time to time he looked around him as if to discover whether the chariot of fire pulled by two winged chimeras, which alone could have borne him so swiftly from Tartarus to paradise, was still there. (HE 113; HF 96)

The aspiring author becomes caught up in a story far more marvelous than he could have thought up, a character in a tragedy that he himself never seems able to read. At a critical moment during his attempt to rescue Esmeralda, he seems to lose track of his moral priorities, mistaking the symbol of tragic success for a resolution to a tragic situation. He chooses to save Esmeralda's goat rather than Esmeralda herself. He recalls that the goat "would be hanged if he were captured, that that would be a great shame, poor Djali." In his mind "he alternately weighed up the gypsy and the goat" and, in a moment when Esmeralda is distracted, he takes the opportunity to "slip away with the goat" (HE 459–60; HF 464). The tragic poet, so enthralled with the prize traditionally awarded to the successful tragedian, seems to miss the point of the tragedy in which he is participating.

The poet unable to grasp the story of which he is a part is blood brother to the living gargoyle who cannot comprehend the building of which he is a part. Quasimodo is in fact unable to comprehend most of the world because he is unable to perceive the world correctly. He is a malformed lens through which only distorted images may pass:

> The impression of objects underwent a considerable refraction before they reached his intelligence. His brain was a peculiar medium: the ideas that passed through it emerged all twisted. The reflections which resulted from this refraction were necessarily warped and divergent. [. . .] The first effect this fatal constitution had was to cloud his vision of things. He received almost no immediate perception from them. To him, the external world seemed much further off than it does to us. (HE 165–66; HF 150)

He cannot read the "granite pages," the "marble letters" that are so readily legible to his protector Claude Frollo, the hieroglyphs of the "theocratic masonry of Egypt" to which the narrator compares Romanesque architecture (HE 191; HF 177).

In one respect, however, Quasimodo is not at all distant from the external world. Though he cannot read the hieroglyphics of Notre-Dame, he can at times merge with them. He and the building come together so intimately that the two are like the snail and its shell or the tortoise and its carapace. The narrator offers these and other metaphors, suggesting the most fundamental sort of connection between Quasimodo and the cathedral, along with the following disclaimer: "There is no need to warn the reader not to take literally the tropes we are obliged to employ here in order to express this peculiar, symmetrical, immediate almost consubstantial coupling [*accouplement singulier, symétrique, immédiat, presque co-substantiel*] of a man and a building" (HE 164; HF 149). If indeed there is no need to warn the reader about the dangers of taking figures literally, why does the narrator bring it up in the first place? What would make him think that the literal reading of tropes ought to be an issue?

One reason, certainly, is that the very notion the argument wishes to convince us of — that two disparate entities such as a man and a building could engage in a "consubstantial coupling" — suggests the possibility of a merger of tenor and vehicle in a trope. The point of a trope is that it brings together two elements that in fact do not "properly" belong together. But the trope necessarily asserts the very thing that its intended figurative understanding must deny, that is, that the two relata are exactly the same. If we believe that disparate entities can really merge, as

Quasimodo and the building are alleged to, we might also believe that metaphors mean literally what they say. We would be in danger of ceasing to be "good" readers, who attend not to the deadly letter of discourse but only to the life-giving spirit.

The authorial voice appears to want to cut off the threat of literal reading he realizes is implicit in his rhetoric, but at the same time he knows that such reading cannot be easily stopped. His statement that there is "no need to warn the reader" might express either confidence in the reader's ability to take care of this matter for him or herself or a confession that the cat is already out of the bag, that there is no point in uttering warnings because literal readings are unavoidable. We cannot dismiss this second possibility because in fact Hugo brings this chapter to its climax with an unforgettable scene which precisely acts out a literal reading of his phrase "strange mating [*accouplement singulier*]" used in the sentence warning against literal readings. Quasimodo enacts a scene of intercourse with one of Notre-Dame's bells. The narrator, as we might expect, prefers not to make explicit the sexuality of the scene he depicts, but it comes through clearly enough:

> Then, suspended above the abyss and launched on to the fearsome oscillation of the bell, he seized the bronze monster by its little ears, gripped it between his knees, spurred it on with his heels, and renewed the fury of its peal with the full weight and impact of his own body. The tower meanwhile was quaking; he shouted and gnashed his teeth, his red hair bristled, his chest sounded like a blacksmith's bellows, his eyes flashed fire, the monstrous bell whinnied, panting, beneath him; and now it was no longer the great bell of Notre-Dame and Quasimodo but a dream, a whirlwind, a tempest [. . .] a strange centaur, half man, half bell [. . .].
> (HE 168; HF 153)

Since the bell has the name of Marie and has already been referred to as Quasimodo's "sweetheart," as his "favourite among this rowdy family of girls," and as member of his "harem" (HE 167; HF 152), the imagery of horse and rider tends to enhance rather than diminish the outright bawdiness of this scene. The hunchback is embracing the bell quite literally, grasping her between his knees with passionate abandon.

There is indeed no need to warn against literal reading of metaphors like "accouplement singulier" *both* because we already know the necessity for figurative reading *and* because we are shown the necessity of literal reading. Reading of every kind is essential to the success of the story, essential, in fact, to its very existence. The learned author, like the scholar Claude Frollo, is able to decipher the hidden, figurative meanings embodied in or scratched upon ancient buildings; he makes a great big book out of reading the one little word ἀνάγκη. But this same author can behave at other times like the unlettered Quasimodo, forget the displaced meanings offered by figurative reading, and act out the unseemly literal significance of tropes. Having found this metaphorical version of the Rosetta Stone on the walls of Notre-Dame, Hugo makes his decipherment of that mysterious script into a tale of things "Egyptian." *Notre-Dame* represents both a literal and a figurative reading of the Gothic hieroglyphs of ἀνάγκη.

It can be no surprise that this tale, which announces itself as the product of one act of reading this word, should include near its center a scene that depicts another. If indeed the book had its beginning in the author's fascination with this inscription, Hugo is almost obliged to make room somewhere in the story for the appearance of this fateful word. Its engraving and first reading become the novelist's version of the dramatist's *scène à faire*. In it, the concerns of the man writing and reading in 1830 on the subject of ἀνάγκη merge with those of the imaginary medieval writer and reader.

Hugo plays openly with the temporal complexity of his chapter titled "ἈΝΆΓΚΗ" by showing us to the place of the medieval inscription by way of a modern one. Jehan Frollo is looking for the cell of his brother Claude, and he finds a likely looking door:

> Those curious enough to visit that door today will recognize it by this inscription, carved in white letters on the black wall: I ADORE CORALIE. 1823. SIGNED UGÈNE [sic]. The word "signed" being part of the text.
> "Phew!" said the student; "this must be it." (HE 270; HF 263)

The juxtaposition of the modern description and the reported dialogue allows for the anachronistic possibility that Jehan has recognized the door by the same inscription by which we modern readers are supposed to recognize it and by which presumably the author has found it on his own visits to Notre-Dame. The modern reader also cannot help noticing that Jehan is visiting his brother's cell — the location of the mysterious Greek inscription — for a purpose entirely consistent with Hugo's in writing his novel: "I need money" (HE 277; HF 271). The stupendous achievement of composing this huge text in a few months' time was motivated in no small way by extreme financial pressure. Thus the author is figuratively present in the archdeacon's cell, reading the fateful word, for just the same reason that leads Jehan to be there literally. The "necessity" that drives Jehan and Hugo may be of a more secular kind than that which drives Claude Frollo, but each still has ample experience of the rigors of ἀνάγκη.

The temporal complexity of this scene of reading is entirely consistent with the concept of literary legibility proposed at the end of "This Will Kill That." The edifice of letters is a structure made out of pieces belonging to various different periods, all of them joined together to form "a vast construction, with the entire world as its base" (HE 201; HF 188). Shakespeare, Byron, Homer, and the Vedas are all bound together in a single anthology. The wall on which Frollo inscribes the fateful word appears as a similar sort of anthology, though on a considerably smaller scale:

Other mottoes had been inscribed in great profusion on the walls, as was the fashion with hermeticists: some written in ink, others carved with a metal point. For the rest, Gothic characters, Hebrew characters, Greek characters and Roman characters all higgledy-piggledy, the inscriptions overflowing haphazardly one on top of the other, the most recent obliterating the earlier ones, and all intertwined with each other like the branches of a thicket or the pikes of skirmishing soldiers. It was, in fact, a somewhat confused skirmish between all the philosophies, the daydreams and lore of mankind [*de toutes les philosophies, de toutes les rêveries, de toutes les sagesses humaines*]. (HE 272; HF 265)

Here, the two alternative images offered earlier, the building as book and the totality of books as a building, come together: the cathedral of Notre-Dame becomes an actual manuscript, a surface on which the "wisdom of mankind [*sagesses humaines*]" appears in written form. But we notice that here the rhetoric is considerably more troubled than it was in the earlier, highly optimistic depiction of mankind at cooperative labor on the construction of "the hive to which all the golden bees of the imagination come with their honey" (HE 201; HF 188). Instead of cooperation there is warfare, instead of bees bringing honey there are soldiers brandishing pikes. In the earlier metaphor literature of previous ages forms the solid base on which the newer literature rests, but here earlier inscriptions are covered over and destroyed by newer ones. Instead of a construction site, the scene of reading and writing is a battlefield.

It might even be something worse than a battlefield. A battle, for all its violence, has some structure, if only that imposed by the distinction between opponents. To Jehan, the wall is so full of writing that it seems utterly chaotic and therefore almost illegible. The abundance of writing is overwhelming; it "helped no little to make the defaced wall of the cell resemble a sheet of paper over which a monkey had drawn an ink-laden pen" (HE 272; HF 265–66). The impression is not one of construction in progress but instead just the opposite, of ruin: "The whole cell presented an appearance of general neglect and decay" (HE 272; HF 266). And in the center of this landscape of ruin sits Claude Frollo, reading, "poring over an enormous manuscript adorned with weird paintings" (HE 272–73; HF 266).

The archdeacon is evidently engaged in studies connected with his alchemical endeavors, in this particular case with the attempt to transform fire or light, presumed to be a "vaporous" form of gold, into the metallic substance. He reads in the great book before him that the power to extract gold from fire might lie in the uttering of "certain women's names," since a "woman's name must be pleasing, soft, imaginary; end on long syllables and resemble words of benediction" (HE 273–74; HF 267). As the reader might expect, one of the names that occurs to him as appropriate to the furtherance of his "Egyptian" science is that of the "Egyptian" girl,

Esmeralda. But Frollo cannot even get the whole name out of his mouth before he checks himself and shuts the book in an attempt to "chase away the idea that obsessed him" (HE 274; HF 267). He thinks of Esmeralda not as the locus of a power that will aid him but as an "obsession which has made my brain shrivel" (HE 274; HF 267).

Shutting the book does not end the scene of reading, however. Frollo takes up a hammer and nail, magical implements that are alleged to have the power to drive a distant enemy into the earth. Frollo has no success with this "magic hammer of Ezechiel" because he lacks "the magic word that Ezechiel uttered." He tries out some words but fails, apparently for the same reason as before: "*Sigéani, Sigéani!* May this nail open up the grave for whoever bears the name of Phoebus! . . . Curse it! Still the same everlasting idea!" (HE 274; HF 268). Frustrated once more by his obsession with Esmeralda, he gives up on the second attempt to find a proper magic word. After a few moments during which Jehan can see only Frollo's "fist clenched convulsively on a book," the archdeacon takes up a compass and inscribes the word ἀνάγκη on the wall (HE 274–75; HF 268).

While Frollo may not have considered this inscription his third attempt to come up with a magic word with the power to transmute light into gold, the living into the dead, it nonetheless succeeds — for the writer Victor Hugo. It does not succeed for Frollo, of course, because he does not see the mystery in the letters he has just drawn. That later reader cited in the prefatory note, however, will find in ἀνάγκη the very thing to turn his reading into ready money, to transform the contents of his ink bottle into a drama of violent death. The author of *Notre-Dame* succeeds, thanks to Frollo's frustrated exclamation of despair written on the wall, where the priest had failed. Frollo, it is clear, does not really want to read the full import of his own inscription, as becomes acutely evident when Jehan gives a performance of his skill at reading Greek in response to his brother's accusation that Jehan's education is deficient:

> "Latin is barely understood, Syriac unknown, Greek so detested that it is not adjudged ignorant even for the most learned to skip a Greek word without reading it, and people say: *Graecum est, non legitur.*"
>
> The student looked resolutely up. "Brother, would you like me to explain in simple French that Greek word written on the wall there?"
>
> "Which word?"
>
> "ΑΝΑΓΚΗ."
>
> A faint blush spread over the archdeacon's yellow cheekbones, like the puff of smoke which is the outward sign of the secret commotions of a volcano. The student barely noticed it.
>
> "Well, Jehan," stammered the elder brother with an effort, "what does that word mean?"
>
> "Fatality."
>
> Dom Claude went pale again, and the student continued heedlessly:

"And that word underneath it, carved by the same hand, Ἀναγνεία, means 'uncleanliness.' You can see we know our Greek." (HE 276–77; HF 270)

The elder brother falls silent and in apparent embarrassment offers no comment on Jehan's proficiency.

Neither the characters nor the narrator mention the odd fact that Jehan has found a kind of miniature thesaurus on the walls of his brother's cell. Next to the recently inscribed ἀνάγκη is ἀναγνεία, an item one would expect to find very near ἀνάγκη in a dictionary. The reader might also remember that earlier Jehan had seen on this same wall, among the many "skirmishing" inscriptions, the word ἀναγκοφαγία, "strict discipline," yet another word beginning ἀναγ — and thus another legitimate entry in this little thesaurus. Since Claude Frollo has been pondering for some time the mystical properties of words, we can reasonably imagine that he has been considering how the structure of relationships between words corresponds to the structure of experience. He has after all devoted his own life to ἀναγκοφαγία only to find himself overwhelmed by feelings which he considers to be evidence of ἀναγνεία. We, along with Jehan, have just witnessed a scene in which the archdeacon's attempts to practice his "strict discipline" are thwarted by repeated outbreaks of emotional "uncleanliness." These two very different qualities do not go well together in a priest's life, but the Greek words that name them do go together very well in a dictionary.

Ἀνάγκη belongs to the same lexicon, where it both names and helps to explain what is happening to the unhappy archdeacon. Both Frollo's "strict discipline" and his "uncleanliness," as well as the relationship between them, are the products of an inexorable force, of a "fatality" that is both "necessity" and "mortality." If Jehan's Greek were as advanced as his brother's, he might have noted that ἀνάγκη carries a powerful connotation of physical violence. Its etymology, according to Liddel and Scott, reveals its origin in the verb ἄγχω, "to compress," but also especially "to strangle, throttle, choke." Since so many of the novel's characters suffer or are threatened with exactly this form of violence, we can only conclude that Hugo composed his story in conformity with the principles suggested by Frollo's miniature lexicon. And if we take seriously the little tale of the novel's origin offered by the prefatory note, then we can only conclude that the varieties of "discipline" and "uncleanliness" the reader witnesses in the story are indeed the products of ἀνάγκη in the sense that the author found in the very letters making up the word suggestions for the matter of his tale.

Hugo has made his character Claude Frollo a participant in the composition of the novel by making him the writer of the miniature text upon which the story is based. But Frollo remains a character in the text and subject to its power because he cannot separate himself from the words he has written. The relationships that obtain among the letters on the wall to a large degree define him, and he cannot escape from that definition. That is his fate. He is embarrassed when Jehan begins to read his Greek dictionary, not because the younger brother thus proves he knows some Greek, but because he threatens to read the essential structure of Claude Frollo's character. The narrator and the reader, safely distant, know that the archdeacon need not have worried: Jehan is not skilled enough to read with that degree of penetration. But we also know that Frollo has good reason to be worried about other readers and about the process of reading — a process that both gives him life and condemns him to a violent death.

Notes

[1] For a discussion of the importance of the notion of effacement and related ideas in *Notre-Dame*, see Brombert 82–85.

[2] That is, into *modern* French. The pun is anachronistic, of course, and probably could not have occurred to Parisians of the late fifteenth century, whose Middle French language would have sounded quite strange to Hugo and his readers. This interweaving of medieval and modern Paris is such a regular feature of the novel that one is justified in thinking that it was the result of a conscious decision on the part of the author.

[3] The role of architecture in the novel has received much critical attention: for some useful discussions, see Nichols; Kessler; Nash.

[4] The notion of a thoroughgoing secularizing trend in British Romanticism has been cast into doubt by Ryan, who understands major writers of the period as revising Christian religion rather than replacing it with purely secular concepts.

[5] Cf. Keats's Greek funerary urn, discussed in the previous chapter.

[6] The theme of hieroglyphics in *Notre-Dame* has been explored in detail by Chaitin.

[7] For more on the figure of the gypsy in *Notre-Dame*, see Hölz.

6: "Spiritual Communication": Gautier's *Spirite*

THE OPENING PARAGRAPHS OF Theophile Gautier's "fantastic tale" *Spirite* (1865)[1] describe in considerable detail a quiet moment of reading in the life of the story's hero, Guy de Malivert:

> Near him a lamp, placed in a stand of old crackled celadon, shed through its groundglass globe a soft, milky light, like moonbeams through a mist. The light fell upon a book which Guy held with a careless hand, and which was none else than Longfellow's "Evangeline."
>
> No doubt Guy was admiring the work of the greatest poet young America has yet produced, but he was in that lazy state of mind in which absence of thought is preferable to the finest thought expressed in sublime terms. He had read a few verses, then, without dropping his book [*sans quitter le livre*], had let his head rest upon the soft upholstering of the arm-chair, covered with a piece of lace, and was enjoying to the full the temporary stoppage of the working of his brain [*il jouissait délicieusement de ce temps d'arrêt de son cerveau*]. (GE 14; GF 35–36)

The relation depicted here between the reader and his book is odd enough to make one pause. The description begins conventionally enough: light, already transformed into a standard Romantic image, "moonbeams through a mist," illuminates a book that was for many, already in 1865 when Gautier wrote this tale, the emblem of a certain sort of old-fashioned Romanticism. There would be no more appropriate light by which to read "Evangeline" than moonbeams through a mist, even if (or perhaps especially if) both the moonbeams and the mist should happen to be totally artificial.[2]

It can be reasonably assumed that Guy de Malivert's creator shared his admiration for Longfellow. There is doubtless no irony intended here. But it is decidedly peculiar that the fruit of reading "the greatest poet young America has yet produced" should be the absence of thought. The rhetoric of the passage insists, however, that this cessation of mental activity does not require the cessation of reading: the phrase translated here as "without dropping his book" is "sans quitter le livre" (more literally "without *parting from* the book"). Somehow, in a way that is not and perhaps could not be specified, Guy remains engaged with "Evangeline" while at the same time enjoying a period of cerebral stoppage ("ce temps d'arrêt de son cerveau").

There is no shortage of readers in our own day who would find no contradiction at all between reading Longfellow and stopping all brain activity. The sentiment that "Evangeline" is the product of a great poet is no longer so widespread as it once was. Such deprecatory opinions aside, however, we ought for the moment to take the narrator's evaluation at face value and accept that, in the world of this fiction, "Evangeline" counts as a repository of "the finest thought expressed in sublime terms." If we can allow Goethe his enthusiasm for the lugubrious Ossian, we can certainly allow Gautier his affection for Longfellow.

The subject matter of "Evangeline" is of considerable relevance to the topic of Gautier's story. Once the reader has digested the whole of *Spirite*, that relevance is evident: Longfellow's poem concerns a pair of betrothed lovers who spend their entire living existence apart but are united in death. A few of the concluding hexameters of "Evangeline" suggest why Gautier makes such prominent reference to it at the commencement of his tale:

> Still stands the forest primeval; but far away from its shadow,
> Side by side, in their nameless graves, the lovers are sleeping.
> Under the humble walls of the little Catholic churchyard,
> In the heart of the city, they lie, unknown and unnoticed.
> Daily the tides of life go ebbing and flowing beside them,
> Thousands of throbbing hearts, where theirs are at rest and forever,
> Thousands of aching brains, where theirs no longer are busy,
> Thousands of toiling hands, where theirs have ceased from their labors,
> Thousands of weary feet, where theirs have completed their journey.
> (1381–89)

Gautier actually takes up Longfellow's figure of the brains that are no longer busy to characterize the mental state of his hero. It is this cessation of brain activity that will allow Malivert access — as we learn later — to the deceased beloved he does not yet know he possesses. There is thus an important narrative reason both for Guy de Malivert's reading of "Evangeline" and for the joyous stoppage of his brain. Evidently, the notion of "reading" at work in Gautier's story must be different from what we usually take it to be.

An arrestingly direct and forceful development of a nonstandard notion of reading appears in one of Kafka's early, unfinished stories, "Wedding Preparations in the Country." The character Raban suggests that "books are useful in every sense," under certain circumstances even those books "whose contents have nothing in common with" the concerns of the reader. Raban cites the example of someone who has some personal project on his mind and who is reading a book that has nothing at all to do with that project. Such a reader "will be stimulated by the book to all kinds of thoughts concerning the enterprise," though these thoughts will have nothing to do with the material being read. But, "since the contents of the book are precisely of utter indifference, the reader is not at all impeded in these thoughts, and he passes through the midst of the book with them, as once the Jews passed through the Red Sea." Raban's proposal outlines a form of reading in which the reader pays no heed at all to the apparent intentions of the author (Kafka 75).[3]

Guy de Malivert's reading of Longfellow is a far more radical process even than Raban's model of "passing through the Red Sea," for instead of being stimulated to thoughts irrelevant to the concerns of the text, Guy is brought to a condition of utter thoughtlessness and profound sensuousness. He forgets not only the contents of the book but everything else as well, lulled by the "sublime" verses into a state of total oblivion that is not very different from death but that is yet a "delicious" pleasure to be enjoyed. The book is still open before him, and he is still "reading" it, but the benefit he gets from the process is one of physical well-being and of mystical union rather than mental stimulation. Raban's model of oblivious reading suggests a process by which one ignores the spirit of the text and instead plunders its letters for material that will feed an altogether different spirit, the spirit of the reader's enterprise. The reader differentiates himself from the material he reads. Guy's mode of reading, on the other hand, leads to a kind of meditative oblivion in which the reader never "parts from" (*quitter*) the book; instead, he becomes very like the material object a book may be thought to be — a set of letters that may be currently empty of spirit but that can be refilled and revivified. Without intending to, Malivert enters precisely the state of spiritual emptiness that typically prepares the mystic for a revelation. And the nature of that revelation — that lovers physically separated in life can be spiritually united in death — will be in keeping with the nature of the book from which he has never truly departed.

Guy does not pass through the Red Sea without getting wet, as Raban's model of reading proposes; he plunges into the water and is dissolved. He forgets the book by merging with it in a union that has more than a slight hint of sexuality. The phrase "il jouissait délicieusement de ce temps" is frankly sensual, and serves to prefigure the sensuality of Guy's later union with the spirit of Lavinia. It prefigures as well the "celestial joy" (GE 254; GF 213) that Malivert will experience in the moment of his death, the very literal "temps d'arret de son cerveau." Of course we know that the hero's brain does not really cease functioning as he sits in his chair immersed in "Evangeline," that the rhetoric of the passage seeks only to inform us that Guy was not engaged in strenuous mental activity, that indeed he was very near to falling asleep. Indeed, we learn a few pages later that he "was beginning to feel in his eyes the golden dust of sleep" (GE 21; GF 40–41) as he reclined in his chair, apparently still clutching his volume of Longfellow. But that rhetoric also begins to stake out the territory that the story will explore in greater detail, introducing us to the crepuscular dreamworld to which one gains access by means of reading. That realm lies on the boundary between life and death, waking and sleeping, attention and inattention, body and spirit.

Malivert's reading of Longfellow is more than a thematic prefiguration of the story to come: it is the physical preparation necessary for the continuation of the plot. One must die — at least a little — in order to be reborn. Guy's body must first accommodate "Evangeline" as a prevenient spirit that takes him over and prepares the way so that another, more powerful spirit — Malivert's kindred Spirite — may take possession of him later on. Obliged to write a short note of apology to Mme d'Ymbercourt for failing to keep his promise to have tea with her, he finds himself strangely unable to complete the simple task:

> Then he paused, and leaned his cheek on his hand, for his inspiration failed him. He remained for some time thus, his wrist in place, his fingers grasping the pen, and his brain unconsciously filled with thoughts wholly foreign to the subject of his note. Then, as if Malivert's body were tired of waiting for the words that did not come, his hand, nervous and impatient, seemed inclined to fulfill its task without further orders. His fingers extended and contracted as if tracing letters. (GE 25; GF 43)

The note gets written during a period of absent-mindedness, and Guy himself does not know what the note "he" has written contains until he reads it:

> "What is this?" exclaimed Malivert, when he read his letter over. "Am I crazy or a somnambulist? What a strange note! It is like those drawings of Gavarni's which exhibit at one and the same time in the subscription the real and expressed thought, the true and the false. Only, in this case the words do tell the truth. My hand, instead of telling the pretty fib [*joli petit mensonge social*] I meant to write, has refused to do so, and, contrary to custom, my real meaning is expressed in my letter [*l'idée sincère est dans la lettre*]." (GE 26; GF 43–44)

It is easy to recognize in this passage a scene of fantastic "automatic writing," a mode of communicating with the spirit world fashionable among believers in the occult from time to time. It is perhaps less evident, though no less important, to recognize that Malivert participates here in a scene of self-reading that launches him on his path toward union with his spectral double, Spirite. One must not lose sight of the fact that it is not only the act of *writing* that is important here, it is more pertinently the act of *reading*.[4] Malivert is, as it were, absent during the process of writing, and he does not even know what the note contains until he reads it, discovering only then that it contains his "real meaning" ("l'idée sincère"). He discovers in reading the full presence of his true feelings, which paradoxically have been allowed to surface only because he has let his fingers write without conscious direction. His spiritual absence during the act of writing makes possible the full presence of his spirit in the text he reads.

Where, one wants to ask, is the real Malivert when he writes automatically? In this instance, the genuine article, "l'idée sincère," resides only in the text as it is read retrospectively by a writer who is not at all certain he is actually the "author" of the words he has written. He had meant to compose something else altogether, "a pretty little social lie [*joli petit mensonge social*]" that would have revealed precisely nothing about his true feelings. His true self, then, can hardly be said to coincide with his intentions. Nor does it coincide with his behavior after he finishes reading, for he suppresses his feelings and decides to keep his engagement with Mme d'Ymbercourt. But in a written text that is the product of a body that seems to want to "dispense with proper order [*se passer d'ordre*]" (GE 25; GF 43) as well as to dispense with obedience to order, the true spirit infuses the inscribed letters: "l'idée sincère est dans la lettre."

The "real" Malivert is embodied in a document and can only be discovered by an act of reading. No one, not even himself, can gain access to his genuine thoughts save by deciphering them out of a text. He is a "legendary" character in the sense that he "must be read" if he is to be known at all.[5] The plot later turns on this feature of his character, for Lavinia's childhood infatuation with him matures into love primarily by way of reading his various writings, which she seeks out assiduously. Although she hardly ever manages to be in the same room with the object of her love, much less speak with him, she forms a deeper and apparently more accurate assessment of his character on the basis of her reading than do those who come into frequent personal contact with him. Malivert in fact appears to prefer to hide his light under a bushel and to present to the world — and even perhaps to himself — the image of a somewhat superficial man of society. It is only after considerable time and effort that Lavinia manages to learn that "the well-bred gentleman in [him] concealed [*cachait*] a distinguished writer," for he publishes not under his own name but "under the Latinized pseudonym of one of [his] given names" (GE 126; GF 117).

That the writer in Malivert is "hidden [*caché*]" and that it is not "Guy de Malivert" but some other persona offered as the author of his writings corresponds exactly with the situation of absent-minded or "automatic" writing through which Lavinia, in the form of Spirite, communicates with her beloved. The possibility of automatic writing becomes the essential premise for Gautier's story, and much of the novella is taken up with "dictées" through which the dead soul Spirite communicates with her living lover. But just as Guy finds his true intentions voiced in a text composed by a spirit external to his own volition, so does Lavinia find in the writings of this author-who-is-*not*-Guy-de-Malivert the distinguished person hidden by the man of society. One of the principal fantastic elements of this "nouvelle fantastique," the spiritual dictation, is in fact a literal acting out of a figurative description proper to Guy's "ordinary" literary activity. *All* his works are written by "someone else." The published works belong to a persona of the pseudonym; now this special set of writings turns out to be composed by an actual other person who takes temporary control of his body. The "automatic writing" he does under the direction of Spirite is a logical development of the gesture implied by writing under a pseudonym. In both cases the corporeal Guy de Malivert is temporarily effaced only to reemerge in the fullness of his spiritual reality in a text, where it is accessible to readers.

"To read a writer is to place yourself in communication with his mind [*lire un écrivain, c'est se mettre en communication d'âme*]," writes Spirite/Lavinia (by way of Malivert) regarding her reading of Malivert's works when she was a living girl (GE 126; GF 117). But if reading is a matter of "spiritual communication [*communication d'âme*]," it may well be that the reverse is also true, that when spiritual communication takes place it is always a matter of reading. In this tale, at any rate, precisely such is the case. The lovers are able to contact each other almost exclusively through reading. They do get glimpses of each other, of course, she of him at a couple of social functions during her lifetime, and he of her in a couple of mystical sightings after her death. These fleeting glimpses, however, only point up the great importance of the scenes of reading in which the two learn to know and love each other. A glimpse across a room or in a mirror may be enough to excite interest, but it is only the beginning of a process of "communication d'âme" that occurs primarily by way of texts. "By dint of reading you," Spirite tells Malivert, "I learned to know you, whom I had seen but once, as well as if I had met you intimately every day" (GE 128–29; GF 119). Reading offers Lavinia an opportunity to penetrate all externals— even externals of the writing being read — to the "intimate recesses of your thought" (GE 129; GF 119) by a means more efficient than personal acquaintance. For the skilled reader ("pour qui sait lire") no difficulty in the text is great enough to obscure for long "the true attitude of the soul" lodged therein (GE 127; GF 117). Such a skilled reader does "not always take literally what the author says," but works her way through the obscuring veils of "literary systems," "fashionable affectations," "style," and whatever else "may modify the exterior form of a writer" (GE 126–27; GF 117). Reading as Spirite describes it is therefore the systematic removal or penetration of everything exterior until the "poet's secret" (GE 127; GF 117), the hidden interior, is revealed.

Spirite engages in reading whenever she wants to understand something thoroughly. Indeed she can think of no better way of explaining the penetrating vision she obtains after her death than to compare it to reading: "I read as in an open book the poem of God, the letters of which were formed of suns" (GE 186; GF 162). God writes in characters that far surpass the lifeless markings of mortal script: His letters are the immense heavenly bodies themselves, not dead matter but a "prodigious life" that populates the skies (GE 186; GF 162). But this living script is legible only to those who have themselves died. Spirite, who longs to play Beatrice to Malivert's Dante (or Lavinia to his Aeneas), wants to share her experience of God's book with her beloved, but she cannot. "Would it were permissible for me to explain some of its pages to you! But you are still living in inferior darkness, and your eyes would be blinded by the dazzling effulgence" (GE 186; GF 162). The phrase "you still live among inferior shadows" offers two potential explanations for the possibility of Malivert's participation, depending on where we imagine the emphasis should be placed. The problem might be "inferior shadows" among which Guy still lives, or it might be that he is still alive (the shadows being a necessary accompaniment to being alive). The rhetoric of the sentence leaves both possibilities open, in part because the story assumes there to be no essential difference between being alive and being afflicted with "inferior shadows."

Death, which translates the shadowy body into bright spirit as it changes Lavinia into Spirite, makes of the soul a perfect reader, able to penetrate even the inferior darkness of living creatures. Where Lavinia had to read Malivert's soul by way of his writings, Spirite now reads his thoughts directly: "My spiritual nature [*ma qualité d'esprit*] allowed me to read in your heart" (GE 187; GF 163). Spirite's supernatural skill at reading corresponds to a desire voiced earlier in the story by Malivert as he puzzles over the mysteries of the note he — or someone — had written to Mme d'Ymbercourt:

> As he noted these details, Guy thought of Edgar Poe's "Golden Bug" and of the wonderful skill with which William Legrand manages to decipher the meaning of the cryptogram used by Captain Kidd to indicate enigmatically the exact spot where he had concealed his treasure. He longed to possess the deep intuition which can guess so boldly and so accurately, which fills up blanks and restores connections [*renoue la trame des rapports interrompus*]. (GE 46; GF 59)

Spirite possesses precisely this skill and she is using it to the very end Malivert had imagined: she is "restoring the weft of interrupted connections" (a more literal translation of "renoue la trame des rapports interrompus") by restoring her own connection to her beloved. She does it by reading him and by transforming herself into a very concrete text accessible to his not-yet-perfect mode of reading. In both cases, she depicts herself as moving away from the externalities of the flesh and toward the pure inwardness of the spirit, though by means of a material medium.

The scene in which Malivert reads Longfellow results in a mystical union with the poem characterized by a state of spiritual openness that is physically pleasurable. It has both a spiritual and a physical aspect. Not all reading has this complex structure, however, as Malivert demonstrates on several occasions. The earth-bound, shadow-dwelling Malivert is not at all averse to reading in a manner that is aggressively superficial. He, like Spirite, reads human beings, but before her intervention in his life he can only treat these living texts as coffee-table books. Finding himself bored with the company at Mme d'Ymbercourt's, he entertains himself by "studying" the various beautiful ladies assembled there: "He leafed through [*feuilletait*] these books of beauty with a nonchalant eye" (GE 37; GF 53). This sort of causal interaction contrasts sharply with the reading that Lavinia/Spirite does of Guy and he, under her tutelage, of her. Malivert reads these women in an oblivious mode, as it were; if they were books, we might well say, with Kafka, that their contents were "precisely of utter indifference" to the man who reads them. He is quite content to enjoy these agreeable exteriors, to read the graceful curve of the letter without worrying about the spirit. It is only with Spirite, who has no body to display graceful curves, that Malivert must move to the opposite extreme and focus entirely on inward, spiritual matters.

The contrast between Malivert's attitude toward the young socialites and toward Spirite emerges sharply when we consider how Spirite makes known to Malivert that she wants him to write. She appears to him as a disembodied hand: "The small, clean, well-turned, high-bred wrist ended in a most soft lace. As if to plainly mark that the hand was there but as a sign, the arm and the body were wanting [*étaient absents*]" (GE 111; GF 107). This is indeed strange, marvelous, and very spiritual, but it is also reminiscent of the scene at Mme d'Ymbercourt's, where Guy engages in his very unspiritual perusal of the ladies: "Guy watched the satiny shoulders covered with rice powder, the necks on which curled stray threads of hair, the white bosoms occasionally betrayed by the too-low epaulets of the bodice" (GE 36–37; GF 52). These women, too, appear as a segmented series of body-parts. But here, of course, the segmentation is all in the rhetoric; later, it becomes part of the reality of the narrative. Spirite, in a sense, makes good on Guy's superficial reading of the "books of beauty" by deepening it, turning a figurative and distinctly erotic dismemberment into something chaste and spiritual. She appears not as a set of shoulders or breasts but as a hand. What was before a physical delight in aspects of bodily grace becomes now denial of the body. Spirite's body is in fact described as "absent."

By transforming Guy's mildly erotic interest in the parts of the female body into a denial of full corporeality, the later passage both undoes and reinforces the earlier one. While it revalorizes the body as no more than a "sign" of spiritual presence, it also reminds us of the possibility of physical dismemberment and destruction that is the precondition for the victory of the spirit. Spirite can appear as a disembodied hand only because she is dead, and the fact of her death cannot be ignored or dismissed. Malivert surely does not dismiss it: "No doubt the spirit or the soul [*l'esprit ou l'âme*] that was entering into communication with Guy de Malivert had borrowed the form of its former perishable body, but such as it is must have become in a more subtile [*sic*], more ethereal region where the ghosts of things alone and not things themselves can exist" (GE 81; GF 85). Guy immediately falls in love with this vision, not because he mistakenly thinks it is alive but because he knows for certain that it is dead. The dismembering rhetoric of his appraisal of the ladies of society already suggests that erotic interest is linked in Guy's mind with physical decomposition. He is drawn to living things that may be understood as dead and to dead things that may be understood as living. That, of course, is why he is drawn to texts and to creatures that appear to him in the form of texts.

The text is the embodiment of Malivert's notion of a perfect object of love. Spirite, who combines in supernatural fashion the qualities of text and of person, is therefore irresistible for him. He realizes that, discovering his love for Lavinia only after her death, he has not lost but rather gained:

> From the way he adored her shadow he understood what a passion the girl herself would have inspired in him. But soon his thoughts took another course; he ceased to reproach himself, and regretted his commonplace grief. What had he lost, since, after all, Spirite had preserved her love beyond the tomb and had come from the depths of the Infinite to descend to the sphere which he inhabited? Was not the passion he felt nobler, more poetic, more ethereal, more like eternal love, since it was thus rid of terrestrial contingencies, and had for its object a being idealized by death [*une beauté idéalisée par la mort*]? (GE 154; GF 139–40)

The phrase "idealized by death" is one of the most revealing in the story. How can a person be "idealized" by ceasing to exist? The answer is of course that in Malivert's conception death does not involve ceasing to exist but rather only ceasing to change. Mortal love is contaminated by mutability, by "its weariness, its satiety, its lassitude [. . .]. The most dazzled eyes see, after a few years, the charms they first adored turn pale; the soul [*âme*] is less visible through the worn flesh and love seeks in amazement its vanished ideal [*et l'amour étonné cherche son idole disparue*]" (GE 154; GF 140). Death fixes a person forever (in our minds, at any rate) in an unchanging book of memory. Dante's Beatrice never grows old and ugly; having died young, she remains (for Dante) young forever. Spirite, the idealized form of Lavinia, will never change: she will always be what she appears to be in the text she dictates to Malivert. She is purged of everything exterior, everything contingent, embodied now only in an utterance that may be read and reread forever through the lens of a love that need no longer feel astonished by irrelevant alterations. The outside, the body of the flesh, is gone, and only the inside, the spiritual body, remains.

The ideal of a pure spiritual relationship propounded by Gautier's novella requires the establishment of a bond based on an interiority purged of everything external. The story enforces such a relationship between its hero and heroine by preventing their physical proximity. They are in the same room with each other only on a couple of occasions, and at those times Malivert does not have the slightest idea who Lavinia is or even that she exists. The intimacy of their bond is helped, however, and not hindered by their physical separation. Reading is the perfect medium for this sort of intimacy, because it is a mode of communication predicated upon absence. "Is not a book," Spirite asks rhetorically, "confidences addressed to an ideal friend, a conversation from which the interlocutor is absent?" (GE 126; GF 117). Lavinia, even before she dies and becomes the ethereal Spirite, makes herself into such an ideal friend not only by acting in the role of a sympathetic reader, but by remaining ever apart from her beloved author. Later, after her death, she makes Malivert into such an ideal friend by making herself into a legendary object, an entity that must be read. She produces, with his help, a set of texts through which he gains access to her. Gautier makes very clear that the process of "automatic writing" by which Guy takes down the spiritual dictation of the ghostly Spirite imparts no knowledge. Guy does not know anything about Lavinia until he reads what he has written:

> Suddenly the impulse that guided his hand stopped, and his own thought, suspended by that of Spirite, returned to him. The faint light of dawn was filtering through the curtains of his room. He pulled them aside, and the pallid light of a winter morning showed him on the table many pages covered with a feverish, rapid writing, the work of the night. Although he had written them with his own hand, he did not know their contents. With ardent curiosity, with deep emotion, he read the artless and chaste confidences of the lovely soul, of the adorable being, whose executioner he had been; innocently, it is needless to add. (GE 151–52; GF 136–37)

The return of the word "confidences" reminds us that the text is looking for the "ideal friend" that Malivert's own writings had found in Lavinia. Guy thus becomes for Spirite what Lavinia had been for the unnamed author of Malivert's works: an absent interlocutor.

The ways in which Lavinia and Malivert are absent, even from themselves, become more and more complex. Lavinia is now absent in what would seem to be the most definitive way possible: she is dead. Her spirit is separated from a body that no longer exists save as a transitory metaphor of her inward loveliness. One would suppose that this permanent separation from the realm of materiality would impose insuperable difficulties on Lavinia's efforts to gain the attention of her beloved. As she says herself, "Between a spirit and an uninitiated living being communications are difficult. A deep gulf separates this world from the other" (GE 188–89; GF 163). But this gulf turns out to be far less difficult to cross for Spirite than the gulf of unconsciousness and inattention that had separated the living Lavinia from Malivert. Hard as it is for Spirite to make contact with her living beloved, it is nonetheless easier than it had been for the living Lavinia to make contact with him. One of the most striking features of Gautier's tale is this paradox: Lavinia's death, the event we would expect to conclude forever her efforts to communicate with Malivert, is not the end of the story but the beginning, much as Beatrice's death was for Dante.

Lavinia's death — aided, later, by Malivert's death as well — opens up the possibility of recovering and improving the past. The actual history of Malivert's relations with the living Lavinia is characterized by failure. Once Lavinia is dead, however, a new opportunity arises to recuperate this failed past and make good on all its missteps and lapses in an ideal, spiritual realm where inattentiveness and unconsciousness are no longer problems. In this new context, they are transformed into positive advantages that allow the disembodied Spirite entry into the temporarily vacant space of her beloved's mind. All the barriers that prevented physical communication in the material world are now metamorphosed into open pathways of the spirit. Once Lavinia is no longer a material girl, the broken past can be healed.

Death translates Lavinia into Spirite and makes of her an entity accessible only by mystical visions and by reading, as Malivert had been for her during her lifetime. Even when she was alive she had described herself in terms of a textual figure: "My heart held but a single page; you had written your name on it unwittingly, and no other was to take its place" (GE 167; GF 148). The image is perhaps truer than its speaker intended. Lavinia is not simply eternally loyal to Malivert; she is in effect nothing else but her love for him. Her character is defined exclusively and completely by her love, a love for which she dies and for which she struggles even as a disembodied ghost. She is a text so brief that it needs far less than a whole page, comprising nothing more than the name of her beloved.

When Guy returns from his mental absence to read the pages dictated by Spirite, what he reads is an elaborate variation on his own name. The "other" who had taken control of his thoughts and directed his hand turns out, on closer inspection, to be a mirror image of Malivert himself. Gautier stresses this aspect of the relation between his hero and heroine by letting Guy obtain his first vision of Spirite in a mirror. The narrator says that what he saw was "the head of a young woman, or of a young girl rather, by the side of whose loveliness earthly beauty was but a shadow" (GE 79–80; GF 84) but later adds in explanation that "what he saw, though it was *like* [*semblable*] the face of a beautiful woman, in no respect *resembled* [*ressemblait*] what, on this earth, is called a beautiful female face" (GE 81; GF 85; Gautier's emphasis). The distinction between "like [*semblable*]" something and "resembling [*ressembler*]" something is hard to discern — perhaps intentionally so — but it is alleged to be crucial. The sentence appears to claim that two things (the image in the mirror and a woman's face) can be alike and not alike at the same time. The coexistence of sameness and difference is the essence of the relation that Guy discovers by looking in the mirror at Spirite, a creature who both is and is not himself. It is precisely this relation that obtains between Malivert and the documents he writes under the influence of Spirite, for one could properly say that he wrote them *and* that he did not.

The experience of Malivert finding in his mirror an image of himself that is also in fact an image of someone else is a figure for the experience of the writer who, upon reading the product of his own hands, finds something that is at once his and yet also fundamentally alien. Malivert's relationship with Spirite, his love for a double of himself whom he only discovers posthumously by way of reading, puts into mythic form the disquieting experience of every author who has ever tried seriously to read his or her own writing. One inevitably discovers important and substantial differences between the person who wrote the document and the person who now reads it, never mind that these two persons are supposed to be identical. One begins to suspect the existence of enormous differences between a *text*, which a powerful cultural tradition assures us contains the spiritual essence of its author, and a living person, whose mutable spirit is not readily separable from a body of flesh and blood. Spirite's reflections on her reading of Guy's writings present the view that reading involves "communication d'âme" in which the "true attitude of the soul at last reveals itself to the real reader [*finit par se révéler pour qui sait lire*]" (GE 127; GF 117). Guy's experience with the letter to Mme d'Ymbercourt and, in even greater measure, the "dictation" of Spirite complicate and enrich that view. When reading his own works the writer may find not simply the essence of his own spirit but also that of another, remarkably different spirit. The liveliness of this other spirit, furthermore, may turn out to be the result of its death.

Gautier's tale puts the most optimistic construction possible on this discovery of a dead/alive self/other in a text that is supposed to be the mirror of one's own soul. The lovers, who are two different people and yet images of a single self, finally overcome all the obstacles separating them, erasing the gap between life and death, male and female, real and ideal. After Malivert's death at the hands of bandits, his friend Baron de Féroë has a vision of the souls of the two lovers:

> They floated side by side in a celestial, radiant joy, caressing each other with their wings and toying with divine endearments. Soon they drew closer and closer, and then, like two drops of dew rolling on the same lily leaf, they finally formed a single pearl.
>
> "There they are, happy forever, their united souls forming an angel of love," said Baron de Féroë, with a melancholy smile. (GE 256; GF 215)

This vision of perfect union, of self and other joined in an unbreakable bond of love through an undying eternity, comes only at the conclusion of a story that offers a much more nuanced picture in the bulk of its narrative. I do not mean to suggest that the happy ending is not true to Gautier's real hopes and intentions; on the contrary, everything we know about him suggests that Gautier did indeed believe in and long to dwell in a pure, ideal realm of undying essences. But the story is haunted by a tenacious doubt that lurks in nearly every paragraph. Even the happy ending is somewhat undercut by the Baron's melancholy smile and his rhetorical question, "But how long have I still to wait?"

Of course, in one sense the Baron will not have to wait long. The termination of physical existence is a dead certainty. But the transformation into pure living spirit depends on our ability to read, and that ability is less reliable, and the results we obtain from its exercise are always subject to further interpretation. We cannot even be sure that the Baron's happy vision is not itself a textual artifact, for it takes place while he is in the midst of reading "that strange and mysterious work of Swedenborg entitled, 'Marriage in the Other Life'" (GE 255; GF 214). Has the Baron seen what actually happened to Malivert and Spirite, or has he successfully spun a Swedenborgian fantasy out of his reading? The story does not permit a definitive answer, because it is itself a Swedenborgian fantasy in which much of the narrative obscures or even obliterates the distinction between actuality and the effects of reading.[6] There may after all be little or no difference between the living souls of the dead lovers in the Baron's vision and the living spirit emerging from the dead letters as he reads Swedenborg's book. In both cases the Baron has performed the exhilarating, terrifying miracle of raising the dead by means of the revivifying word.

Notes

[1] The publication date of Gautier's novella serves as a useful reminder that the boundaries of the "Romantic century" cannot be set definitively at 1750 and 1850. McFarland, for example, defines the limits of the period in terms of the work of such authors as Rousseau at the beginning and Baudelaire at the end (15). There is no dispute among literary historians about Gautier's participation in the late phase of French Romanticism: he was closely associated with Romantic figures like Victor Hugo and was himself a leading poet and novelist of the 1830s and 1840s. *Spirite* is best understood as an autumn blossom in the Romantic garden, late in arriving but unquestionably the product of the summer season.

[2] Longfellow's poem was published in 1847. A translation into French alexandrines by Pamphile Lemay appeared in Quebec almost exactly contemporaneously with *Spirite* in 1865. It would have been difficult, though perhaps not entirely impossible, for Gautier to have seen the translation while he was writing his novella; but

his enthusiasm for the poem would be difficult to understand unless he had at least some acquaintance with the English original. Although Longfellow himself praised it (with some reservation), Lemay's translation would not have been likely to elicit such interest.

[3] For more on this passage from Kafka and on the theory of reading it implies, see Koelb, *Kafka's Rhetoric* 86–89; for more on the "oblivious" mode of reading, see Koelb, *Incredulous Reader*, 143–57.

[4] For an analysis of Gautier's story that foregrounds the theme of writing, see Ziegler.

[5] This notion of a text or textual element as "legendary" is developed further in Koelb, *Legendary Figures* 1–27.

[6] The name of Swedenborg already appears much earlier in the narrative, e.g., in chapter 4 (GE 66; GF 75), as if to alert the reader to the tale's intellectual background. And of course Gautier has arranged for his hero's closest friend, Baron de Féroë, to be a Swede.

Part III
The Incarnate Word

7: "Eat This Scroll": Kleist's "Michael Kohlhaas"

Romantic protagonists not only revived the dead past by reading; they also often achieved spiritual revivification by incorporating texts into their physical bodies. We have seen how Goethe's character Werther seeks to make himself one with a set of texts, principally the poems of Homer and "Ossian." He reads his way into these texts so thoroughly that he seems to have consumed them, and indeed at times he even appears to have figuratively eaten his way into them. The merger of self and text, both wished for and dreaded by Romantic protagonists, is also inevitably a crossing of the border between life and death. Werther, Claude Frollo in Victor Hugo's *Notre-Dame de Paris*, and even Keats's Endymion all traverse this boundary or reside in its immediate vicinity. They are primarily concerned with the recovery, recuperation, and revivification of the past. Other figures, like Mary Shelley's Frankenstein (along with his demonic creature) and many of Poe's characters, are more urgently concerned with the closely related pleasures and terrors that accompany transforming the dead word into living flesh. One of the most interesting of these protagonists is the title character of Heinrich von Kleist's story "Michael Kohlhaas" (1810).

Kleist's famous tale is both one of the most admired and one of the most frequently censured works in the modern German canon. There is nearly universal admiration for the story of Kohlhaas's attempt to obtain redress for an injustice done to him by the Tronka family, for his excesses in taking the law into his own hands, and for his final vindication for the former and condemnation for the latter. But this simple, powerful tale is complicated by what many critics refer to as a "sub-plot" in which Kohlhaas comes into possession of a prophecy regarding the Elector of Saxony and, by destroying the paper on which this prophecy is written, avenges the Elector's injustices. This prophecy plot has received sharp criticism from many quarters and, in spite of a number of attempts to defend it, continues to provoke critical displeasure.[1] David Luke and Nigel Reeves — to cite just one example from the many available — find the story "as Kleist might have completed it," without the prophecy material, to be wholly admirable. They call it "the story of individual grievance developing, with fascinating and dreadful realism, through ever-increasing complexities until it becomes a major affair of state and is then brought to a paradoxical but impressively logical resolution." But when Kleist finally completed in 1810 the project he had started perhaps as early as 1804, it went in another direction. "Unfortunately, [. . .] Kleist was not content to finish 'Michael Kohlhaas' on those lines, but introduced a bizarre and fantastic sub-plot which seriously damages the artistic structure of an already long and complex narrative" (Luke and Reeves 27). Luke and Reeves follow the precedent of, among others, Georg Lukács, who saw in the novella a potentially successful realism suffering a "derailment" (*Entgleisung*) in the last quarter of the text. Lukács therefore simply omits the prophecy material from his discussion, and other interpreters have clearly wished they could do the same.

It is worth asking ourselves why so many of us are uncomfortable with the story as Kleist wrote it. It cannot be the mere fact that Kleist has made use of fantasy, since he does so in other tales without provoking similar discomfort. No one objects, for example, to the intrusion of the supernatural in "The Beggar Woman of Locarno" or "St. Cecilia." The judgment of Luke and Reeves is once again typical: "The irruption of the inexplicable into an otherwise explicable world is here again [in 'St. Cecilia' as in 'The Beggarwoman'] very far from seeming to be a mere whimsical and stylistically alien digression: instead, it is once more the precise centre and appalling *pointe* of the whole tale" (Luke and Reeves 33). But why is the confrontation between natural and supernatural, explicable and inexplicable, seen to be "whimsical" and "alien" in the one case but central in the others? What is different about "Michael Kohlhaas" that sets the stage for such large-scale critical disappointment?

One answer certainly lies in the disposition of many readers, particularly those in the twentieth century, to read the story as a "realistic" chronicle gone astray. Kleist, after all, seems to distinguish between "Kohlhaas" and "St. Cecilia" by describing the former as "From an old chronicle [*Aus einer alten Chronik*]" and the latter as "A legend [*Eine Legende*]." This might suggest to some that supernatural elements could well be expected in the latter but not in the former. Modern readers hold "chronicles" to a higher standard of verisimilitude than "legends," and they therefore suppose — wrongly, as it turns out — that "Kohlhaas" will measure up to this standard. In any case, engagement with the story evidently produces a set of expectations that are frustrated by the actual course the plot finally takes. Such readers, assuming they are reading a story that turns on the issue of Kohlhaas's horses, find the rug pulled out from under them by the "whimsical" addition of the issue of the prophecy. A tale that seemed to be about one thing (the horses) suddenly swerves away from that established topic to go haring off after something else entirely. Disappointment, or at best puzzlement, is the result. Even those who defend the plot as Kleist wrote it see the story as divided into two sections marked prominently by the change in narrative attention from horses to prophecy. One of the most radical of recent defenses, the Lacanian reading offered by Helga Gallas, provides a psychoanalytic motivation for the division, whereby the scrap of paper bearing the prophecy functions as a figurative substitute for the horses. In Gallas's view, then, the division is only formal and superficial, since both the horses and the paper with the prophecy are already themselves metaphors of the phallus; but the division is still there and indeed figures very prominently in her analysis. One could go so far as to say that Gallas's analysis actually depends upon the presence of a division, since the process of metaphorical substitution and metonymic displacement according to which the tale is said to function can only be glimpsed precisely because Kleist staged so openly the move from one "object" to another.

All of these readings, whether they attack or defend, assume that there is a prominent change in narrative attention. But this change may be more a feature of the critical tradition attached to this text than a structure somehow embedded in it. If we listen at least as carefully to the *rhetoric* of the narrative as we do to the things narrated, we discern a unity that is perhaps otherwise obscured. A rhetorical reading of Kleist's story discloses a set of concerns that remain unchanged from beginning to end.[2] The rhetorical analysis offered here suggests that structures embedded in and foregrounded by the text as Kleist wrote it give it an unmistakable coherence, that there is no change at all in narrative attention, and that the story is explicitly "about" the same topic all the way through. Not only need we not assume that Kleist went astray, we need not even assume that he set up a structure of figurative substitution and displacement.

There is plenty of textual evidence to suggest an underlying unity binding together the whole narrative. The considerable narrative space between the incident about the permit and the introduction of the theme of the gypsy's prophecy is filled to overflowing with documents that replace each other, answer each other, or cancel each other out. Nearly every turn of the plot is associated with some sort of *Schrift* initiated by Kohlhaas, the officials of the governments involved, or other parties involved in the dispute. There are contracts, writs, letters, receipts, petitions, edicts, declarations, resolutions, notices, proclamations, certificates, inquiries, passports, notes, reports, dispatches, sentences, verdicts, and more. When one begins to reckon up all the documents that figure in the story, one is prompted to exclaim, as Judge Adam does in Kleist's play *The Broken Jug*, that they seem to be piled as high as the Tower of Babel. Certainly they seem to speak with a confusion of tongues equivalent to that which the Lord imposed upon the Tower builders and to lead Kohlhaas no closer to divine authority — not, that is, up until the end.

The question of the relation of the texts to divine authority is opened up early in the narrative, though the story does not offer an example of divine Scripture until the tale of the gypsy woman is told. The question is in fact implicit in the very historical setting — the Reformation — and in the appearance among the dramatis personae of Martin Luther himself.

Luther, author of the doctrine *sola scriptura*, is Kohlhaas's spiritual leader, since Kohlhaas and his wife had been among the early converts to Lutheranism. The great work of translating the Bible into German was, of course, motivated by the belief that Scripture could serve as the sole means by which the individual could establish a personal relation with God, unmediated by doctrine, clergy, and other institutions of the Church. No doubt that when Kohlhaas promulgates his first edict and declares that he does so "by virtue of the powers vested in him at birth [*kraft der ihm angebornenen Macht*]," his reasoning derives in part from the Protestantism he has embraced. When he speaks with the great reformer face to face and hears him ask, "Who gave you the right to attack [. . .] in pursuance of the decrees issued on no authority but your own?" he is unable to offer more than an apologetic "No one, your Reverence" (KM 152; KW 45). The reader, however, is at liberty to supply the answer Kohlhaas fails to give: "You, Martin Luther, gave me the right to find divine authority in myself."

Kohlhaas is perhaps wise in his reticence. Luther could not have accepted such an answer and would surely have replied that it is very difficult to be sure when it is the voice of God one hears within and not that of the devil. The theologian is not certain whether the horse dealer is in touch with divine order or diabolical disorder, though Kohlhaas's actions incline him toward the latter. The former possibility cannot be dismissed, however, and Luther has to acknowledge that "if the circumstances really are as public opinion has it, then what you demand is just" (KM 154; KW 47).

Holy Scripture makes its way into this mass of documents not only by implication, through the presence of Luther, and not only because as a good Lutheran Elizabeth has the Bible read to her on her death bed, but perhaps most importantly because Kohlhaas's final act of vengeance against the Elector of Saxony is an acting out "word for word" of a set of scriptural commandments. In the Old Testament it is Ezekiel who hears the voice of divinity offer him a text that he is supposed to eat: "Then I saw a hand stretched out to me, holding a scroll. He unrolled it before me, and it was written all over on both sides with dirges and laments and words of woe. Then he said to me, 'Man, eat what is in front of you, eat this scroll [. . .].' So I ate it, and it tasted as sweet as honey" (Ezekiel 2:9–3:3). In the New Testament the Revelations of John echo this figure: "The voice which I heard from heaven was speaking to me again, and it said, 'Go and take the open scroll [. . .] and eat it. It will turn your stomach sour, although in your mouth it will taste as sweet as honey.' So I took the little scroll from the angel's hand and ate it" (Revelations 10:8–10).[3] When Kohlhaas eats the paper bearing the prophecy, then, he is doing more than simply keeping it from the elector; he is incorporating it into himself, making himself one with it. It is the physical fulfillment of and a figure for the act of reading he has just completed. The biblical texts just quoted are clearly intended as allegories of a kind of successful reading in which the reader assimilates so thoroughly the material he reads that it becomes part of him. Kohlhaas, by eating the prophecy, incorporates the mysterious text into himself, including especially that part of himself that is supposed to survive the death of the flesh.

Many readers fail to notice the central importance of textual incorporation in "Kohlhaas," perhaps because they tend to read the first half or three-quarters of the story as centering on Kohlhaas's horses. They do so, naturally enough, because Kohlhaas himself makes so much out of them and because they function for him as the master trope standing for both injustice and justice, both power and impotence, both obedience and rebellion. Kohlhaas literally makes a federal case out of his horses and projects onto them all of his fears and desires respecting his relation with the community. It is quite understandable that Gallas should see in them the locus of anxiety equivalent to Freud's conception of castration anxiety, given the enormous charge of emotion with which Kohlhaas invests them. The reader, however, need not accept as the issue of Kleist's story the object Kohlhaas has chosen to make the issue of his struggle with the state. One of the principal effects of the prophecy material, in fact, seems to be to deflect attention away from the matter of the horses and bring it back to what was intended all along to be the central issue, the possession of authoritative documents.

If we turn to the crucial opening scene in which Kohlhaas comes into conflict with the Tronka family, we find that the horses come into play principally as stand-ins (that is, as collateral) for a missing document. It is Kohlhaas's lack of a *Paßschein* ("permit") that starts all the trouble:

> The warden, still fastening a waistcoat across his capacious body, came up and, bracing himself against the wind and rain, demanded the horse-dealer's permit [*Paßschein*]. "My permit?" asked Kohlhaas and added, a little disconcerted, that so far as he knew he did not possess one, but that if the warden would kindly explain what on earth such a thing was [*was dies für ein Ding des Herrn sei*] he just might possibly [*zufälligerweise*] have one with him. (KM 115; KW 10)

Kohlhaas's reaction to the warden's demand deserves careful attention. He does not simply state that he does not have the document in question; he claims that he does not know what sort of "Ding des Herrn" a *Paßschein* would be. Kohlhaas's language is on the one hand merely the use of a commonplace expression, an emphatic trope properly translated as "what in the world?" Kleist, however, frequently practiced a kind of complex rhetoric in which both tenor and vehicle in a figurative expression signify with equal force. It was Kleist, after all, who had his heroine Penthesilea chew on the body of the slain Achilles and later remark that she was simply putting into practice "word for word [*Wort für Wort*]" the everyday hyperbole that says "I love him so much I could eat him up." Kleist evidently thought this one of the most important features of his play, for when he wrote to his cousin Marie von Kleist in the autumn of 1807 to announce that he had finished the work, he reminded her of its subject matter with a single sentence, "She loved Achilles so much that she really did eat him up [*Sie hat ihn wirklich aufgegessen, den Achill, vor Liebe*]" (KW 796). One has reason to suspect, then, that when Kleist's characters use tropes one had better attend to their literal as well as to their figurative meanings. In this case, the suspicion that the permit the warden wants might be a "Ding des Herrn" in the literal sense is confirmed when he explains to Kohlhaas that "without a state permit a dealer bringing horses could not be allowed across the border" (KM 115; KW 10). So this permit really is a "thing of the lord" in that it is issued by the appropriate "Landesherr." What the text does not express explicitly but nonetheless urges us to consider is that a document might also be a "thing of the Lord" claiming its authority not merely from the will of a secular ruler but from the divine order itself. As the story develops, it becomes ever more clear that indeed the issue really does center upon Kohlhaas's relation to both the secular and the divine systems of order.

We must also read carefully Kohlhaas's apparently ironic request to be told what a *Paßschein* might be so that he might look to see whether he was provided with one "by chance [*zufälligerweise*]." This is, to be sure, an example of ironic self-deprecation where the assertion that the speaker is "just a poor ignorant country boy" (or the like) is used to put the other party at a disadvantage. Kohlhaas implies that a permit must be a thing of such minute importance that he might have one lying about somewhere and not even know about it. At the same time, though, his language proposes the notion that this "Ding des Herrn" might come into a person's possession quite by chance, and in this story (as it turns out) we must take that possibility very seriously. Kohlhaas does gain possession, by chance, of a document by means of which he can bring the scales of justice into better balance. This document, the gypsy woman's scrap of paper, belongs to a realm clearly different from that to which the requested *Paßschein* belongs, since it has a supernatural rather than a secular origin. Each document, however, may be properly described as a "Ding des Herrn."[4]

The issue of the permit remains central to the plot, its meaning however steadily complicated by the rhetoric of its presentation. The text explains, for example, that Kohlhaas is required to leave his two fine black horses with Wenzel von Tronka "as surety that he would get the permit [*Ein Pfand, zur Sicherheit, daß er den Schein lösen würde*]" (KM 117; KW 12).[5] Although he suspects that the requirement of such a permit is illegal, the horse dealer is prepared to fulfill the clearly intended meaning of the phrase "den Schein lösen" by leaving the horses and purchasing a permit in Dresden. As it turns out, though, he acts out an entirely different significance of these words when he "dissolves the appearance" by learning, to no great surprise, that "the story about the permit was a mere fabrication [*die Geschichte von dem Paßschein ein Märchen sei*]" (KM 118; KW 13).[6] The word "Märchen" implies that the permit demanded by Tronka belongs to the realm of the (literary) imagination and not to the legal structure governing the everyday world. Kohlhaas's horses, then, have been held to guarantee the production of a document that neither exists nor can exist under the prevailing legal system. The absence of the permit, so mightily deplored by the Junker's warden, is irremediable — except perhaps in the realm of "Märchen."

For now, Kohlhaas can only temporarily remedy this absence by a bizarre bureaucratic shuffle in which he obtains a different document certifying that the first document (if it existed) would have no legal standing. He persuades a disgruntled Dresden official to issue "a written certificate of its [the permit's] groundlessness" (KM 118; KW 13), which he duly carries back to Tronka castle and shows to the warden. Having thus procured a document that properly ought to serve as a replacement for the one initially demanded, Kohlhaas expects to get in return the *other* replacement, the horses. What he gets, however, is to his way of thinking another set of stand-ins that are in fact absolutely inadequate. Instead of the sleek, healthy, well-fed horses he had left with the Junker, he is given "a pair of scrawny, worn-out nags, their bones protruding like pegs you could have hung things on" (KM 119; KW 13). He declines to accept these horses as his and tells the Junker boldly, "Those are *not* my horses, my lord; those are not the *horses* that were worth thirty gold florins! I want my healthy, well-nourished horses back!" (KM 121; KW 16). The horse dealer's language asserts that the horses offered are for all practical purposes non-horses. The narrator's description subtly substantiates that claim by figuratively transforming the animals in question from living creatures into dead objects, "pegs you could have hung things on." Instead of vital steeds who can carry living riders, Kohlhaas is offered dead things capable of carrying only other dead things.

There is a symmetry in this turn of events, even if it is not exactly justice. Kohlhaas has offered a non-permit in place of the document demanded, and he has been offered non-horses in place of the horses he requires. It comes close to balancing out and Kohlhaas himself, in spite of his justifiable anger, is prepared to "accept the loss of the horses as a just consequence" (KM 121; KW 16), provided it indeed turns out that his groom Herse had failed to perform his duty, as the Junker's people charged. But that charge, too, proves to be completely baseless: Kohlhaas learns instead that Herse had been mistreated without cause while trying to take care of the horses at the Tronka estate, and he feels consequently that he has no alternative but to take further action. The action he takes, perhaps not surprisingly, answers precisely the demand that initiated the problem, the demand for a document. He sets about producing a variety of documents seeking remedy in the courts of law for the mischief done by the earlier (non)documents. "With the aid of a lawyer [. . .] he drew up a statement in which he gave a detailed description of the outrage committed against him and his groom Herse by Junker Wenzel von Tronka. He demanded punishment in accordance with the law" (KM 127; KW 21). After months go by without any action, he produces more documents, all to no avail. He sends letters, receives letters, composes petitions, and receives more letters. At last he gets a letter transmitting a resolution from the Chancellery that directs Kohlhaas to desist from his litigation about a pair of horses that the Junker von Tronka was quite prepared to return to him.

The rhetoric of the horse dealer's response to this resolution is instructive: "Since for Kohlhaas the horses were not the issue — he would have been equally aggrieved had they been a couple of dogs — this letter made him foam with rage [*er schäumte vor Wut*]" (KM 130; KW 24). Both dogs and horses may be said to "foam" ("schäumen"), though under very different circumstances: horses when they are overheated, dogs when they are wildly aggressive. Persons do so only figuratively in the everyday cliché "vor Wut schäumen" that Kleist uses here. The sentence shows itself to be ironic by offering rhetorical evidence that the explicit statement it makes is not true. If horses/dogs are not the issue, why does Kohlhaas immediately behave like a (metaphorical) horse/dog? The irony actually preserves both conflicting propositions, as irony always does when it explicitly states the opposite of what it means. A person who makes the ironic observation "Lovely weather!" in the middle of a blizzard necessarily offers the possibility that the listener might assume the speaker enjoys blizzards. Both constructions — that the weather is terrible and that it is wonderful — inhere in the structure of the discourse. It is therefore profitable to seek to understand how both terms in this ambivalent structure are valid. In what way, we might wonder, is it correct to say that the horses both are and are not the issue? The sentence that in effect poses the question also offers the way toward an answer. The horses are not an issue in themselves, just as Kohlhaas asserts, but they become an issue as metaphors for other matters of importance to the story — of Kohlhaas's powerful emotions, for example, or for justice itself, or even (as Gallas would have it) of phallic potency.[7] For this to happen, however, the horses must first be transformed into a text. That is, of course, exactly what occurs in the opening scene when the warden proposes that Kohlhaas offer the horses in lieu of the missing permit.

The chronicle material offered Kleist the occasion for enlarging upon a figurative equivalence of horses and texts that was already a part of his linguistic experience. In early January of 1808, at the time of the first publication of the literary journal *Phöbus*, in which Kleist printed portions of *Penthesilea*, Jean Paul declared himself ready to contribute: "I will provide the best [horse] I can to hitch to the team of your *Phoebus* — no hobby-horses of any sort — and if I cannot help either the team or myself, at least my [horse] can run along side, the way people have single horses do in Naples, letting them trot along with the team just for the fun of it" (KW 805). By publishing "Kohlhaas" in *Phöbus* later that year, Kleist could well have bragged with Penthesilea that he had made Jean Paul's metaphor good "word for word." The figurative horses he puts in harness for his publishing enterprise are the "real" horses inscribed so prominently in the center of the tale of the justice-seeking horse dealer.

"Kohlhaas" is a story that connects horses and texts by both metaphor and metonymy, by both representing horses (contribution to *Phöbus*) and containing them (characters in the narrative). The horses were already textual artifacts before Kleist wrote his story. The story in fact fills the space of a missing "horse" in that it occupies a place in the "Gespann" proposed by Jean Paul's figure. It is little wonder, then, that the horses in the story act as stand-ins for a missing but necessary text, the permit that Kohlhaas later discovers is only a "Märchen." At the story's beginning, this "Märchen" marks a space occupied at first by nothing, then by the horses, and then by a lengthy series of texts beginning with the "written certificate of its groundlessness" and ending only with the gypsy's prophecy and the reader's discovery that this tale is not the realistic narrative it first appeared to be but is instead the missing text, the "Märchen" indirectly demanded by the warden of the Tronka castle.

The tale's end also keeps the reader's attention focused on documents. It is important to remember that the final scene of the story is not only or even primarily the narrative of Kohlhaas's execution. The execution itself does not even take up the whole of a single sentence. Most of what goes on in that scene is various acts of reading. After the sentence of death is read to Kohlhaas a few days before the actual execution, he receives a letter from Luther, the contents of which are unavailable to the chronicler and reader. It was "without a doubt a very remarkable communication, all trace of which, however, has been lost" (KM 210; KW 100). He also reads a note from an old woman, apparently the gypsy woman, but closed with the signature "Your Elizabeth." Although all the words of the note are delivered to Kohlhaas and to the reader, an essential paratextual element gets lost. Kohlhaas, naturally enough, wants to know where the note came from, but when the man who brought the note is asked for more information, a gap opens up: "But just as the castellan was answering: 'Kohlhaas, the woman . . ., only to falter strangely in mid-speech, the horse dealer was swept along in the procession [to the place of execution] which moved off again at that very moment, and could not catch what the man, who seemed to be trembling in every limb, was saying" (KM 210–11; KW 101). When he reaches the hill where the sentence is to be carried out, he is given the document containing the verdict of the court in Dresden, and he "read it through, his eyes wide and sparkling with triumph" taking special note of "a clause condemning the Junker Wenzel von Tronka to two years' imprisonment" (KM 212; KW 102). When he spies the Elector of Saxony in the crowd he "strode up close to him, took the locket from round his neck, took out the piece of paper, unsealed it and read it; then fixing his gaze steadily on the [Elector] who was already beginning to harbour sweet hopes, he stuck it in his mouth and swallowed it" (KM 213; KW 103).

All of these acts of reading, culminating in the reading/eating of the prophecy, serve to establish reading as the means by which the story reaches its resolution. Kohlhaas does not simply decipher the marks in the various documents he reads: he makes himself one with their meaning and thereby puts himself in intimate contact with a power outside himself. It is in this union with a power beyond himself that he achieves a significant victory over the Elector of Saxony. Paradoxically, the outcome of Kohlhaas's execution, in which the horse dealer's body is literally dismembered, is that the Elector becomes, as Kleist's narrative puts it, "zerissen an Leib und Seele" — "physically and mentally a broken man" (KW 103; KM 213). Kohlhaas, in other words, "gets it all together" while the Elector "falls apart." The executioner's severing axe is thus of relatively little consequence in comparison to the act of unifying reading, and the narrative space devoted to the two processes reflects this valorization precisely.

The equation between eating and the spiritual incorporation of a text had already occupied Kleist's mind for some time when he began work on "Kohlhaas." We cannot forget that a climactic act of eating also marks the moment of greatest stress and significance in *Penthesilea*. In *Penthesilea*, too, the issue is not simple revenge but more importantly the protagonist's attempt to make a text an active part of life. By chewing Achilles's body the Amazon queen not only performs a figurative act of love ("Küsse, Bisse, das reimt sich") but also puts a text to work ("einen vor Liebe aufessen"). Penthesilea's frenzied attempt to eat the body of her enemy/lover is certainly deranged, but it does follow its own rigorous logic. Achilles himself exists for Penthesilea first as a discourse, a text of authority, handed down by Otrere. Her desire for him is first and foremost the desire to incorporate into her life the maternal word delivered in Otrere's dying moments. She does not choose Achilles out of selfish desire; he is chosen for her by maternal (and royal) commandment. Her task is to put maternal discourse into action, to incorporate into her life this text called "Achilles." When Penthesilea chews on Achilles's body, she conflates in her frenzy two texts that ought to remain separate, the commandment of Otrere to possess Achilles and the commonplace hyperbolic expression that posits eating the beloved as the highest proof of love (cf. Koelb, *Inventions* 65–79).

Love and justice serve analogous functions in *Penthesilea* and "Kohlhaas" in that each is presented as a transcendent value approachable in this world only by disastrously fallible acts of interpretation.[8] In both the play and the story, the central issue is the protagonist's urgent desire to be in contact with a transcendent text recognizable principally by the emptiness left by its absence. Penthesilea tries with all her might to fill the void left by the death of Otrere and to remain in firm contact with the textual trace the queen has left behind. Kohlhaas discovers the void left by the absence of divine justice when he is required to present an unobtainable document. Kohlhaas, like Penthesilea, does not retreat from this void but tries instead to fill it with substitute documents, with horses, and finally even with his own body. His body at last does succeed in filling the void, but only because it has first been filled up with a "Ding des Herrn," a text of divine authority.

The allegedly "derailed" material about the gypsy woman and her prophecy is a semi-secularized Holy Scripture that is absolutely essential to the project of the novella. It represents a genuinely authoritative document that can finally answer the demand made of Kohlhaas at Tronka castle. We must recognize, however, that much of its claim to authority for us the readers rests on the mystery of its contents and on the mystery surrounding the unheard words of the castellan regarding the gypsy woman's identity. Neither the reader nor Kohlhaas knows for sure if the gypsy is in fact Elizabeth somehow returned to life, so that she and her prophecy hover on the boundary between the natural and the supernatural. Kohlhaas knows, but the reader does not, what the letter from Luther said and what the prophecy concerning the Elector ordained. When the narrator surmises about the former that it was "doubtless quite remarkable [*ohne Zweifel sehr merkwürdig*]" his comment applies equally well to the latter, or perhaps even better. A message that is unavailable to us must be very important indeed, rather like the "Imperial Message" of Kafka's little parable. Kafka's story drives home the point that the ultimate guarantee of a text's transcendent authority is its literal unavailability. "You" to whom the message is directed can only "sit at your window when evening falls and dream it to yourself." The text that cannot be possessed physically may be spiritually accessible though the imagination. The poor Elector of Saxony is in just this position, possessed of the certain knowledge that a text of the highest importance has been sent in his direction but that he can only imagine its contents.

Kohlhaas achieves a perfect symmetry — and therefore, in a sense, a perfect justice — by placing the Elector in exactly the same position that the Elector (through his servants and vassals) had placed him. Each is faced with the necessity of filling an essential void in the center of an authoritative document. A text that has been emptied out of content must be filled up, possibly by imagination, possibly by incorporation. As the story presents these alternatives, incorporation is at least the equal of imagination as a generative force of remarkable fecundity. Not only does Kohlhaas produce an enormous quantity of documents, most of which survive and become incorporated into the body of the story "Michael Kohlhaas," he produces as well a significant number of human progeny who survive and produce in their turn descendants, so that Kohlhaas's line apparently outlives the Elector's. The final sentence of the novella notes that "in Mecklenburg some hale and hearty descendants of Kohlhaas were still living in the century before this" (KM 213; KW 103). The story of the Elector, for which the reader is referred "to history," remains a blank to be filled in.

Kohlhaas pays a high price for achieving unity with an authoritative text. Transcendence is uncompromising. It "goes beyond" this world and therefore takes out of this world anything or anyone that incorporates it. It is not simply to heighten the drama that Kleist delays until the execution Kohlhaas's reading of the prophecy; he means rather to emphasize again the close relation between transcendence and emptiness. Having incorporated the Scripture and thereby having made himself one with it, Kohlhaas no longer belongs in this world. He belongs wherever Elizabeth is and wherever that *Schein* the Junker's warden demanded is: in the world of *Märchen*.

Kleist's story stages a drama of deep ambivalence about those objects, texts, which offer both the promise of unity, order, and fullness, and the threat of chaos, dismemberment, and emptiness. A key element in that drama is the paradox that the solution to the horse dealer's problem, the gypsy's scrap of paper, belongs exactly to the same category as the problem's origin, the required permit. This story of justice is just as much a tale of reading and writing. There can be little doubt that it puts into play an issue of urgent existential importance for the man Heinrich von Kleist, who was evidently hoping desperately to resolve through literature a crisis brought on by his commitment to literary activity. Kleist's choice of an intellectual rather than a military profession set him apart and outside of the aristocratic Prussian society into which he had been born. He was considered a renegade and a ne'er-do-well by his own family, not least for devoting himself to a literary career that tended to use up rather than produce financial resources. Still, even though he was "a totally useless member of society in their eyes" (KW 884), precisely because he spent his time writing, he nonetheless hoped "to give them joy and honor from my writing labors" (KW 883).[9] Literature was to be the homeopathic cure for an ill brought on by literature.

The chronicle of Kohlhaas, like the patriotic drama *Prinz Friedrich von Homburg*, attempts to reinscribe Kleist's literary efforts within the circle of Prussian aristocratic society. The plot is set up so that Brandenburg, through its Elector, comes out looking far superior to the shabby Saxony, its neighbor and enemy. The surprising result of the horse dealer's career of apostasy from the norms of good citizenship is that his family actually rises socially. No sooner is Kohlhaas's body laid in the coffin than "the Elector [of Brandenburg] sent for the dead man's sons and, declaring to the High Chancellor that they were to be educated in his school for pages, dubbed them knights forthwith" (KM 213; KW 103). These boys, now presumably called "von Kohlhaas," take up precisely the place in the Brandenburg (that is, Prussian) social system from which Kleist had retreated in favor of first science and then literature. The rebel's descendants thrive as honored members of a thriving and honorable state. Many commentators have recognized the political intention behind the prophecy material, but frequently they imagine it to be, like the "sub-plot" itself, "artistically extraneous" (Luke and Reeves 28). Far from being extraneous, it goes to the heart of the matter by offering an ameliorative and healing role for literature. As the gypsy's text helps Kohlhaas to achieve union with the order from which he has been alienated, so does the text of "Kohlhaas" seek to bring Kleist's literary activity into concert with a career of service to the state from which literature had apparently alienated him. Writing "Michael Kohlhaas" is to be the cure for the affliction of being the writer of "Michael Kohlhaas." The text of the story repeats the paradox of the texts in the story. It is a text that, in every way, incorporates other texts. It is a scroll that has eaten scrolls.

Kleist's powerful investment in the notion of textual incorporation demonstrates how much he participates in one of the central concerns of European Romanticism. The Romantic desire to recuperate and revivify the dead past by imaginative reading finds one of its most dramatic expressions in "Michael Kohlhaas." Kohlhaas performs a secularized version of the Christian "dying into a new life" by making himself one with a text belonging to a transcendent realm. He dies *and* he becomes more vigorously alive in the same moment, actualizing both sides of the ambivalence about texts made so memorable by Paul: "for the letter kills, but the spirit gives life." Kleist's story demonstrates in narrative what Romantic aesthetics proposed in theory: letter and spirit, life and death, can merge into one another. The document that kills may be in every respect identical to one that gives life, and an act of reading may be both destructive and revivifying at the same time.

Notes

[1] For a discussion of the question of the relation of the prophecy plot to the rest of the story, along with a useful survey of negative critical opinion, see Bernd. For the sake of convenience I will cite here only the recent but typical comments of Luke and Reeves.

[2] The terms "rhetoric" and "rhetorical reading" refer here both to classically rhetorical matters — figurative language and the formal deployment of discourse —

and to issues deriving from more recent rhetorical theory, particularly the concern for language that is readable under more than one interpretive convention. As discussed below, the phrase "Ding des Herrn," the word "Paßschein," and even various locutions involving "horses" are all examples of rhetoric in the latter sense. See Koelb, *Inventions* (esp. 10–13).

[3] The biblical parallel is also discussed by Lange (218), by Gallas (89), and by Dietrick (171) in her chapter on "Kohlhaas," one of the most stimulating and important treatments of the story to date. Dietrick notes the complication that "to nourish is also to destroy, to partake of life's abundance is also to take away from it." Kohlhaas's incorporation of the paper is also its physical destruction, its absolute removal from the secular world.

[4] Dietrick (158) also suggests a close relation between the *Paßschein* and the gypsy's scrap of paper, though her analysis moves in a somewhat different direction from mine. She also notes that Best (187) refers to the gypsy's paper as a "Papier der Papiere, das Kohlhaasens geschriebenen, Briefe und Anschläge füllenden Streitdialog mit der Obrigkeit zugleich zeichenhaft überhöht," though Best never connects it with the *Paßschein*.

[5] Dietrick (183) points out in a note that the word *Pfand* (surety, collateral), in the form of the compound *Unterpfand*, is also used in connection with the roebuck that plays such an important role in the prophecy plot.

[6] Ellis (39) notes the importance and ambiguous significance of the frequently repeated verb "lösen."

[7] Graham (214–16) sees the horses as symbols of justice, but as "exceedingly primitive" ones that are not really up to the task of representing Kohlhaas's conception. Primitive symbols they may be, but they are certainly powerful. We find magical horses in fairy tales, romances, folklore, poetry, and all sorts of modern fictions. Kafka took up the figure of Kohlhaas's horses and transformed them into the erotically powerful residents of the Country Doctor's pigsty (Koelb, *Kafka's Rhetoric*, 199).

[8] Kleist presents both love and justice in a similar fashion in other works. *Die Familie Schroffenstein* could serve as a paradigmatic example.

[9] From a letter of Nov. 10, 1811; see P. B. Miller 201.

8: "I Sickened as I Read": Mary Shelley's *Frankenstein*

Mary Shelley's account of the genesis of her famous novel is now familiar to nearly every reader of English literature: the immediate occasion for the composition of *Frankenstein* (1818) was a literary game suggested by Lord Byron in the summer of 1816. Byron, the Shelleys, and John William Polidori were on holiday in Switzerland. During a spell of bad weather, the company amused themselves by reading "some volumes of ghost stories, translated from German into French" they had chanced upon, and Byron suggested as a further amusement a sort of literary contest in the manner of the *Decameron* in which each member of the company would write a ghost story.[1] In her account of fifteen years later, the introduction to the edition of 1831,[2] Shelley recalls that she had difficulty coming up with an idea for a story "to rival those which had excited us to the task" and that she suffered from a "blank incapability of invention" that embarrassed her. She had to reply with a "mortifying negative" to inquiries as to whether she had as yet thought of a story (SF 226). Her writer's block was overcome, she says, by a conversation between Byron and Percy Bysshe Shelley about the possibility of discovering the fundamental principle of life. They speculated on the consequences of such a discovery: "Perhaps a corpse would be re-animated; galvanism had given token of such things: perhaps the component parts of a creature might be manufactured, brought together, and endued with vital warmth" (SF 227).[3]

This story of the genesis of Mary Shelley's novel is intriguing in its own right, even if the report is not historically accurate in every detail.[4] It is a story of the desire, stimulated by reading, to create something similar to what has been read, of a blockage frustrating that desire, and of the sudden removal of the blockage by an accidental inspiration. At least as intriguing as Shelley's account of her novel's beginning is an aside inserted in the midst of that account:

> Everything must have a beginning, to speak in Sanchean phrase; and that beginning must be linked to something that went before. The Hindoos give the world an elephant to support it, but they make the elephant stand upon a tortoise. Invention, it must be humbly admitted, does not consist in creating out of void, but out of chaos; the materials must, in the first place, be afforded: it can give form to the dark, shapeless substances, but cannot bring into being the substance itself. In all matters of

discovery and invention, even of those that appertain to the imagination, we are continually reminded of the story of Columbus and his egg. Invention consists in the capacity of seizing on the capabilities of a subject, and in the power of moulding and fashioning ideas to suggest it.

(SF 226)

Shelley recalls that the conversation that inspired her had concerned bringing together the "manufactured" parts of a creature. Her digression on poetic invention, however, explicitly affirms that creation takes place by a process of putting together parts that have not so much been manufactured for the purpose as found and appropriated to a new and different end. Indeed, "the materials must, in the first place, be afforded."

This principle of poetic creation applies not only to the story of *Frankenstein*'s genesis but also to the creation, in the novel, of Frankenstein's demon. "The dissecting room and the slaughter-house furnished many of my materials" (SF 50), confesses the unhappy scientist. One of the most significant aspects of the monster's creation seems to have had its beginning, not in the conversation that allegedly made that beginning possible, but in the author's reflections upon such beginnings. While Shelley recalls the conversation as discussing a creature made of *manufactured* parts, her novel proposes a creature assembled from pre-existing organic materials — the recycled parts of dead bodies. The making of the monster is — significantly and indeed frighteningly — no coherent process of total manufacture but a molding and fashioning of chaotically scattered substances gathered from graves, dissecting rooms, and other places of death. It seems as if Shelley's feeling of being "mortified" by her inability to begin her story — that is, her sense of being embarrassed, as we might say, "to death" — were transformed into the very stuff necessary for beginning her story. Victor Frankenstein begins his work with materials that have been literally mortified.

The parallel between the story related in the introduction of *Frankenstein*'s inception and the story related in the novel of the monster's creation is intriguing, but all the more so when we discover that another unmistakable parallel is embedded in the description of how Frankenstein came to be involved with "that passion, which afterwards ruled my destiny" (SF 32). Compare these two passages, the first from the introduction of 1831, the second from the early pages of the novel:

> But it proved a wet, ungenial summer, and incessant rain often confined us for days to the house. Some volumes of ghost stories, translated from the German into French, fell into our hands. (SF 224)

> When I was thirteen years of age, we all went on a party of pleasure to the baths near Thonon: the inclemency of the weather obliged us to remain a day confined to the inn. In this house I chanced to find a volume of the works of Cornelius Agrippa. (SF 32)

In both the story of *Frankenstein* the book and the story of Frankenstein in the book, the primal scene that sets everything into motion is a scene of reading. The impressionable mind comes by chance upon a book, the reading of which will initiate a chain of events leading to an act of creation.

That Shelley intended the reader to recognize the implicit analogy between Victor Frankenstein and herself is clear enough, and it is clear as well what at least one element in her motivation must have been. The figuration of the poet as a divine creator was a common topos in the late eighteenth and early nineteenth centuries, and Shelley was engaged in exploring the demonic underside of that topos. But it may not be so clear, initially at least, why she insists on the importance of acts of reading. The Romantic topos of divine/poetic creation, as for example in Goethe's poem "Prometheus," does not regularly include the necessity to read. The "old" Prometheus of the myth, as he is depicted in Goethe's poem, can simply "make people" almost casually; the "new" Prometheus, Frankenstein, must study books.

Without books, Frankenstein would never have conceived the idea of making a person.[5] Frankenstein assures Walton that if his father had carefully explained to him why Cornelius Agrippa was "sad trash" upon which a young man should not waste his time, things would have turned out differently:

> I should certainly have thrown Agrippa aside, and, with my imagination warmed as it was, should probably have applied myself to the more rational theory of chemistry which has resulted from modern discoveries. It is even possible, that the train of my ideas would never have received the fatal impulse that led to my ruin. But the cursory glance my father had taken of my volume by no means assured me that he was acquainted with its contents; and I continued to read with the greatest avidity.
>
> When I returned home, my first care was to procure the whole works of this author, and afterwards of Paracelsus and Albert Magnus. I read and studied the wild fancies of these writers with delight. (SF 33)

The seductive and "fatal impulse" produced by reading the "wild fancies" of Agrippa, Paracelsus, and the rest arise because Victor was reading Agrippa and the others from a vantage point of ignorance: "It may appear very strange," he confesses, "that a disciple of Albert Magnus should arise in the eighteenth century; but our family was not scientifical, and I had not attended any of the lectures given at the schools of Geneva. My dreams were therefore undisturbed by reality" (34). Mary Shelley's tale is thus a story not of excessive knowledge but of revivifying the supposedly dead knowledge of the past.

Victor Frankenstein has at least a retrospective awareness of the potential for harm that inheres in such a rite or revivification. His awareness comes far too late, of course, to do him any good. It helps the reader of his narrative, however, to understand from the outset that the creative impulse that produces the demon, the "fatal impulse," arises out of a particular mode of reading. The great and intriguing paradox of Frankenstein's achievement is that his success is the result of a kind of reading that some would call misreading, that he makes something new because he has reread something old in a way that brings it back to life. Frankenstein emerges as one who reads in a manner associated with the figure of Eve, according to a tradition established by the Church fathers. We find one of the principle texts of this tradition in the *Breviloquium* of Saint Bonaventure:

> There is a double book, one written within, which is the eternal art and wisdom of God, and the other written without, namely the sensible world. [. . .] Man was given a double sense and appetite with respect to the two books [. . .] so that he could turn to whither by reason of his freedom of choice; woman, by giving her ear to the suggestion of the serpent in the exterior book, did not turn back to the interior book [. . .] but yielded to the sensual in the exterior book and began to negotiate for the exterior good. (quoted in Koelb and Noakes 346–47)

The result of Eve's mode of reading is the disruption of the world order of Eden and the imposition of a new dispensation according to which women will be bearers of children and thus producers of further images of God, but with the unpleasant proviso that this production of new life will be accompanied by pain.

Young Frankenstein is as much a new Eve who produces his offspring in pain and as a result of a certain mode of reading as he is a new Jehovah who makes an Adam out of the materials of the earth. This may in part account for his ultimate refusal to attempt the production of a female companion for his monster: this new Adam does not really need an Eve, since she already exists. "She" has given figurative birth to an offspring who deserves to bear the mark of Cain, a murderer of the "brother" (in this case, Frankenstein's brother and not the monster's, but a brother all the same). "She" has participated in an act of reproduction about which "she" has every reason to feel ambivalent. Mary Shelley's protagonist is a man who reads and gives birth in pain like a woman, a version of God the Father reconstrued through the figure of Eve the Mother. Reading is so important to Victor because it is a concept in which spiritual reproduction has as much importance as physical reproduction, if not more.

Frankenstein is surely a metaphorical Eve who reads the world by paying more attention to one of its "books" than the other, but the book Victor privileges is just the opposite from the one Bonaventure's Eve attends to. She ignores the book of the "mind" and of the eternal "wisdom of God" in favor of the external book of the body, of the "sensible world." Frankenstein, on the other hand, favors the interior book of "dreams" over the exterior one of "reality." The difference is interesting but not so enormous as one might think. For, if we take Bonaventure seriously, both cases are clear-cut examples of reading in the feminine mode, since the male is supposed to have a "double sense and appetite" that directs him equally to both books. While Frankenstein does not misread in just the same way Bonaventure's Eve does, then, he still misreads according to Bonaventure's paradigm of Woman's deficient perspective. There is no reason to suppose that Shelley was unaware of the irony of putting her male protagonist in this traditionally female posture. The entire premise of the novel, after all, involves a male attempting to take on a female function — with catastrophic success.

Consciously or not, Shelley plays upon the topos of woman as misreader. Although she perhaps did not know it through the particular passage from Bonaventure I have cited, she surely knew it in one of its historical permutations, as for instance in Sterne's *Tristram Shandy*. These and other instances have been well documented in feminist scholarship.[6] The allusion is important because it complicates and enormously enriches the notion of a "new Prometheus," so dear to Romanticism in all its forms, and invests it with a mythic power. The act of creation associated with a rhetoric of patriarchy is reproduced here, but with that rhetoric doubled back on itself. *Frankenstein* may thus be understood as pushing the logic of traditional accounts of creation so far that the patriarchal perspective will no longer hold, even as it serves as the foundation for everything that happens in the story.[7]

We see this same kind of double gesture in the episode that Victor calls "the catastrophe of th[e] tree" (SF 35). During a severe thunderstorm, the fifteen-year-old Frankenstein witnesses the destruction of an oak tree by a stroke of lightning:

> As I stood at the door, on a sudden I beheld a stream of fire issue from an old and beautiful oak, which stood about twenty yards from our house; and so soon as the dazzling light had vanished, the oak had disappeared, and nothing remained but a blasted stump. When we visited it the next morning, we found the tree shattered in a singular manner. It was not splintered by the shock, but entirely reduced to thin ribbands of wood. I never beheld any thing so utterly destroyed. (SF 35)

The incident turns out to be a failed epiphany on the one hand and a successful metaphor of Victor's future on the other. In both cases it invokes the image of the Tree of Knowledge and the mythology of the Fall of Man. The fruit of this particular tree is interest in electricity. This has the benefit of diverting Frankenstein for a time from Agrippa and the others, and in the edition of 1831 Victor proposes that this diversion prompted by the catastrophe of the tree was "the immediate suggestion of the guardian angel of my life — the last effort made by the spirit of preservation to avert the storm that was even then hanging in the stars, and ready to envelop me" (SF 239). The figure of "averting the storm" already displays the ineffectiveness of the angelic sign, since the literal storm has long since unleashed its power. In any case, the Old Testament has instructed us that the fruit of the tree does not bring salvation; it brings death. Knowing this, Victor adjusts his account to the Genesis narrative by seeing in the fate of the tree his own future. Chapter 1 closes in the 1831 edition with the assertion that, in spite of the "strong effort of the spirit of good," destiny had "decreed my utter and terrible destruction" (SF 239). The echo of "utterly destroyed," the description of the shattered oak, in "utter [...] destruction," the predicted fate of Victor, can hardly be missed.

But there is more to this story of the tree. Just as medieval readers found in the Tree of Knowledge a prefiguration of the cross of Jesus and thus of the life-giving sacrifice, so does Shelley's Frankenstein understand the destruction of the oak as a prefiguration of the creation of the monster. Another rhetorical echo reinforces the parallel, for when Victor finally succeeds in bringing his assembly of dead flesh to life, he exclaims: "How can I describe my emotions at this catastrophe, or how delineate the wretch whom with such infinite pains and care I endeavored to form?" (SF 52). Here is a second catastrophe connected with lightning, since the "spark of being" that the creator infuses in his creature during a rainstorm appears to be a form of electricity. Here again, the power of the "spark" is ambiguous. As before the lightning stroke had been both a sign of life (meant to save Frankenstein from the storm of destiny) and the bringer of death, here the spark is both the bringer of life and the immediate cause of catastrophe.

The image of the blasted tree forges a powerful figurative link between Victor Frankenstein and his creature. Both the creator and the monster are, like the tree, little more than shattered remnants — in Victor's case, emotional and moral fragments of a "glorious spirit" (as Walton describes him [SF 216]) torn asunder by a pitiless destiny; in the monster's case, actual corporeal fragments of formerly living bodies. More than that, though, the image forcefully suggests the relation of Mary Shelley's tale to that of the creation and fall of man in the Old Testament. Just as Frankenstein's creature comes into being in part by acts of grisly dismemberment of formerly vital bodies, so does Shelley's creation come into being in part by similar acts performed on the once almighty text of the Bible. The oak tree blasted to fragments in the peaceful garden of Frankenstein's boyhood is therefore both a metaphor standing for the Tree of Knowledge and a metonymy standing for the whole of the Bible, indeed, for much of the body of the literary canon.

The story of Frankenstein's obsession with the idea of creating life begins quite understandably, then, with a complex scene of reading. The logic of the project embodied in the novel calls insistently for such a scene, and upon analysis is seems almost inevitable. Inevitable, too, is a corresponding scene that occurs in the monster's narrative of his own early development, during the first encounter between Frankenstein and his creation (after the "catastrophe" of the initial life-giving act) high in the Alps, on the edge of a great glacier. Though Frankenstein has no inkling the monster is there, the reader is given fair warning when we learn that "pallid lightning" was flashing above Mont Blanc. The creator and his demonic offspring take shelter from the rain in a little hut, and there the monster tells his tale. The external circumstances, particularly the rain and the (earlier) lightning take us back to two decisive moments earlier in the novel, the destruction of the tree and the infusion of life into the creature.

The infusion of life is not complete, of course, until the creature has a psyche. The demonic offspring mimics his "father's" developmental trajectory by engaging in psychologically formative acts of reading. In a stunning reversal, however, the horrible monster turns to books Shelley and her readers would surely have found far superior to Agrippa, Paracelsus, and Albert Magnus: he reads *Paradise Lost, Plutarch's Lives*, and that paradigmatic novel of reading, Goethe's *Werther*.[8]

It is useful to examine how the creature comes to have physical and intellectual access to these books. One of the most remarkable capabilities of Frankenstein's monster is an intellect with an apparently inherent understanding of semiotic processes. As the creature tells it, he actually grasps the principle of reading *before* he can fully understand speech:

> As there was little to do in the frosty season, [Felix] read to the old man and Agatha.
>   This reading puzzled me extremely at first; but, by degrees, I discovered that he uttered many of the same sounds when he read as when he talked. I conjectured, therefore, that he found on the paper signs for speech which he understood, and I ardently longed to comprehend these also; but how was that possible, when I did not even understand the sounds for which they stood as signs? (SF 109)

Although the creature perceives speech simply as a set of incomprehensible noises, he understands that in the act of reading those noises are produced in accordance with marks on paper. He understands, in short, the principle of the sign before he has much of any success in linking particular signifiers with signifieds. The monster is a sort of grammatologist *avant la lettre* — a monster indeed.[9]

But the chief importance of this scheme of reading lies not so much in its semiotic theory as in its establishment of a desire for reading in the creature. "I longed to comprehend," he tells Frankenstein, and that longing establishes him as his creator's spiritual if not corporeal progeny. Frankenstein, too, has a natural love of reading. "We learned Latin and English," he tells Walton, "that we might read the writings in those languages; and so far from study being made odious to us through punishment, we loved application, and our amusements would have been the labours of other children" (SF 31). The creature, as is perhaps only fitting, must get his education second hand by observing in secret as Felix instructs the Arabian girl Safie. He boasts that he was able to learn far faster than the girl and that he could "imitate almost every word that was spoken. While I improved in speech, I also learned the science of letters, as it was taught to the stranger; and this opened before me a wide field for wonder and delight" (SF 114). Here again the creature associates himself with his creator in that his increasing reading skills are described as the mastery of a "science."

The book Felix uses to instruct Safie and, indirectly and unknowingly, the creature is Volney's *Ruins of Empires*. The creature explains the importance for him as providing "a cursory knowledge of history" and of geography, politics, religion, and even racial prejudice ("the slothful Asiatics" are contrasted with Greeks possessed of "stupendous genius"; SF 114–15). The title suggests to Shelley's readers, though, the carefully constructed analogy between the origins of the creature's body and those of his mind. His physical self is composed of the "ruins" of dead persons, while his mind is furnished with the ruins of empires. In both cases dead remnants serve as the material out of which something living and whole may be fashioned. The extraordinary vigor of the creature's powerful body appears to be in part the result of a kind of anthologizing activity: Frankenstein has taken only what he considers the most suitable body parts to make his new Adam. In an analogous fashion, a vigorous mind results from the "wonderful narrations" culled from the *Ruins of Empires*, and we soon see the creature wrestling with profound ethical and religious questions. "What was I?" he wonders (SF 117), and what was "man [. . .], at once so powerful, so virtuous, and magnificent, yet so vicious and base?" (SF 115).

The apparent answer to the question "What was I?" is suggested by the information the creature gathers by way of Felix's reading, and it is not a happy one. While the monster knows that he is more physically robust than the normal human, he also knows that he is "hideously deformed and loathsome." In fact, he is utterly bereft of the things Felix's readings tell him are the most valued by human society: "I learned that the possessions most esteemed by your fellow-creatures were, high and unsullied descent united with riches" (SF 115). A miserable monster with no money and no "descent" at all must be miserable indeed. In his misery, the creature regrets ever having acquired the knowledge that now afflicts him, for now he knows that he is miserable:

> Of what a strange nature is knowledge! It clings to the mind, when it has once seized on it, like a lichen on the rock. I wished sometimes to shake off all thought and feeling; but I learned that there was but one means to overcome the sensation of pain, and that was death — as a state which I feared yet did not understand. [. . .] Miserable, unhappy wretch! (SF 116)

Once again the reader is tacitly invited to compare the creature to his creator, to contrast the deadly knowledge that Frankenstein obtains through his reading with an equally deadly but different sort of knowledge the creature obtains thanks to reading conducted by Felix. Frankenstein's reading incites in him a sense of capability, a desire for achievement; the creature's (secondhand) reading incites in him a sense of utter worthlessness and incapacity.

Further scenes of reading only add to the monster's anxiety and self-hatred. By chance he comes into possession of three books, "*Paradise Lost*, a volume of *Plutarch's Lives*, and the *Sorrows of Werther* [sic]. The possession of these treasures gave me extreme delight" (SF 123). The delight, however, proves to be short-lived, in part because he makes a fundamental mistake about the nature of the books: he reads them literally as "histories" (SF 123) rather than as literary constructions. He conceives of Werther, for example, as an actual person whose life and death can serve as a model for his own. More important, though, is that these writings become his Scripture, the lessons of which he seeks to apply to his own situation. The monster proves to be a zealous and agile practitioner of *applicatio*, finding in the readings chance has sent his way a wealth of information relevant to the conduct of his existence: "As I read, I applied much personally to my own feelings and condition" (SF 124). That is what one is supposed to do with Scripture, and the creature seems to have an instinctive grasp of the principle.

The most important feature of Goethe's *Werther*, he realizes at once, is that it deals with death by suicide.[10] "The disquisitions upon death and suicide were calculated to fill me with wonder. I did not pretend to enter into the merits of the case, yet I inclined towards the opinions of the hero" (SF 124). He admits to weeping over Werther's suicide, though he confesses that he did not "precisely" understand it. He understands enough, however, to realize that suicide is an option for him as well, and indeed one that calls urgently for consideration. He also understands that there are some limits to the applicability of Goethe's text for him:

> I found myself similar, yet at the same time strangely unlike the beings concerning whom I read, and to whose conversation I was a listener. I sympathized with, and partly understood them. But I was unformed in mind; I was dependent on none, and related to none. "The path of my departure was free"; and there was none to lament my annihilation. (SF 124)

The line quoted by the creature is not from Goethe, of course, but from Percy Bysshe Shelley's poem "On Mutability." Apparently the demon eventually read much more than the three books he found in the leather portmanteau. In any case, the audience of the creature's tale — both Shelley's readers and the fictional audience, Frankenstein himself — should readily recollect the quoted line, since Victor had cited several lines, including this one, from "On Mutability" only a few pages earlier, as part of his description of the ascent of Montanvert. Overwhelmed by the somber majesty of the landscape, he had considered the limitations on human freedom: "If our impulses were confined to hunger, thirst, and desire, we might be nearly free" with the freedom that comes with thoughtlessness and lack of sensitivity (SF 92–93). The impact of the mountain scene on his mind reminds Victor of how susceptible every human mind is to each passing impression. This puts him in mind of "On Mutability":

> We rest; a dream has power to poison sleep.
>   We rise; one wand'ring thought pollutes the day.
> We feel, conceive or reason; laugh or weep,
>   Embrace fond woe, or cast our cares away;
> It is the same; for, be it joy or sorrow,
>   The path of its departure still is free.
> Man's yesterday may ne'er be like his morrow;
>   Nought may endure but mutability! (quoted in SF 93)

Frankenstein's quotation implicitly contrasts the freedom of dreams, thoughts, and moods to come and go as they will with the constraints placed on human beings by those very moods. Thought may be free, but the humans who think them are not; they are, rather, the prisoners of their dreams.

The dream of which Victor Frankenstein is both the victim and the prisoner is now standing before him and telling him its tale. By equating himself with Percy Shelley's evanescent but yet powerful dreams, the creature acknowledges himself to be Frankenstein's creature, a dream come to life. His thoughts of suicide in response to reading *Werther* open the question of the superior freedom and power of the dream over the dreamer. But the question is by no means settled, since the monster proves to be far more enduring than the mutable moods invoked in Percy Shelley's poem. Is the "path of his departure" really free, or is he now bound up as well in the prison of human dreams? He who was once a dream now has dreams of his own. He who was once a text must now wrestle with trying to understand other texts. In fact, the creature's confrontation with the possibility of death shows how far he has come from his previous condition of death.

It also shows how much of his creator he carries in him. Mary Shelley's audience is not likely to miss the irony in the repetition of the creator's quotation by his creature, nor the additional irony that Percy Shelley is the author whom both cite. Though only the demon is in physical reality an assembly of pieces of other people's bodies, both the monster and his maker are intellectually assemblies of other people's thoughts and utterances. Frankenstein's demonic creation is far more like his progenitor than either realize or would care to admit, for both construct their autobiographies to a large extent as histories of reading — Agrippa, Paracelsus, and so on for Frankenstein; Goethe, Petrarch, and Milton for the monster. The creation of a human psyche is in this regard no different from other sorts of creation: in the words of the introduction to the third edition, "the materials must, in the first place, be afforded." The appearance of Percy Bysshe Shelley's poetry among the intellectual materials used to make both Frankenstein and the monster reminds us of the story of the genesis of the novel as told in that preface, of the conversation between Byron and Percy about the reanimation of corpses. Mary Shelley's account of the impact of that conversation on her recalls the imagery of her husband's poem, for she describes herself as the prisoner of powerful thoughts: "My imagination, unbidden, possessed and guided me [. . .]. The idea so possessed my mind, that a thrill of fear ran through me" (SF 227–28). The path of their departure was free, but Mary Shelley herself was not free of them until she had made them permanent in her book.

The creature's mind is possessed and ultimately shaped by the books he reads, as he learns from Goethe to question the conditions of his existence, from Plutarch to love virtue and hate vice, from Milton to see himself as both a new Adam and a second Satan. But none of these authors has as deep or as abiding an impact on him as the author of a manuscript the creature finds in the pocket of some clothes he had taken from Frankenstein's library:

> It was your journal of the four months that preceded my creation. You minutely described every step you took in the progress of your work; this history was mingled with accounts of domestic occurrences. You, doubtless, recollect these papers. Here they are. Every thing is related in them which bears reference to my accursed origin; the whole detail of that series of disgusting circumstances which produced it is set in view; the minutest description of my odious and loathsome person is given, in language which painted your own horrors, and rendered mine ineffaceable. I sickened as I read. (SF 128)

Of course the reader of such a journal, finding himself to be its subject matter, can do little else but try to fit his own story into the context of those other stories he had been reading. It is little wonder he finds himself more miserable than Werther, more vicious than Romulus and Theseus, more accursed than Adam or even Satan.

The monster's reading of Frankenstein's journal is a kind of figural precursor of a Freudian primal scene: the offspring observes the "disgusting circumstances" that lead to his coming into being. My concern here is not with the psychosexual implications of this figuration but with the fact of its mediation by means of a text.[11] The creature quite literally "finds himself" described in the book, and that book's rhetoric has a decisive impact on its reader's (that is, the creature's) evaluation of its central character (once again, the creature himself). We have a very specific idea of what that rhetoric was, not only or chiefly because the creature alludes to "language which painted your own horrors," but because we recall the descriptions Frankenstein had given in an earlier chapter of the "miserable monster" that so appalls its creator that he repeatedly runs away from it: "Oh! no mortal could support the horror of that countenance. A mummy again endued with animation could not be so hideous as that wretch. [. . . It was] a thing such as even Dante could not have conceived" (SF 53). A literal reader such as the creature, one who takes all books as "histories," could only feel utterly overwhelmed by the force of rhetoric such as this. The monster's consequent hatred for his creator is a mirror image of the creator's hatred of his creation, and the language the creature uses to describe himself is drawn from the text inscribed by his maker.

The terrible consequences that follow upon almost every act of reading presented in *Frankenstein* are not at all what Mary Shelley or her audience had been educated to expect. The reading of Albert Magnus and Paracelsus may be somewhat distressing, but surely one would not expect a man such a Victor, who could read Latin and Greek, as well as English and German, and who filled his hours as a teenager "in acquiring and maintaining a knowledge of this various literature" (SF 36), to have his life shattered because of what he read. On the contrary, such careful attention to the classics is supposed to produce a paragon. The creature, lamenting the creator he has murdered, calls his victim "the select specimen of all that is worthy of love and admiration among men" (SF 219). The golem manufactured by this model of European learning is no less well read, but with no less catastrophic results. The reader of Goethe, Plutarch, and Milton becomes a murdering fiend. He does not wish to become one — indeed he despises himself for what he is — but he does so all the same, prevented not a whit by his mastery of humane letters. What has gone wrong?

Much of the problem, surely, has to do with various forms of misreading, of mistaking the husk for the kernel, the dead letter for the living spirit. Frankenstein tends as a young man to have too much regard for the book of the mind and too little for the book of the body. With his successful reanimation of the assembled creature, however, his fault suddenly turns to the opposite: he is so overwhelmed by the bodily ugliness of his creation that he never even attempts to read the book of its mind. In this deficiency Frankenstein is not alone. Indeed, every character in the story who comes in contact with the creature, with the brief exception of the blind old De Lacy, attends so exclusively to his hideous appearance that his acquaintance with the works of Goethe and Milton never gets a chance to play a role. As the creature says of such people to his blind host, "a fatal prejudice clouds their eyes, and where they ought to see a feeling and kind friend, they behold only a detestable monster" (SF 130). To some extent, then, the creature is a great spirit trapped in a miserable body, a noble book bound in a repulsive cover, doomed to be forever misread because unread.

But only to some extent. First of all, there is more than enough evidence to make us doubt the pure nobility of the creature's spirit. Frankenstein gives voice to a thought that must surely cross the mind of every reader of the creature's history: "You swear [. . .] to be harmless; but have you not already shewn a degree of malice that should reasonably make me distrust you?" (SF 143). If there is indeed only a "feeling and kind" soul inside that hideous body, why does the soul exult so in the murder of Frankenstein's little brother? Perhaps some of the less noble characters that appear in Plutarch and Milton have had a decisive influence on the creature's mind after all. But even if they had not, even if the apparent monster is the kind and sensitive spirit he depicts himself to be, it is by no means certain that external appearances alone are responsible for his misery. We, the readers of Mary Shelley's book, know this especially well, as should the creature himself, having been instructed by Goethe's novel of the sorrows to which a "feeling and kind friend" is liable. Werther is the very model of a sensitive and caring friend to Charlotte and Albert, and they are equally caring and sensitive in return. But even in this atmosphere, so thoroughly saturated with kindness and sensitivity that every character seems to drip with it, Werther suffers emotional pain so terrible that he takes his own life. He does not strangle children, to be sure, but the violence he perpetrates on himself is brutal and horrifying. He acts so as to cause as much acute and lasting pain as possible.

Frankenstein's monster is, in this crucial respect, a revised version of Werther. He is the sensitive hero turned demonic. It is easy to recognize the ways in which the creature is a new Adam and a new Satan but perhaps less easy to see his deep kinship with Goethe's lovesick young reader of Homer and Ossian. That kinship, though, is just as important as the more apparent ties to Milton's biblical characters. Indeed it may be more so. Mary Shelley's novel, closer in time and in spirit to Goethe than to Milton or Plutarch, makes an enduring mythic image out of a literal reading of the metaphor that guides so much of *Werther*: a new man is made by putting together revitalized pieces (texts) of dead men. Werther is the "new" man cast in the mold offered by the revolutionary system of taste just coming into being in the late eighteenth century. Goethe's contemporaries recognized his character as representative of the new aesthetic, and we recognize him as the prototype of the developing Romantic hero. In *Frankenstein* we find that hero split in two: the Faustian, Promethean element is embodied in Victor, while the sensitive, suffering spirit is housed in the powerful but hideous body of the creature.

The story of the monster's education underlines one of the novel's main points: the creature is deadly not because he is insensitive or lacking in moral judgment, but because deadliness is the foundation of his being.

His inception is bound up with deadly acts of revivifying reading, acts that contaminate the realm of life by introducing reanimated fragments of the dead past. Perhaps one of the most frightening characteristics of these living fragments is their remarkable durability. Because they come from the land of the dead they are, as it were, inoculated against mortality. Not only is the monster incredibly strong and nearly impossible to kill, Frankenstein himself seems to possess a similar resistance to death. Upon learning of Henry Clerval, Frankenstein falls into a fever, lingering for two months on the point of death: "Why did I not die? [. . .] Of what materials was I made, that I could thus resist so many shocks, which, like the turning of the wheel, continually renewed the torture[?]" (SF 174). This is one of the clearest indications in the text suggesting a physical similarity between Frankenstein and his creature. Both are composed of "materials" that make them tough to kill. The materials in question could not be the literal fragments of dead bodies used to make the monster, for Victor is obviously a naturally born human. The materials they have in common are evidently spiritual ones, the same sort of thing Mary Shelley was talking about when she wrote of her own creative enterprise that "the materials must, in the first place, be afforded." The emblem of all such spiritual material, in this novel as in so many other forms of Romantic fiction, is reading matter.

Spiritual material clings tenaciously to life, for as the apostle proclaimed, the spirit giveth life. But the vehicle that carries that spirit is the letter, or something very like the letter, and the letter kills, if not properly read. The paradox of Frankenstein and of his monster is that of the letter endued with spirit. Such an inspired letter must always be as full of death as it is of life. Indeed the very arrival of life in the dead vehicle of literal flesh has to be at least as horrifying as it is exciting, and the hand that fosters and achieves such a union of spirit and matter will be instantly overwhelmed by regret: "He would hope that, left to itself, the slight spark of life which he had communicated would fade: that this thing, which had received such imperfect animation, would subside into dead matter" (SF 228). But it does not. It hangs on to its spark of life with far greater success than other, more "perfect" examples of animate nature. It is really hard to know what is worse about dead matter reanimated by the living spirit: that it is so deadly to all those who come into contact with it; or that it is so persistently, so impertinently alive. Both are horrifying, because in both cases the boundary between life and death becomes uncertain. Each becomes contaminated with the other, and with contamination come uncertainty and fear.

Mary Shelley's novel highlights, toward the end of the narrative, the close relation between Frankenstein's reanimation of dead flesh and the parallel process of animating dead letters when Walton's enframing letter to his sister resumes. Walton had been recording for his own later use a set of notes based on Frankenstein's account of his life:

Frankenstein discovered that I made notes concerning his history: he asked to see them, and then himself corrected and augmented them in many places; but principally in giving life and spirit to the conversations he held with his enemy. "Since you have preserved my narration," said he, "I would not that a mutilated one should go down to posterity." (SF 207)

Victor does with Walton's text just what he had done with the materials he had obtained from graveyards: he gave them "life and spirit." But now he proposes to do a better job, for the result of his efforts is to be a textual body saved from mutilation instead of the mutilated looking body he had produced when he made the creature. It does not seem that either his immediate audience, Walton, or his own creator, Shelley, believes he has succeeded. Walton describes the narrative he has made from these notes in exactly the same terms Victor uses to describe his monster. He calls it a "strange and terrific [that is, terrifying] story" that will make his sister feel her "blood congealed with horror, like that which even now curdles mine" (SF 206–7). This reaction contrasts sharply with the joy he anticipates the tale will afford his sister and himself. "This manuscript will doubtless afford you the greatest pleasure: but to me, who know him, and who hear it from his own lips, with what interest and sympathy shall I read it in some future day!" (SF 25). Walton's feelings about his narrative make a close parallel with Frankenstein's feelings toward his act of creation, about which he feels "enthusiasm" and "unremitting ardour" (SF 49) when he commences but only "horror and disgust" (SF 53) when he is done. Later, when he tries at the monster's urging to create a female companion, an Eve for his demonic Adam, he recalls the feelings he had felt before: "During my first experiment, a kind of enthusiastic frenzy had blinded me to the horror of my employment" (SF 162). One of the horrors he seems to be sensitive to now is the textual nature of his work. He does not speak of an act of creation here, but of composition: "I found that I could not compose a female without again devoting several months to profound study and laborious disquisition" (SF 147). There is a sly irony here in the implicit suggestion that it might just be more difficult to "compose" a female than a male. But the story is quite direct in its insistence on the analogy between Frankenstein's work and the work of those who compose texts. Perhaps most telling of all is the language used to describe Victor's final refusal to complete the creation of a female: "I thought with a sensation of madness on my promise of creating another like to him, and, trembling with passion, tore to pieces the thing on which I was engaged" (SF 164). This rhetoric of tearing up a piece of work is of course familiar to every writer and perhaps even more appropriate to a writer's destruction of a manuscript than to Frankenstein's dismemberment of the body he had been assembling.

It is not at all surprising, then, that as the tale nears its conclusion the demon becomes more and more a text that Frankenstein must decipher.

Having vowed to destroy the monster he had created, Victor pursues his enemy with furious zeal. The creature knows he is being pursued and even encourages his pursuer with messages left along the trail:

> What his feelings were whom I pursued, I cannot know. Sometimes, indeed, he left marks in writing on the barks of trees, or cut in stone, that guided me, and instigated my fury. "My reign is not yet over" (these words were legible in one of these inscriptions); "you live, and my power is complete. Follow me; I seek the everlasting ices of the north, where you will feel the misery of cold and frost, to which I am impassive. You will find near this place, if you follow not too tardily, a dead hare; eat, and be refreshed. Come on, my enemy; we have yet to wrestle for our lives; but many hard and miserable hours must you endure, until that period shall arrive." (SF 202)

Although he hears reports of a gigantic creature, and though he catches glimpses of the creature from a great distance, his only significant contact with his creation takes place by way of these messages. The being that was "composed" out of "materials" like a text now becomes in fact accessible only as text, only as reading matter that Victor finds scattered in fragments along his path.

It is also worthwhile to point out here that Shelley appears almost to have gone out of her way to offer her readers a text that is formally mutilated, a set of fragments assembled into a rough organism. It begins in a familiar fashion, as if it is going to be a standard epistolary novel in the eighteenth-century style (like *Werther*, perhaps). The first part of the text is divided by the headings "Letter I" through "Letter IV." In the course of Letter IV, however, the nature of the text changes. Walton has met Victor Frankenstein, rescued from the arctic ice by Walton's ship, and has been seized by an intense fascination with the stranger. Though his writing is still addressed to his sister Margaret, Walton no longer refers to it as a letter but rather as "my journal concerning the stranger" (SF 22). No further division by letter headings is made in the remainder of the text. No sooner has the "journal" regarding Frankenstein commenced than it too breaks off, interrupted by the "manuscript" of Victor's life story. This section of the text — the bulk of the novel — is divided into chapters. In the edition of 1818 there was a further division brought about by the three-volume format: the number sequence of the chapters began anew at the beginning of each volume. The organization of the text follows this pattern until chapter 7 of the third volume (the last one), in which Frankenstein's "manuscript" ends and Walton's "journal" resumes. This transition is marked formally by the insertion of a new section heading, "Walton, in continuation," but the "journal" text slips unheralded back into the epistolary format with the entry labeled "September 2d," which opens with a conventional greeting and even announces itself as a letter with the words "I write to you" (SF 210).

Although this formal heterogeneity is not especially intrusive, it does make an impression on the reader of a certain fragmentation. While it would be easy to assume that Shelley was somewhat careless about the formal presentation of her novel, such an assumption is not very persuasive when one considers the striking and extremely apt analogy to be made between the fragmented structure of Shelley's text and the piecemeal assembly of Frankenstein's monster. That the author was aware of and interested in that analogy cannot be doubted. In the introduction of 1831 she takes up the rhetoric of her character Victor to describe her book, about to appear in a third edition: "And now, once again, I bid my hideous progeny go forth and prosper" (SF 229). The ambivalence of this statement is perhaps as striking as the analogy it proposes. She loves and hates this reading matter, this scene of the raising of the dead, which is in her own memory full of life and full of death: "I have an affection for it, for it was the offspring of happy days, when death and grief were but words, which found no true echo in my heart [. . .] when I was not alone; and my companion was one who, in this world, I shall never see more" (SF 229). In 1831, as we can well imagine, Mary Shelley must have felt far more in common with Victor Frankenstein than she would have cared to suppose in 1816. The happiness that she had in her act of creation is now mingled with regrets for the terrible losses associated with it. "But this is for myself," she asserts; "My readers have nothing to do with these associations" (SF 229).

But readers cannot help but have to do with these associations. The lesson Romantic fiction drives home for us is that the act of reading itself is the inevitable scene of these associations. And there is no better teacher of that lesson than Mary Shelley's hideous progeny.

Notes

[1] Among the fruits of this contest were, in addition to *Frankenstein*, Polidori's *The Vampyre* and Byron's "A Fragment" (1816).

[2] I cite the 1818 edition throughout save for those instances, clearly indicated in the text, in which I discuss the introduction or other revisions to the edition of 1831. For a discussion of the materials introduced in 1831, see O'Rourke; for an argument in favor of the superiority of the 1831 edition, see Crook; also Ketterer, especially 107–10. Ketterer is particularly critical of Rieger, whose edition I use.

[3] The relation of *Frankenstein* to Romantic science has been extensively studied and commented upon; see, for example, Hindle. Mellor offers an influential feminist reconsideration. My argument here has a very different focus: the issue is not so much the scientific background as the way in which reading functions in crossing the boundary between life and death. This is not meant to diminish the importance of the scientific background, which is in fact assumed.

[4] For an account of the inaccuracies of Shelley's 1831 introduction, see Rieger, xvi–xviii.

[5] A detailed account of the texts that form the novel's intellectual background can be found in Pollin.

[6] Feminist approaches to *Frankenstein* have dominated the vast body of scholarship on Mary Shelley since the 1980s. For an overview of feminist readings, see Hoeveler. Spivak's influential essay on "Three Women's Texts" offers both a feminist reading and a challenge to feminist scholarship by stressing the relation of *Frankenstein* to the history of British imperialism.

[7] One might well refer to this process as the "feminization of Romanticism." The phrase and the concept were introduced by Poovey.

[8] For an examination of the creature's reading from the point of view of the history of education, see McWhir.

[9] One critic who has been especially sensitive to the relation between the creature's monstrosity and his rhetorical talent is Brooks. He points out that "the Monster is eloquent. From his first words he shows himself to be a supreme rhetorician of his own situation" (592). It is possible for the creature to display such semiotic sophistication because such notions were abroad in the land already in the late eighteenth century. The rhetorician Hugh Blair wrote in 1785: "Words, as we now employ them, taken in the general, may be considered as symbols, not as imitations; as arbitrary, or instituted, not natural signs of ideas" (57; I am grateful to J. H. Koelb for directing me to this citation).

[10] Shelley's use of *Werther* in *Frankenstein* has received critical attention from scholars of both British and German literature. For a recent discussion from an English-speaking scholar, see Burwick; for a view from the German side, see Braune-Steininger.

[11] Psychoanalytic approaches to *Frankenstein* have had a significant impact on scholarship; for a classic study on the Oedipal theme by a prominent scholar, see Veeder. London, on the other hand, emphasizes the psychosexual implications of the novel from the perspective of gender theory. Brown suggests in "*Frankenstein*: A Child's Tale" that Shelley's novel anticipated by a century Freud's acknowledgment of the *Grausamkeit* of childhood, while at the same time "masking the nature of its insights under the veil of a silly 'ghost story' or 'hideous phantom'" (170). Sherwin proposes that a genuinely Freudian reading of the novel must reject the "orthodox psychoanalytic rendering" in favor of "the true Freudian space — a place where Freud joins the company of such alienists as Blake, Milton, and Kierkegaard" (891). Obviously there are many mansions in the house of Freudian criticism.

9: "Those Who, Being Dead, Are Yet Alive": Maturin's *Melmoth the Wanderer*

LIKE GOETHE'S *WERTHER*, Kleist's *Kohlhaas*, and Shelley's *Frankenstein*, Charles Robert Maturin's gothic romance *Melmoth the Wanderer* (1820) exposes the demonic underside of a resurrection of the flesh and a death that brings one into life. *Melmoth* emphasizes the unnatural quality of a form of life that belongs to death; the novel makes the reader share in what Maturin's character Monçada calls "the horror of being among those who are neither the living nor the dead" (MM 205). In the first chapter, Old Melmoth, John Melmoth's uncle, hovers on the boundary between life and death and leads the reader into that realm of horror. He dies before the chapter is done, dies definitively and permanently, providing by means of his death the promise of an inheritance and therefore a comfortable life for his nephew. Before he dies, however, he brings up the topic of one who should have died but who lives on. In fact, Old Melmoth proposes that his death is a direct result of the living-on of that other, an ancestor depicted in an old portrait kept in a closet:

> "John, they say I am dying of this and that [. . .] — but, John," and his face looked hideously ghastly, "I am dying of a fright. That man," and he extended his meagre arm toward the closet, as if he was pointing to a living being; "that man, I have good reason to know, is alive still." "How is that possible, Sir?" said John involuntarily, "the date on the picture is 1646." "You have seen it, — you have noticed it," said his uncle. [. . .] "You will see him again, he is alive." (MM 21)

The interweaving of life and death is already thick, and the novel has hardly begun.

Old Melmoth's death, through which John Melmoth is to be delivered from a kind of living death into a new life of freedom, is occasioned by the old man's fear at seeing alive his ancestor Melmoth the Wanderer, who should have been dead long since. One begins to grasp the complex irony of the epigraph from Shakespeare posted at the head of the first chapter: "Alive again? Then show me where he is; / I'll give a thousand pounds to look upon him." The quotation comes from act 3, scene 3 of *2 Henry 6*, where the villainous Cardinal Beaufort is depicted in the grip of mortal illness, confessing to his crimes in a fevered delirium. The cardinal is apparently referring to the Duke of Gloucester, whom he had strangled in his bed. Gloucester is definitively not "alive again," though the cardinal might have well wished he were. Maturin uses the quotation to refer to all of the Melmoths at once: John, who finds himself figuratively "alive again" thanks to his inheritance from his uncle; Old Melmoth, who would not in life give a thousand pounds for anything at all, but who bestows in death that and more on his nephew; and Melmoth the Wanderer, who is alleged to be not so much alive "again" as alive "still," though the distinction becomes unimportant here. What is most relevant about Beaufort's words is that they are in the form of a question. Is anyone in this story "alive again"?

Melmoth explores the terrifying uncertainty of dwelling on the boundary between life and death, a boundary that is also the hazy border between the literal and the figurative, the body and the spirit. It is a story that wonders whether we have a choice about dwelling on that boundary, about living lives that are contaminated with death and experiencing deaths that are strangely tinged with life. It displays an urgent concern with the wonderful and terrible effects that follow upon acts of raising the dead, always leaving open the question as to whether revivified corpses are fully rescued from death, and thus genuinely alive, or remain fatally contaminated by the touch of the grave. The dramatic narrative arising out of such strong concerns will contain, we expect, a number of powerful scenes in which corpses are brought to life.

Readers of Maturin's gothic novel may have a difficult time identifying these scenes because, unlike *Frankenstein* or *Endymion*, *Melmoth* does not offer any episodes in which those who have been dead become literally "alive again." But the figurative movement from death to life, the metaphor of something dead becoming alive again or threatening to do so, dominates the narrative. Indeed it is not too much to say that the novel is organized principally around such scenes of figurative revivification and that they make up a substantial portion of the narrative space. As we have learned by now to expect, they are scenes of reading.

Much of *Melmoth* is devoted to depicting acts of reading, some of them containing additional acts of reading embodied within. The manner in which these readings are presented is calculated to associate them firmly with the "horror of being among those who are neither the living nor the dead." One is likely to be struck when reading the novel, for example, by the focus on the physical condition of the manuscripts that play so important a role in the story. Reading is not often easy for the characters in Maturin's novel, for the texts they must bring back to life by reading are mostly semi-decomposed corpses. It is a wonder that they are legible at all—and from time to time they are not. The first major manuscript to appear, the story of Stanton, is introduced with these words:

> The manuscript was discoloured, obliterated, and mutilated beyond any that had ever before exercised the patience of a reader. Michaelis himself, scrutinizing into the pretended autograph of St. Mark at Venice, never

had a harder time of it.[1] — Melmoth could make out only a sentence here and there. (MM 32)

The implied comparison to an animate (or once-animate) body comes across with particular force in the word "mutilated," which we rarely use to describe objects that we think of as merely physical. One can mutilate the body of a person or animal; one may even mutilate a painting; but one does not speak of a "mutilated house" or a "mutilated mountain" unless one wishes to imply that these objects have some animate quality. The implication of spirituality is heightened by a further implied comparison, this one to the text of the Gospel of St. Mark. Stanton's story is hardly Holy Scripture, but it does concern the relation between God and man (or between God's adversary and man) and could reasonably claim to possess spiritual value.

If we put together the figures of mutilated body and gospel text, we can detect the presence of an even more deeply buried comparison: the manuscript is like the body of Jesus, the spiritual body that was dead and then rose again. This implication lingers in the distant background, of course; it is not the major point the sentence makes. But in a novel that opens with the words (borrowed from Shakespeare) "Alive again?" it cannot be dismissed as a figment of overzealous interpretation. Furthermore, the mention of the "pretended" autograph Gospel of Mark brings up a vitally important controversy in biblical scholarship, already hot in the early nineteenth century and certainly familiar to an educated Anglo-Irish Protestant clergyman such as Maturin: did the Gospel end at 16:8, as the oldest manuscripts attest? If it did — if it ended with Mary Magdalene and the other women running in terror from the empty tomb — then it offers only highly ambiguous witness to the resurrection. This "mutilated" Mark concludes in effect with the question, "Alive again?" without offering any answer.

In Maturin's novel, the reading of Stanton's mutilated manuscript shows how a text that looks very dead and is already partially decomposed can become miraculously alive again. We are forced to consider it miraculous, since a document that is only legible "here and there" somehow manages to recover nearly all of its vivid detail in the course of Melmoth's reading. The process of reading performs a miraculous raising of the dead as it reassembles and revivifies the dismembered body of the text.

Though the fragmented narrative comes to us, Maturin's readers, in its reassembled form, it takes care to show us its still gaping wounds. The vivid story of Stanton lapses from time to time into illegibility: "Here the manuscript was illegible for a few lines" (MM 35); "Another defect in the manuscript occurred here" (MM 37); "after a few blotted and illegible pages" (MM 44); "only these words were legible in the manuscript" (MM 61); "several pages . . . were wholly illegible" (MM 65). There are so many reminders of the difficulty Melmoth has reading Stanton's text that our attention is almost as much on the drama of textual reconstruction as on the tale of Stanton's encounter with the Wanderer.[2] The story of Melmoth's reading is intertwined with Stanton's, and the two bind together so tightly that they become difficult to separate. As Melmoth reads Stanton's distressing text, so does Stanton take up in the midst of his (reconstructed) narrative a "volume in manuscript" (MM 52) containing various mad proposals, odd drawings, and other fragments produced by a "powerful but prostrated intellect" (MM 53). Stanton's adventure blends with that of young Melmoth not only formally but also thematically, for it eventually becomes clear that both stories could share the same title: "The Quest for the Wanderer." The horrifying yet intriguing person whose likeness hangs in Old Melmoth's room, John Melmoth's ancestor, is the object of obsessive fascination for both Stanton and John. The pursuit of Melmoth the Wanderer becomes Stanton's unique vocation: "I have sought him every where. — The desire of meeting him once more, is become as a burning fire within me, — it is the necessary condition of my existence" (MM 66). John is afflicted by a similarly fiery curiosity, frustrated not by physical separation but by textual decay:

> The conclusion of this extraordinary manuscript was in such a state, that, in fifteen mouldy and crumbling pages, Melmoth could hardly make out that number of lines. No antiquarian, unfolding with trembling hand the calcined leaves of an Herculaneum manuscript, and hoping to discover some lost line of the Aeneis [sic] in Vergil's own autograph, or at least some unutterable abomination of Petronius or Martial, happily elucidatory of the mysteries of the Spintriae, or the orgies of the Phallic worshippers, ever pored with more luckless diligence, or shook a head of more hopeless despondency over his task. He could but just make out what tended rather to excite than assuage that feverish thirst of curiosity which was consuming his inmost soul. The manuscript told no more of Melmoth. (MM 65–66)

What could Stanton hope to obtain from the demonic Wanderer if not some fragment of forbidden knowledge such as the "antiquarian" hopes to find in an ancient manuscript and John seeks vainly in the pages of Stanton's document? We never learn what Stanton hopes to accomplish by pursuing Melmoth, and we cannot be sure that Stanton himself knows. We also never learn just why John is so intent on tracking down every trace of his ghastly ancestor. What is certain is that the object of their inquiries belongs properly to the boundary-world between life and death, a world that is figured in the novel by the decomposing, fragmentary, yet somehow revivable text.

It is no coincidental detail that the quest for the Wanderer becomes inseparable from acts of reading. The demonic Melmoth is a creature of *legend* in the oldest sense of that term: he is something that "must be read," something that belongs to the distant past, thus to the realm of the dead, and therefore something that can only be brought back to life by rescuing him from the tomb of the dead letter.[3] No matter that the story presents an apparently living Melmoth in the flesh at several points in the narrative; that living presence serves only to confirm an impression gleaned principally from reading. It is also worth remembering that the textual Wanderer is — until the very last few pages of the novel — a far more substantial figure than the "actual" man whom John occasionally sees. Young Melmoth's first sight of his demonic ancestor takes place in the room where the old uncle lies dying. The nephew is sitting in the corner at some distance from his uncle's bedside when the door opens and "a figure" appears whom he recognizes as "the living original of the portrait" hanging in the room. He reassures himself that there is nothing alarming about "a resemblance between a living man and the portrait of a dead one," but his alarm returns when the figure reappears (MM 23). He is about to investigate the matter when the uncle dies, diverting everyone's attention. He encounters the figure again, during the storm that wrecks Monçada's ship and that nearly drowns Melmoth himself, but he later refers to the incident as "a horrid dream" (MM 76). He also sees the Wanderer during the night after he finishes reading Stanton's manuscript, after he has burned the portrait. But again the scene is set in such a way as to cast doubt on the reality of John's experience:

> The wind was high that night, and as the creaking door swung on its hinges, every noise seemed like the sound of a hand struggling with the lock, or of a foot pausing on the threshold. But (for Melmoth never could decide) was it in a dream or not, that he saw the figure of his ancestor at his door? (MM 67–68)

The rhetoric of this passage is characteristic of the whole of the novel, including the author's preface. The reader is offered only uncertainty, and much of that uncertainty comes from the clever use of a rhetorical question. The narrator does not assert that John saw the Wanderer; he only reports, in a sort of *style indirect libre*, the question in the character's mind. While strong evidence is offered many hundreds of pages later, at the novel's close, that the apparition was not a dream, the uncertainty hangs over almost all the rest of the story. Even when the course of the narrative leaves no doubt that the Wanderer is actually there, a palpable physical presence, it opens up other questions no less basic and no less troubling about his ontological status. We may be assured that the demonic Melmoth is no dream, but what else is he? Who is he? Where did he come from? What does he want? Is he a man or a supernatural being? Is he alive or dead? Why does he behave as he does? Does he (or do we) have any choice?

The rhetorical uncertainty that creates so much of the novel's atmosphere extends even to the most basic matters, such as the identification of the characters. To put it bluntly, it is often difficult to tell who is who in the novel. The narration thus puts at risk one of the structures the readers of novels most rely on when they read, that is, the reference-structure of the cast of characters. Who is meant, for example, when the text refers to "Melmoth"? There are three different characters by that name. Again and again the text seems to play upon the potential of misidentification inherent in the ambiguity created by having three persons with a single name among the *dramatis personae*. Here is an example from a particularly important scene in the first chapter, one already alluded to above, in which John gets his first glimpse (perhaps) of his ancestor:

> John, greatly shocked, retired from the bed-side, and sat down in a distant corner of the room. The women were again in the room, which was very dark. Melmoth was silent from exhaustion, and there was a death-like pause for some time. At this moment John saw the door open, and a figure appear at it, who looked round the room, and then quietly and deliberately retired, but not before John had discovered in his face the living original of the portrait. (MM 23)

It is impossible to determine for certain just who was "silent from exhaustion." It was almost certainly not the Wanderer, who has not yet entered the room, but that is as much certainty as the reader can hold on to. The simple name "Melmoth" is regularly used in these opening pages to refer to the nephew, while the uncle is called "Old Melmoth." Here, however, the narrator seems to be making a distinction between "Melmoth" and "John," implying that the uncle and not the nephew was silent. But of course the passage makes clear by the mention of the "death-like pause" that *everyone* was silent for a while, so that the sentence remains as apt a description of John as of the dying uncle. The ambiguity here may seem trivial, since it does not matter much in the greater scheme of things whether the nephew or the uncle is silent from exhaustion, but its introduction at just this point is worth noting. The text sets up an uncanny moment of uncertainty in the reader at the very moment that it first offers the uncanny appearance of the improbably living ancestor, that *other* Melmoth, the one who ought to be silent as the grave and "exhausted" in the Latin root meaning of "emptied out." The reader's little moment of uncertainty moves quickly into one of the story's chief moments of gothic horror. The passage both presents and exploits the connection between the problem of reading an uncertain text and the moral-philosophical problem presented by the Wanderer's uncertain life-in-death. The two uncertainties seem deeply related.

Maturin goes much farther in his exploitation of the uncanny potential of such moments of indecidability. He uses it even when there is really no question of actual confusion as to the identity of the characters:

> The narrative, when Melmoth was again able to trace its continuation, described Stanton, some years after, plunged in a state the most deplorable.

> He had always been reckoned of a singular turn of mind, and the belief of this, aggravated by his constant talk of Melmoth, his wild pursuit of him, his strange behaviour at the theatre, and his dwelling on the various particulars of their extraordinary meetings [...] suggested to some prudent people that he was deranged. (MM 50–51)

In the context of the narrative, the reader has no difficulty guessing that the first Melmoth is young John and that the second is the Wanderer whom Stanton had encountered. But even so, the potential for confusion has an effect of silently equating the two identically named characters. A Melmoth is a Melmoth is a Melmoth. Young John Melmoth and his demonic ancestor begin to look like specular doubles of each other, each pursuing the other in a complex but quite symmetrical movement. This symmetry finds another expression in this passage, where the phrase "his wild pursuit of him" offers a pair of matching pronouns with ambiguous antecedents ("his . . . him") that could refer to Stanton's pursuit of the Wanderer or the Wanderer's pursuit of Stanton. Because of the reference to an unspecified "Melmoth," one is also reminded that young John is pursuing the Wanderer through this text and that the Wanderer appears as well to be pursuing John. All this reduplication is, of course, typical of Romantic fiction in the German ("gothic") tradition, where twins, shadows, ghosts, and other sorts of mirror-image characters are a regular feature, and where protagonists are often involved in quests for their proper identities.

There is another doubling under way here, one that is ultimately even more troubling than any of the others. The reader of the novel called *Melmoth* is functionally doubled in the story by a character named Melmoth who serves mainly as a reader of texts concerning another character named Melmoth. The reader of Maturin's "romance" actually seems to be at least as much inside the novel as regarding its contents from the outside — not only or most importantly because the narrator explicitly addresses this reader in the middle of the book, but also and chiefly because acts of reading comprise so much of the action. The two characters who serve as intermediaries bringing the story of the Wanderer to us, John Melmoth and Alonzo Monçada, do so chiefly by reading various documents. Indeed, there are enough manuscripts incorporated (in part or whole) into the novel that the narrative seems at times more like an anthology of fragments, a collection of literary *disjecta membra*, than a novel. This does not make the text easy to read, but it does make its formal structure an appropriate metaphor for the uneasy relation between dead part and living whole that evidently troubled its author. It also implicates the (external?) reader of the novel in the (internal?) actions of its characters, blurring further the boundary between "inside" and "outside."

It is remarkable with what consistency the documents in *Melmoth* are presented as offering severe difficulties of decipherment. They are damaged, faded, written in bad handwriting or illegible script and must be labored over to yield any information whatever.[4] Manuscripts need not be old, like Stanton's narrative, to be hard to read. A letter Monçada receives from his brother Juan is at times as obscure as the supposed autograph of St. Mark: "After these lines several were unintelligible to me, apparently from the agitation under which they were written; — the precipitancy and fiery ardor of my brother's character communicated itself to his writings. After many a defaced page I could trace the following words" (MM 135). Paradoxically, the very vitality that causes the brother to write turns his text — at least partially — into a set of dead letters that the addressee cannot bring back to life. The paradox is especially striking since the passage urges us to consider the written text as a metonymy for the spirit of the person who wrote it. This same figure occurs again when Monçada receives another letter from Juan reporting terrifying events whose effects "could easily be traced in the broken and irregular lines in which he vainly tried to describe" them (MM 194). This letter, too, is "much defaced": "a great part of it was illegible, from being crushed amid the stones and damp clay contiguous to the door" (MM 194). As it turns out, the mutilation, defacement, and death presented as belonging to the condition of letters are prophetically accurate figures for the condition of Juan himself, who soon lies in a premature grave. The texts collapse time in their figurative commingling of life and death, reflecting both the present "fiery ardor" of Juan's life and the future "damp clay" of his tomb. Are the letters themselves alive or dead? How can one choose between the two? Is there any choice?

The complexity of the uncertainty appears only to grow when we consider that these letters from Juan to Alonzo, whose illegibility indicated both the life and death of the writer, find their own death and life in the reader. Alonzo, who brings the dead letters back to life by reading them (and re-presenting them for us to read) must also destroy them as completely as possible to prevent them falling into the wrong hands. He disposes of these letters and other letters as best he can, frequently by eating them. "I swallowed the first [paper] the moment I had read it," Monçada tells Melmoth, and later comments that one of the letters was so short that "I found no difficulty in *swallowing it* immediately after perusal" (MM 144, 196; Maturin's emphasis). It is hard to say whether this action permanently destroys the letters or in fact preserves them. The biblical figures of reading as eating, surely familiar to Maturin the curate, urge the possibility that eating a text is the best way to incorporate its spirit permanently into the living body, as in Ezekiel. Monçada becomes one with the (textual) body of his brother, providing a literal tomb for the body of the dead letters but a figurative haven for the fiery ardor of their spirit. In a novel where so many characters exist principally by way of textual revivification, where indeed Juan appears chiefly as a living presence in his letters, we cannot dismiss the suspicion that Monçada's act of swallowing results more in preservation than in destruction. Alonzo, after all, is able to report these texts word for word to Melmoth, thus demonstrating their continued vitality.

Perhaps the liveliest and deadliest of all the many texts incorporated into the structure of *Melmoth* (as if this great book had swallowed dozens of lesser documents to sustain its growth) is the "Tale of the Indians." This narrative, long enough to be a novel in its own right, is contained in a manuscript belonging to Adonijah the Jew, who shelters Monçada from the Inquisition. The manuscript's physical character, its location, and the circumstances in which Alonzo reads it all contribute to an atmosphere of death so powerful that the narrative it contains cannot help but seem a corpse come back to life. The text resides in a chamber accessible only by a dark passage that falls only slightly short of being "as long and intricate as any that ever an antiquarian pursued to discover the tomb of Cheops in the Pyramids" (MM 291) and that contains in addition to a number of parchment scrolls "*four* skeletons, not in cases, but in a kind of upright coffin, that gave their bony emptiness a kind of ghastly and imperative prominence, as if they were the real and rightful tenants of that singular apartment" (MM 292). Monçada notes that the scrolls are "inscribed with large characters in red and ochre-coloured ink" (MM 292), and Adonijah later describes the documents as "scrawled as it were with the blood of man" (MM 295). The Jew may be speaking figuratively, but Monçada and the reader both know that victims of the Inquisition did indeed from time to time compose documents (often their "confessions") in their own blood when the ink supplied by the authorities proved insufficient for the scope of their piety.

Adonijah wants Monçada to transcribe a manuscript the Jew himself had written, not in the Roman alphabet but in "a character unknown to this idolatrous people." Alonzo immediately recognizes it as ordinary Spanish written in Greek letters, "a mode of writing that, I easily conceived, must have been as unintelligible to the officers of the Inquisition as the Hieroglyphics of the Egyptian priests" (MM 301). This second allusion to the tombs and monuments of ancient Egypt — a matter of intense current interest in the early years of the nineteenth century — links Adonijah's manuscript even more firmly to the realm of death, to an effaced and crumbling remnant that can only be brought back to life by means of decipherment. Deciphering and copying the Jew's text turns out to be an easy matter for Monçada, though it is not a task he takes up happily, knowing as he does that the story it records treats of the Wanderer, from whose terrible temptation Monçada had barely escaped. The Spaniard recognizes and fears the fatal power such a document must contain, fearing especially the vital relevance of its deadly letters for his own situation. Adonijah realizes what Alonzo is thinking and makes this important observation:

"Does thy hand tremble still?" said Adonijah; "and dost thou still hesitate to record the story of those whose destiny a link, wondrous, invisible, and indissoluble, has bound to thine. Behold, there are those near thee, who, though they have no longer a tongue, speak to thee with that eloquence of living tongues. Behold, there are those around thee, whose mute and motionless arms of bone plead to thee as no arms of flesh ever pleaded. Behold, there are those who, being speechless, yet speak — who, being dead, are yet alive — who, though in the abyss of eternity, are yet around thee, and call on thee, as with a mortal voice. Hear them! — take the pen in thine hand, and write." I took the pen in hand, but could not write a line. Adonijah, in a transport of ecstasy, snatching a skeleton from its receptacle, placed it before me. "Tell him thy story thyself, peradventure he will believe thee, and record it." And supporting the skeleton with one hand, he pointed with the other, as bleached and bony as that of the dead, to the manuscript that lay before me. (MM 302)

The skeletons, the manuscript, and the demonic Wanderer are all equally terrifying in their character of beings "who, being dead, are yet alive." The decaying or illegible text, the barely decipherable hieroglyphics found in ancient tombs, the dangerous papers that must be ingested by the body as well as the mind — all these are the potent emblems of the terrifying force that stalks the world of *Melmoth*.

But we immediately realize that this force ought not to be terrifying at all. The one who, having been dead, is yet alive is also the Word made flesh, the incorporate *logos*, the one who promised salvation for those like Alonzo Monçada who kept the faith. Yet no sign of Christian hope appears in this rhetoric of living corpses. The emphasis is instead on terror and on the threat posed by a dead document (the manuscript) to overwhelm a living soul (Alonzo) with its deadly eloquence. The language used by Adonijah and the narrator so thoroughly equates the manuscript with the skeletons that both appear to proclaim terrifying and dangerous messages of doom. The skeletons, like the document, "speak" without being alive. Indeed they "speak" without actually speaking at all, for both remain eternally silent, communicating only as traces of living presences long since departed. Bones and pages both seem to offer the same lesson to the beholder: You, too, are no more than this. The equation is so complete that the language of the passage at times prevents readers from knowing for certain whether it is the skeleton or the manuscript that is under discussion. When the Jew says, "Tell him thy story thyself," holding the skeleton in one hand and pointing with the other at the book, it is impossible to say whether he is addressing the papers or the bones. And because the narration proposes that Adonijah himself belongs to the company of the dead (his hand that points to the manuscript is "bleached and bony as that of the dead"), we cannot be entirely sure that he might be addressing himself as well. As one who has escaped the Inquisition but still is threatened by it, he might properly be described as one who, being dead, is yet alive. Monçada, of course, shares this experience of the Inquisition and has himself returned from the dead, having resided at length in a subterranean tomb. Adonijah could be telling Monçada to tell his story to the skeleton (or to the manuscript) as well as directing the bones (or the document, or himself) to report to the Spaniard. The passage allows, even encourages this ambiguity because all the possible addressees of Adonijah's command are equally appropriate.

The difference between these living-dead figures assembled in Adonijah's chamber and the figure of the resurrected Jesus with whom they appear to have so much in common has to do with the nature of the boundary between life and death. The story of Jesus proclaims that the Nazarene crossed that boundary, that he died and came to life again. The story told over and over again in *Melmoth* proclaims that the boundary is uncertain. The Jew speaks very precisely and properly of those who, "being dead, are yet alive," while the gospel narratives tell of one who, *having been dead*, yet lives. The boundary between life and death remains clear for the writers of the canonical New Testament, except perhaps for the "mutilated" Gospel of Mark, which ends with the women fleeing in terror from the empty tomb. The miracle reported most unambiguously in the other gospels is that the boundary was crossed, and that miracle brings hope. The miracle implicit in every aspect of *Melmoth* is that the boundary is vague and uncertain, that death and life may coexist in a single entity. That miracle offers not hope but horror.

The horror the novel offers is not, however, the spine-tingling excitement we might expect from horror fiction. "*Romantic gothic fiction is not exciting*," writes Marshall Brown (*Gothic* 3; Brown's italics). Although not everyone who has read *Melmoth* would be inclined to agree, Brown is surely right in attributing the lack of excitement he finds in Maturin's novel to its sharp narrative focus on "the soul, not the body" as the locus of all the narrative interest (*Gothic* 135).[5] The tale hinges on spiritual matters, on the misuse or downright perversion of religious faith, not on heart-stopping adventures of the flesh; and even when it succeeds in eliciting from its readers a shudder of gothic horror, the reaction comes only rarely from a terrifying scene of physical action but most often from yet another example of religious faith gone awry. Indeed, so much of the novel is taken up with the depiction of misdirected religious zeal that one might almost suppose that Maturin had nothing else on his mind. It is interesting, then, to discover that the author's account of the genesis of his story suggests that his attention lay elsewhere. He speaks not of the evil done by perverted religious practices but of the enormous power of religious scruples:

> The hint of this Romance (or Tale) was taken from a passage in one of my Sermons which (as it is to be presumed very few have read) I shall take the liberty to quote. The passage is this.

> At this moment is there one of us present, however we may have departed from the Lord, disobeyed his will, and disregarded his word — is there one of us who would, at this moment accept all that man could bestow, or earth afford, to resign the hope of salvation? — No, there is not one — not such a fool on earth, were the enemy of mankind to traverse it with the offer!
>
> This passage suggested the idea of "Melmoth the Wanderer." The Reader will find that idea developed in the following pages, with what power or success *he* is to decide. (MM 5; Maturin's italics)

Melmoth becomes the emissary of the "enemy of mankind," traveling the world and offering the exchange mentioned in Maturin's sermon. "*I have traversed the world in the search, and no one to gain that world, would lose his own soul!*" (MM 601; Maturin's italics). The pain, poverty, grief, and abject misery from which Melmoth would promise rescue with his offer of exchange were as extreme as can be imagined, but religious scruple always triumphed.

The resolution of the paradox is perhaps obvious, but it is worth considering: Maturin's story sets up a very orthodox, even pious opposition between external and internal piety, leaving no doubt that inward and spiritual grace has nothing at all to do with the outward signs of religious observance. Religion necessarily goes astray when it "substitutes external severities for internal amendment" (MM 143). Maturin's Melmoth, like the Faust of the Spiess chapbook and Marlowe's tragic drama, tests the limits of Protestant insistence upon the priority of the internal over the external. According to the novel, the individual human soul, offered the choice between external, secular well-being and internal, spiritual salvation, always chooses the latter; but human institutions, including especially the Church of Rome, divert natural piety by focusing exclusively on external matters. Thus the paradox that a novel that devotes so much of its narrative to excoriating religious institutions can correctly claim to celebrate the triumph of religion.

The distinction between the internal and the external is unquestionably one of the chief intellectual foundation stones of Maturin's novel, but it is not presented without considerable ambivalence. While one aspect of the novel appears to insist on maintaining that distinction, another appears to insist that doing so is impossible. One need look no further than the formal organization of the narrative itself, tale within tale like Chinese boxes, to find a powerful denial of the easy separability of inside and outside.[6] Alonzo Monçada's narrative, which makes up a large portion of the novel's physical bulk, is on the one hand, "inside" the omniscient narrative frame but, on the other, "outside" other embedded narratives, such as the "Tale of the Indians" and the additional stories that it contains in turn.[7] One finds, furthermore, that the boundaries between the various tales in the nested structure are readily permeated by the omniscient narrative voice, so that the "outside" perspective reveals itself as vigorously present even within the center of the most deeply embedded tale.

One particularly dramatic example of an "external" perspective making its way into the "inside" of the book can stand for many. Approximately in the middle of the "Tale of the Indians," in a manuscript that Monçada is compelled by its author, the Jew Adonijah, to copy, its heroine Immalee/Isadora learns that she must marry a man she does not know or love. The narrator comments on Isadora's horrified reaction:

> To the mere reader of romance, it may seem incredible that a female of Isadora's energy and devotedness should feel anxiety or terror in a situation so common to a heroine. She has only to stand proof against all the importunities and authority of her family, and announce her desperate resolution to share the destiny of a mysterious and unacknowledged lover. All this sounds very plausible and interesting. Romances have been written and read, whose interest arose from the noble and impossible defiance of the heroine to all powers human and superhuman alike. But neither the writers or readers seem ever to have taken into account the thousand petty external causes that operate on human agency with a force, if it not be more powerful, far more effective than the grand internal motive which makes so grand a figure in romance, and so rare and trivial a one in common life. (MM 413)

Who, one might well wonder, is speaking here? These words appear to come not just from outside the frame of Adonijah's manuscript tale, or Monçada's narrative of reading that manuscript, but from outside the perspective of the fiction as a whole. And to whom are they addressed? The reader of Adonijah's tale (Monçada) is no "reader of romance," nor is Monçada's interlocutor (young Melmoth), since both believe absolutely in the veracity of the narratives offered to them. The only reader of romance present at this scene of reading is Maturin's reader, and the only voice entitled to address that reader is the author of Maturin's book.[8]

It is little wonder that the explicit argument proclaimed by this authorial voice insists on the priority of the external over the internal. The external narrative perspective has muscled its way into the internal workings of the text to assert that "petty external causes" do more to determine the course of actual events than the "grand internal motive" important in works of fiction. The authorial voice appears to enjoy (and seems to invite us to enjoy as well) the irony that he must defend the truth of his romance by casting doubt on the conventional truths defined by the romances of others. The "mere reader of romance" may not be capable of swallowing the unsugared pill of reality, but whoever reads *this* must be another sort altogether, one who knows that external trivia carry more weight in the world than internal motives.

There is, of course, an additional irony that this particular authorial voice does not and could not enjoy: a reader who shares the point of view asserted in this passage would be urged by logic to question the assumption, on which the novel is built, that internal religious motives regularly carry more weight than external "severities." The explicit assertion that "external causes" have priority over "internal motives" contradicts the equally explicit claim that internal motives trump external observances. The contradiction mirrors another, already apparent in the author's preface. The text of the sermon that allegedly served as the "hint" from which the novel was developed proclaims unreservedly that "there is not one — not such a fool on earth" who would trade his chance for salvation in exchange for even the most desirable secular rewards. The novel, on the other hand, offers in the character of Melmoth precisely the individual whose existence the sermon denies. It is quite true that no other character in the book chooses to share Melmoth's fate, no matter how terrible the events that urge him or her to do so. But the great spiritual resolve of Stanton, Monçada, Immalee/Isadora, and the rest can be tested and found firm only by assuming the existence of one who had given in, one who had proved to be just that "fool" who is supposed not to exist.

This is not a minor matter. Maturin could easily have structured his fiction differently by simply following more closely the suggestion of his own sermon, in which it is not a damned soul but the "enemy of mankind," the devil himself, who wanders the world offering the exchange. The Faust story offered an adaptable literary framework that he could have modified so as to have a Faust-like figure (or series of them) confront and overcome the temptation offered by Mephistopheles. But Maturin declined to follow this path and chose instead to build his narrative around a character who is both Faust and Mephisto combined, both tempter and temptation's victim.[9] While one can imagine a host of reasons why Maturin might have preferred having a human rather than a supernatural being as the chief figure in his romance, none of them seems anywhere near as pressing as the thematic imperative offered in the sermon and carried out in every other aspect of the novel. We are still left with the question of why a story proclaiming the priority of internal motives, the power of religious scruples, and the impossibility of choosing secular gain over spiritual salvation should rely so heavily on elements of character, action, and rhetoric that seriously question that priority.

The novel does not gloss over these contradictions. On the contrary, *Melmoth* appears to emphasize the very points at which they appear. But why does it do so? What does the novel accomplish by presenting its theme of the overwhelming superiority of internal, spiritual power in a context dominated by demonstrations of external, secular power?

Historical-biographical explanations can help only to a limited extent, though the particular circumstances of the novel's composition prompt useful speculations. It seems clear, for example, that the opposition between internal spirituality and external worldliness was an urgent and personal one for the author, particularly in the period in which he wrote *Melmoth*. Here was a man of apparently worldly tastes who had nonetheless chosen the life of a cleric, one who was now driven by ill fortune to rely on his secular talents as a writer of romances to support his family. The author's preface that begins with citing the sermon ends with an apology:

> I cannot again appear before the public in so unseemly a character as that of a writer of romances, without regretting the necessity that compels me to it. Did my profession furnish me with means of subsistence, I should hold myself culpable indeed in having recourse to any other, but — am I allowed the choice? (MM 6)[10]

The necessity for a fallen protagonist in a novel that wishes to celebrate a universal resistance to a temptation to fall surely has something to do with these personal circumstances that force Maturin to become an "unseemly" writer of romances. One has to suspect that the author, feeling himself driven away from the seemly profession of full-time cleric, would have considerable sympathy for his fallen hero. One suspects, too, that a powerful ambivalence must have informed every line Maturin wrote, as he sought as best he could to succeed in an enterprise that he considered unworthy. We can never be certain of the author's mental processes, but we can be sure of the lack of certainty that the text itself proclaims. Indeed, there seems nothing more powerful in this novel than its atmosphere of insecurity. The certainty offered by the sermon, the bold assurance that no one would ever trade worldly benefit for a chance at eternal salvation, is utterly lacking.

The final words of the preface offer only an apparently rhetorical question: "am I allowed the choice?" At first glance it seems clear enough that the author's question is indeed rhetorical and that its figurative import denies the possibility of choice. He seems to be telling us that he might consider his fiction-writing morally wrong *if* his financial circumstances allowed him the option of not writing. It is telling, however, that the language used here does not in fact insist that no option exists, it only asks the question. Maybe the question "Am I allowed the choice?" is genuine, and maybe the proper answer is "Yes, indeed you are." The rhetoric of the passage is such as to allow for such a reading, even if it does not explicitly invite it. And if one were to invert the expected procedure and read the novel before the preface, one would surely arrive armed with a great deal of narrative evidence that, when it comes to issues involving the possibility of moral culpability, there is always a choice, no matter how pressing external exigencies might seem.

Is there a choice, or is there not? That is the question that the novel poses and that it steadfastly refuses to answer. Whenever an answer appears plausible, the story evades or refutes it. The novel, of course, deals with choices that must appear to the reader to be far more basic than the one with which Maturin closes his preface. The novel treats matters of life and death, indeed *eternal* life and death, while the last paragraph of the preface is concerned with the relatively transitory question of how a particular Irish cleric is to support his family. One can easily see, though, that the terrible choice (or non-choice) confronting Maturin could have appeared just about the equivalent of a life-or-death choice in the eyes of the author. To the aristocratic Maturin, unaccustomed to worrying about financial matters, the loss of status that came with his father's dismissal from the civil service and the consequent need to subsist on a total income of eighty pounds a year must have seemed very much like the approach of death. The preface suggests that the distressed author, faced with the prospect of physical poverty and the real possibility of physical suffering, elected to put at risk his spiritual well-being by appearing "in so unseemly a character as that of a writer of romances."

Ambivalence is abundantly attested by the text. One can even detect the presence of a link between Maturin's personal ambivalence and that which informs the story of the Wanderer in the opening sentence of the first chapter: "In the autumn of 1816, John Melmoth, a student in Trinity College, Dublin, quitted it to attend to a dying uncle on whom his hope for independence rested" (MM 9). The narrator reports at the end of the opening paragraph that young Melmoth regarded his uncle with a "mingled sensation of awe" informed by a "sensation both attractive and repulsive" as a "being who [. . .] holds the very threads of our existence in his hands, and may prolong or snap them when he pleases" (MM 9). A matter of life and death, then, informs the onset of the narrative.

The very mundane circumstances that provide the setting for the frame story in which the narrative of the Wanderer is embedded already suggest the horror of living on past one's appointed time. They suggest also the paradoxical joy that an appropriate death can bring. Such a paradox is entirely familiar to the Christian tradition and appropriate in a book that addresses that tradition, but the direction in which this novel drives the paradox is not quite so familiar. The paradox here is that the joyful gospel of Jesus might participate in the horrifying uncertainties and deformations inevitable in a world inhabited by those who, being dead, are yet alive. That such a thing could happen — indeed has happened — is asserted by Melmoth to Immalee (later renamed "Isadora"[11]) in the course of the narrative Monçada reads in Adonijah's tomblike chamber. The innocent young Immalee/Isadora seeks instruction from the strange traveler about life in the marvelous countries of Europe, which she has never experienced. He instructs her on many topics, including religion, portraying the Western world in terms that horrify the poor girl. Christianity does not fare any better in Melmoth's account than anything else, as indeed one might have expected in the discourse of an agent of the archfiend. The reader quickly realizes, though, that even the devil must be given his due when it comes to pointing out the abuses of religion:

> They have such a [mild and peaceful] religion, but what use have they made of it? Intent on their settled purpose of discovering misery wherever it could be traced, and inventing it where it could not, they have found, even in the pure pages of that book, which, they presume to say, contains their title to peace on earth, and happiness hereafter, a right to hate, plunder, and murder each other. Here they have been compelled to exercise an extraordinary share of perverted ingenuity. The book contains nothing but what is good, and evil must be the minds, and hard labour of those evil minds, to extort a tinge from it to colour their pretensions. (MM 341)

The great problem of Christianity, then, is the legibility of the Bible. Jesus no longer walks the earth; all that remains is a set of dead letters that may, or may not, provide access to the living spirit of divine grace. The pages of the book are pure, their contents "nothing but good," but the pages themselves are inert and can have no effect until someone reads them. Unfortunately, the process of reading is such that there is nothing to prevent an evil mind from turning the good and pure text to an evil purpose. As Boccaccio pointed out in the "Author's Epilogue" to the *Decameron*, "No word, however pure, was ever wholesomely construed by a mind that was corrupt" (*Decameron* 830). The inevitable result is that even the Word of the living God is constantly at risk of bringing about death. Christ's message of eternal life becomes the text upon which fanatics preach sermons calling for murder.

The demonic Melmoth is, oddly enough, more than ready to grant the essential goodness of the Bible. Those who battle over the meaning of the Bible, he contends, "have never been able to extract a subject of difference from the *essential* contents of that book" (MM 341; Maturin's emphasis). Its essence is to be found in its spirit, however, and not in its letters: "They dare not deny that the spirit that book inculcates and inspires, is a spirit whose fruits are love, joy, peace, long-suffering, mildness, and truth. On these points they never presumed to differ" (MM 342). But they manage to differ on almost everything else, and to such a degree that they often enough come to blows over their differences. If the spirit of the book is so patently clear, perhaps the source of the trouble lies in the letters. Melmoth makes a statement about the language of the Bible that seems to suggest otherwise:

> One point is plain; they all agree that the language of the book is "Love one another," while they all translate that language, "Hate one another." But as they can find neither materials or excuse from that book, they search for them in their own minds, — and there they are never at a loss, for human minds are inexhaustible in malignity and hostility; and when they borrow the name of that book to sanction them, the deification of their passions becomes a duty, and their worst impulses are hallowed and practiced as virtues. (MM 342)

The Wanderer, who at times certainly speaks for the devil, proposes that neither the spirit nor the "language" of the Bible offer any grounds for disagreement; only the fundamental malignity of human nature can be the culprit.

Of course, even allowing for a large dose of irony in the author's insistence in a note appended to this section of the novel that "the sentiments ascribed to the stranger are diametrically opposed to mine" (MM 338 n.) readers need to be suspicious of opinions uttered by emissaries of Satan.[12] We cannot take the devil at his word, not even by imagining that the exact opposite of everything he says is true. We know that Maturin does not agree with Melmoth's belief that all human beings are essentially evil because the novel shows people consistently refusing the diabolical exchange offered by the Wanderer. On the other hand, we cannot accept the author's glib assurance that his own views are "diametrically opposed" to those voiced here by his demonic character. We know that Maturin in fact stands behind most of the criticism Melmoth levels against sectarian rivalries and religious intolerance. The reader is compelled to concur with the Wanderer that in many cases the "pure pages of that book" have given rise to enormous horrors. But if the origin of those horrors is not the evil nature of human beings, where does it lie?

The hint of an answer is embedded in Melmoth's rhetoric, in his insistence on making a distinction between what the language of the Bible "is" and what it is "translated" to mean. The problem in a nutshell is that the "pure pages" are readable, are open to translation. As a matter of fact, they have to be read. There is no other way to their "spirit" or even to their "language" save through reading. If there were some way to apprehend the book directly, without engaging in any "translation" at all, perhaps there would be no violence in the Christian world. Melmoth's formulation may suggest that one can know the language of the Bible directly, without translating it, and that translation is therefore an option that ought to be foregone. The novel, however, argues forcefully that translations are fundamental in our constructions of meaning. Almost every significant event in the story is mediated by acts of reading, many of which are also translations of one kind or another.

In the case of reading, the answer to the question "Am I allowed the choice?" is always both yes and no. No, one does not have any choice concerning whether or not to read: the most significant experience (as it is presented in the novel) only comes by way of reading. But then, having accepted the necessity of reading, one is confronted by an overwhelming abundance of choices. It is easy to say that the Bible clearly says, "Love thy neighbor," but it is painfully difficult to decide what that injunction means. All in all, it would be best if one did not have to choose, if one could simply appeal to the letter of the text and claim that it means "just what it says." Such a claim, however, merely begs the essential question by giving up on that task of reading. Once one takes up the challenge of finding meaning, whether it be in the Bible or in a gothic novel written by an impecunious Irish curate, one is implicated in the diabolical and deadly choices that come with reading. The great strength of *Melmoth the Wanderer* is that is poses that challenge and explores its implications with unremitting zeal.

Notes

[1] This is the same Michaelis who is mentioned by Hamann in the *Aesthetica in nuce* as one of the "scribes of worldly wisdom." See chapter 1, n. 4.

[2] Maturin may well have expected his reader to notice the parallels here with the way Petrach presented his own quest to reassemble the *disjecta membra* of classical Latin literature.

[3] See Koelb, *Legendary Figures*, especially xi–xxviii.

[4] Hennelly stresses the importance of failed communication in *Melmoth* (674–76), but from the perspective of his assertion that the novel displays a very modern concern with existential themes that link Maturin's work with "*Notes from the Underground, The Trial*, and *Lord Jim*" (665).

[5] Among those who might be inclined to disagree with Brown are critics such as Dawson, who argues that the gothic novel is based on a paradoxical enjoyment of fear (623) and comprises "an uninhibited sensational literature" (632).

[6] Many readers have noted this feature of the novel: Kennedy, for example, comments on "its 'Chinese Box' structure" (41). Critics disagree, however, on the significance of this complexity. Kennedy argues that it "mirrors the illogicality and shifting emphasis of the dream" (41). I propose, on the other hand, that the complex structure does not reflect so much dreamlike illogic as the author's desire to foreground the process of reading by mounting (fictional) documents within documents.

[7] Praz points out that part of the story of Alonzo Monçada (chapters 5 and 6 of *Melmoth*) was adapted by Maturin from Diderot's *La religieuse*. In places, Praz argues, "Maturin has followed his model so closely as to translate it literally in many passages" (430).

[8] Sage seems to confirm the emergence of Maturin's own voice in this aside to the reader when he says that the passage "reflects the pressure after *Fatal Revenge* (1807) on Maturin from Scott [. . .] to write in a more 'modern' (i.e., 'realistic') fashion" (Notes 646).

[9] Interest in Goethe and his drama *Faust* was a prominent feature of the English literary scene at the time Maturin was writing *Melmoth*. See Conger for a thorough discussion of the German background; M.-C. Vuillemin examines Maturin's novel as a version of *Faust*.

[10] Some scholars believe that the straightened fininacial circumstances alluded to in the author's preface explain many of the peculiarities of the novel: see especially Oost.

[11] The novel displays a remarkable interest in the connection between name and identity. Just as several persons can share a single name, as in the case of "Melmoth," discussed above, so can one person have several names. For more on the implications (especially policital) of multiple names for a single person, see Lew.

[12] Sage comments that Maturin's disclaimer in the note "leaves the reader uneasy" (Introduction xxvi) and cites Fowler (524) as sharing the nearly universal discomfort readers experience with this passage.

10: "This Hideous Drama of Revivification": Poe and the Rhetoric of Terror

THE NARRATOR OF "BERENICE" (1835), surely one of Edgar Allan Poe's most horrifying tales, presents himself as a man afflicted by a pathological "intensity of interest" so acute that he is utterly taken up "in the contemplation of even the most ordinary objects of the universe." Among the activities symptomatic of his peculiar condition he notes the following:

> To muse for long unwearied hours, with my attention riveted to some frivolous device on the margin or in the typography of a book; to become absorbed, for the better part of a summer's day, in a quaint shadow falling aslant upon the tapestry or upon the floor; to lose myself, for an entire night, in watching the steady flame of a lamp, or the embers of a fire, to dream away whole days over the perfume of a flower; to repeat, monotonously, some common word, until the sound, by dint of frequent repetition, ceased to convey any idea whatever to the mind. (PT 20)

He goes on to say that his condition, though perhaps not unprecedented, seemed to defy "anything like analysis or explanation." This rhetoric of negation is surely meant to awaken the imp of the perverse that sleeps in every reader and to provoke an attempt to produce the very explanation that the narrator forecloses.

The peculiar ailment suffered by Berenice's cousin can be described by a modern reader as a kind of semiotic obsession. Though these are not terms Poe would have used himself, the concepts behind them were surely familiar to him. The object of the cousin's intense interest is evidently the relation between signifier and signified and more especially the contingent yet uncontrollable nature of that relation. Ordinary and even frivolous objects, such as the typography of a book or a shadow on the floor, can become so saturated with meaning that hours can be devoted to their contemplation. On the other hand, objects ordinarily replete with meaning, such as words, can be stripped of all significance by an unrelenting attention to their surface forms.

The signifier that takes firmest hold on his imagination is his cousin's dentition, the "white and ghastly *spectrum* of the teeth," as he calls it. He is possessed by these teeth and wants in turn to possess them:

> The teeth! — the teeth! [. . .] For these I longed with a frenzied desire. All other matters and all different interests became absorbed in their

single contemplation. They — they alone were present to the mental eye, and they, in their sole individuality, became the essence of my mental life. [. . .] I shuddered as I assigned to them, in imagination, a sensitive and sentient power, and, even when unassisted by the lips, a capability of moral expression. Of Mademoiselle Sallé it has been well said, "*Que tous ses pas étaient des sentiments [that every step she took was a sentiment]*." And of Berenice I more seriously believed *que tous ses dents étaient des idées [that all her teeth were ideas]*. [. . .] *Des idées!* — ah, *therefore* it was that I coveted them so madly! I felt that their possession could alone ever restore me to peace, in giving me back to reason. (PT 23)

The teeth, past which all spoken words enter the world, become the single signifier capable of encompassing all meaning.[1]

If the reader has not been infected by the narrator's disease, he or she will have noticed the potential for significance lurking in the phrase "their possession could alone ever restore me to peace." This phrase, like the teeth it refers to, is so highly charged with meaning as to become a source of anxiety.[2] The words "their possession" point in several directions at once, since we cannot be certain whether the pronoun "their" is to be construed as a possessive or objective genitive, and thus cannot tell whether the issue is the narrator possessing the teeth or the teeth possessing the narrator. The readings are not mutually exclusive, especially in the present context, since it is his obsession with the teeth — his being possessed by them — that leads him to want to have them as his property. A further ambiguity is that the antecedent of "their" is uncertain: it usually refers back to the "them" of the previous sentence, but the antecedent of "them" could be either "des idées," the most recently mentioned noun, or the teeth, unquestionably the central topic under discussion. This ambiguity is of some moment because of the important difference between the physical possession of an object and the intellectual possession of ideas. The latter is really a figurative turn of phrase based on the former, for we all know that possessing a concept is by no means the same thing as possessing a hat. The ambiguous antecedent creates an implied syllepsis in which two incompatible notions are brought together in a single verbal construct. Just as Pope makes literary hay out of the confrontation between literal and figurative meanings when he dryly describes the young lady worried lest she "stain her honor, or her new brocade," so does Poe find the stuff of a story in the syllepsis of "possessing" and being possessed by teeth and ideas.[3]

It is clear enough that Berenice's cousin wants to have ideas, that he is in fact in love with the very idea of having ideas, which for him means making and breaking connections between signifiers and their meanings. He is an obsessive observer of signs, the components of which he then breaks apart and recombines.[4] The language in which he describes his first view of Berenice's teeth already shows this process at work. He tells how her "thin and shrunken" lips parted, so that "in a smile of peculiar meaning, *the teeth* of the changed Berenice disclosed themselves slowly to my view" (PT 22–23; Poe's emphasis). Two important characteristics of the teeth are brought into prominence here. First, they appear in such a way as to open up the possibility of finding in them a metonymy of pure significance; that is, they seem to be full of meaning, but no one knows exactly what this meaning is. They are associated with a smile of indefinite but potent significance, a "peculiar" meaning that the narrator does not even attempt to specify. This metonymy suggests a further possibility, realized later, for outright identification of the teeth with meaning. The second characteristic worth noting is that the teeth are not passive objects in this description but active agents: Berenice does not show her teeth, but rather the teeth show themselves. Not only do the teeth embody meaning, they are also capable of becoming as it were disembodied. Any reader prone to reading literally the metonymy of the first half of the sentence will have no trouble reading equally literally the second. Language implies that Berenice's teeth are vessels of meaning with no necessary connection to the rest of Berenice's body. Language also implies that "possessing" ideas and possessing objects can be understood as similar actions.[5]

The terror of Poe's tale results from putting such literal readings into action. Signifiers take over control of this fictional world and put human agency into a subordinate role. Indeed, human agency actually plays no role, on the narrative level at least, in the climactic event of the story in which the narrator obtains literal possession of Berenice's teeth. There is simply a gap in the narrative, after which the narrator discovers himself sitting alone in his library feeling as if he had "newly awakened from a confused and exciting dream" (PT 24). The gap in the narrative marks a gap in the narrator's experience, or at least in the understanding of his experience, and he can only guess at its contents. With striking appropriateness he tropes his memory as an illegible text that nonetheless must be read: "It was a fearful page in the record of my existence, written all over with dim, and hideous, and unintelligible recollections. I strived to decypher them, but in vain [. . .]" (PT 24). The narrator's great facility at reading, which had suggested the absolute importance of obtaining the teeth, is now replaced by an inability to read the story of how he obtained them. But the fault lies not in the self as reader but in the self as text. The narrator still reads obsessively, but his role as reader has so taken over his being that there is no room left in him for anything else. There is nothing inside him that remains legible, and in order to understand what has happened he must again read something else.[6]

The "something else" that presents itself to his attention is, naturally enough, a book. After noting the presence on his table of a small box, the narrator finds himself shuddering without knowing why:

These things were in no way to be accounted for, and my eyes at length dropped to the open pages of a book, and to a sentence underscored therein. The words were the singular but simple ones of Ebn Zaiat: — "*Dicebant mihi sodales si sepulchrum amicae visitarem, curas meas aliquantulum fore levatas [my companions said to me that, if I were to visit the tomb of my lady friend, my cares would be somewhat relieved].*" Why, then, as I perused them, did the hairs of my head erect themselves on end, and the blood of my body become congealed within my veins? (PT 24)

We learn the answer to this rhetorical question almost immediately, for a servant enters to report that Berenice's grave had been found violated, her body in it disfigured but still alive. The narrator suspects that the little box holds the answer. He fails to open it, but it falls from his grasp onto the floor, breaks apart, and discloses "some instruments of dental surgery, intermingled with thirty-two small, white, ivory-looking substances that were scattered to and fro about the floor" (PT 25).

What Berenice's bookish cousin discovers in the lines of Ebn Zaiat is yet another text upon which he has made good. He has already taken the advice offered by the Ebn Zaiat's comrades and visited the grave in order to alleviate his cares. The cousin's particular cares, however, include especially the lady's teeth and "their possession." The illegible text of experience is becoming clear, but it is composed — horrifyingly — of dismembered pieces of other texts. Most dismaying of all is the piece of discourse that suggested the separability of the teeth from the lady, but even that fragment is here as well in terrible fulfillment. Unwittingly the narrator has carried out in full the literal meaning of the trope and separated the teeth not from a lifeless body but from a living person. The reading of the Latin text here in the library makes the narrator's hair stand on end because it reproduces another scene of reading at the gravesite, a more faithful and thorough reading that makes reality conform to the letter of the text. The library is the most appropriate location for the final scene of the story because it foregrounds reading as the activity upon which the plot turns.

The library replaces the gravesite because what happens to Berenice's body is simply a version of what happens regularly in the library. As the graveyard is the place where the bodies of those who once were living have been stored, perhaps one day to come to life again, so is the library the place where dead letters, the embodiment of once living thoughts, are stored in the expectation of experiencing revivification through reading. The world inhabited by Poe's characters enacts precisely a theory of nature that insists on the interpenetration of life and death in every substance, and insists therefore on the impermanence of both being alive and being dead.

The ultimate horror with which Poe confronts his reader, however, appears only obliquely in the tale's final few words. We learn that the enterprise in which Berenice's cousin has thought himself engaged — that is, the recovery of an ideal sign, a signifier fully saturated with universal meaning — has failed completely. When the broken box, dismembered as if in sympathy with Berenice's body, reveals its contents, no great meaning emerges. One could argue that almost no meaning at all emerges, since the narrator is now unable to even name the objects he sees scattered on the floor. He sees only "small, white, ivory-looking substances." We are not for a second allowed to suppose that this inability is the result of inattention resulting from distraction. Quite the contrary. The narrator notes with precision the number of these white objects, thirty-two, but the number does not prompt him — as it surely does us — to name the objects so carefully counted. We are left with the impression that he no longer knows what they are, let alone what they might mean. Instead of putting him in possession of the pure idea, the acquisition of Berenice's teeth has brought the narrator only a terrifying absence of meaning.

Poe's character finds himself at the end of the story in a position remarkably similar to that of a figure in one of Franz Kafka's little stories, "The Top." This brief parable tells how a philosopher becomes fascinated with spinning tops, how he becomes in fact so obsessed with the phenomenon that he hangs about children at play in the hopes of catching a glimpse of this marvelous activity. His behavior is motivated by pure philosophical curiosity:

> For he believed that the understanding of any detail, that of a spinning top, for instance, was sufficient for the understanding of all things. [. . .] Once the smallest detail was understood, then, everything was understood, which was why he busied himself only with the spinning top. (Kafka 444)

Like Berenice's cousin, then, this philosopher imagines that a universal meaning can be discovered in an otherwise trivial object. He hopes to catch the top while spinning and thereby grasp its meaning:

> as soon as the top began to spin and he was running breathlessly after it, the hope would turn to certainty, but when he held the silly piece of wood in his hand, he felt nauseated. The screaming of the children, which hitherto he had not heard and which now suddenly pierced his ears, chased him away, and he tottered like a top under a clumsy whip. (Kafka 444)

As in the Poe story, grasping an object is not the same thing as grasping a concept. Kafka's philosopher learns again and again that a signifier examined up close and naked may have no significance whatever. It is only a dumb piece of wood, or a set of thirty-two ivory-looking substances.[7] The philosopher, the story suggests, is no more than such an object himself.

The terror of "Berenice" emerges from the double possibility that a sign might harbor an entire universe of meaning or, on the other hand, might mean nothing at all. The process of playing with the sign relation that the narrator describes early in the story, his filling and emptying of signifiers, offers a program for rhetorical terror. It is the discovering in language of the unsettling convergence of life and death that Poe's stories so often depict. Does discourse offer the lively spirit, full of significance, or only the dead letter? The apostle Paul readily distinguishes between the letter that kills and the spirit that gives life in the second letter to the Corinthians, but Poe's characters, unlike the fortunate apostle, are not so confident about their mastery of the distinction between letter and spirit. The letters of the texts they read are occasionally indistinguishable from pure spirit, as Berenice's teeth become indistinguishable from ideas in the mind of her cousin. The teeth retain their living spirit even when Berenice herself is dead, but paradoxically they are reduced to dead objects when she is discovered to be still alive. The spiritual life that the narrator finds in the teeth can survive Berenice's death — indeed they seem totally independent of her existence — but they cannot survive her survival. The unspoken implication of the dreadful discovery that Berenice was buried alive is that death and life are easily mistaken for each other. If the living Berenice may be taken for dead, then it is also possible to take dead things for living, to mistake the letter for the spirit, and to see worlds of meaning in a set of thirty-two ivory substances. The reversibility of life and death may not be separated from the reversibility of rhetoric.

Poe's tales of terror are all built on this reversibility. Sometimes it is made explicit in the plot, sometimes not, but it is always present in the structure of the language. It is easy to see that the horrifying conclusion of "The Masque of the Red Death" (1842) essentially repeats the ending of "Berenice," though it puts the issue perhaps even more directly. The mysterious mummer whose appearance at the Prince's ball causes such a sensation is assumed by all present to be a living person who has assumed the appearance of death. His taste may be atrocious, but his costume is wonderfully effective:

> The figure was tall and gaunt, and shrouded from head to foot in the habiliments of the grave. The mask which concealed the visage was made so nearly to resemble the countenance of a stiffened corpse that the closest scrutiny must have had difficulty in detecting the cheat. (PT 141)

This figure of death, however, behaves like a living person, and the partygoers assume that the costume's external meaning is only an appearance thrown over a plenitude of life. But, as we all know, the costume turns out to be empty. The "grave cerements and corpselike mask" reveal themselves to be "untenanted by any tangible form" (PT 141). What everyone, including the reader, thought was full of living meaning is quite empty. The meaning on the surface was all the meaning there was, and the spirit of the letter is nothing more than the letter itself. The mummers of the "Red Death," like the narrator of "Berenice," are left with only objects emptied out of any meaning save the terrible suspicion that fullness and emptiness, death and life, meaning and meaninglessness, are all hopelessly contaminated one with the other.

It is perhaps self-evident that the discovery of death and emptiness where we thought there was life and plenitude provokes terror. It is less evident, but just as true, that the opposite is equally or more terrifying. The presence of life is by no means always reassuring, especially when we have been certain that no life at all was to be found. The discovery that Berenice is still alive repeats a familiar gesture in Poe's fiction, what we can call, using a phrase from "Ligeia" (1838), "this hideous drama of revivification" (PT 50). The resurrection of the dead ought to be a wonderful, indeed glorious event, according to one of the most powerful stories told in our culture, but in Poe's tale the joy in a Christian rebirth is completely effaced by horror. The reason is clear enough: the Christian account of the world posits that death is temporary and that life can return uncontaminated by any trace of morbidity; while Poe's stories suggest that life and death are always intermingled, never to be securely separated. The "drama of revivification" is always "hideous" because it is never complete. Lady Rowena comes back to life over and over again, but always only to lapse once more into "a sterner and apparently more irredeemable death" (PT 50). Berenice emerges from the grave, but she is now a poor, mangled creature whose body cannot for very long support life. Lady Madeline of Usher emerges from the tomb only to die in the act of killing her brother.

It is a striking fact that the climax of "The Fall of the House of Usher" (1839), like that of "Berenice," is part of a scene of reading. The narrator attempts to calm the agitated Roderick Usher by reading to him from "the Mad Trist of Sir Launcelot Canning" (a story that Poe made up for the occasion) in hopes that it will distract the poor man from the "ghastly" storm outside. The storm is frightening, we should note, mainly because the clouds, dead objects though they are, possess "life-like velocity" in their motion. Roderick, the narrator feels, should not behold such things. He listens instead to the reading of a tale with a "wild overstrained air of vivacity" that surprises and — at first — pleases the narrator. But the reading is in a way all too successful: Roderick's vivacity in listening seems to infect the story. The dead letters come to life, not only or most importantly in the narrator's giving them voice, but in the actions belonging to the world exterior to the story. When Ethelred, the hero of the "Mad Trist," breaks down a door with his mace, the narrator and Roderick hear "what might have been, in its exact similarity of character, the echo (but a stifled and dull one certainly) of the very cracking and ripping sound which Sir Launcelot had so particularly described" (PT 76). When the narrator reads of the shriek made by a dragon slain by Ethelred, he hears in the house of Usher a "most unusual screaming or grating sound — the exact counterpart of what my fancy had already conjured up for the dragon's unnatural shriek as described by the romancer" (PT 76).

When a falling shield in the story makes "a mighty great and terrible ringing sound," the narrator and Usher hear "a distinct, hollow, metallic, and clangorous, yet apparently muffled reverberation" (PT 77).

This act of reading, in which the structure of the text actually seems to come to life, provokes in Roderick a "strong shudder" of anxiety (PT 77). The story of Ethelred has not distracted him at all but has revived and intensified the agitation the narrator had hoped to ease. "*We have put her living in the tomb!*" he exclaims (PT 77; Poe's emphasis), adding that his acute senses had heard his sister's "first feeble movements in the hollow coffin" many days ago but that he had dared not speak of it (PT 77–78). Now, he says, in the very instant that the narrator was reading about "the breaking of the hermit's door, and the death-cry of the dragon, and the clangor of the shield" (PT 78), Madeline was breaking out of her coffin, opening the iron hinges of her tomb, and flailing against the copper lining of the vault. He fears she is on her way to take vengeance on her brother for his unseemly haste in burying her. He concludes by shrieking at his friend "*Madman! I tell you that she now stands without the door!*" (PT 78; Poe's emphasis).

The narrator at first had difficulty understanding what Roderick was saying. He speaks in "a low, hurried and gibbering murmur" so that only by "bending closely over him" can the friend "at length [drink] in the hideous import of his words" (PT 77). When the discourse reaches its conclusion, however, such strenuous efforts are no longer necessary. The world makes good on Roderick's language, just as it had on the narrator's act of reading. It is as if the vehemence of Roderick's utterance brings his statement to life: "As if in the superhuman energy of his utterance there had been found the potency of a spell [. . .] without those doors there *did* stand the lofty and enshrouded figure of the lady Madeline of Usher" (PT 78). As the dead letters of Sir Launcelot Canning's book have come to life, so has the lady Madeline. It is a "hideous drama of revivification" on two counts.

This resurrection is only temporary, however, and it turns out to be quite deadly. Madeline returns to the realm of the living only to suffer "violent and now final death-agonies" and to literally frighten her poor brother to death. Moreover, the Usher mansion, now turned into a metaphorical tomb for its two inhabitants, echoes the previous action in which the coffin was rent apart and falls into fragments. The narrator had noticed, when he first saw the building, "indication of extensive decay." He suggests that "a scrutinizing observer might have discovered a barely perceptible fissure" extending from the roof to the foundation (PT 64). Now the light of the moon can be seen shining "vividly through that once barely-discernible fissure"; as the narrator watches the crack widen, the "entire orb of the satellite" becomes visible (PT 78). In a moment the mighty house of Usher disappears under the waters of the tarn.[8]

The moon shining through the fissure in the mansion's walls makes for a wonderfully ambivalent image. Is it life or death that one glimpses through the crack and is allowed to escape through it? The light is described as the "radiance" of "the full, setting, and blood-red moon" (78), and it is hard to say whether positive or negative values predominate. The words "radiance" and "full" suggest life and plenitude, whereas "setting" and "blood-red" suggest death and violence. Ambivalence also infects the relation between the moon and the collapsing mansion. The narrator says that, as the house fell, "the entire orb of the satellite burst at once upon my sight" (PT 78), leaving open the question as to whether the moon simply comes into view as the building tumbles down or if it does not somehow bring about the catastrophe by "bursting" through so violently. Compare this language to the following equally troubling rhetoric from "Ligeia":

> Without Ligeia I was but a child groping benighted. Her presence, her reading alone, rendered vividly luminous the many mysteries of the transcendentalism in which we were immersed. Wanting the radiant lustre of her eyes, letters, lambent and golden, grew duller than Saturnian lead. (PT 42)

These eyes, elsewhere in the story referred to as "orbs" (PT 40), have the power to bring life or death to a text. As Ligeia grows ill, her eyes "shone less and less frequently upon the pages," but they do not grow dim. On the contrary, her "wild eyes blazed with a too — too glorious effulgence" (PT 42). The brightening of Ligeia's eye-orbs, like the sudden brightening of the moon shining on the house of Usher, signifies the approach of death. But this same light is the power that brings life, renders "vividly luminous" the otherwise dead letters of books in which she and her lover are "immersed" (PT 42) and "buried" (PT 38).[9]

When the light of the "orb" penetrates the container of a mystery — a house, a coffin, a little box, a book — it may find a living sign or only a dead signifier. The horror of Poe's tales resides in the fact that one does not know which he or she will find, that at any moment one's expectation of one or the other may suffer a shocking reversal. It is hard to know which is worse for the narrator of "Berenice," the discovery that the contents of the coffin are unexpectedly alive or that the contents of the little wooden box are unexpectedly dead and devoid of meaning. Is it more horrifying that the house of Usher is a place of death or that the house enacts its own death scene and thereby asserts that it had in fact been a living thing? This question propounds the paradox that Kafka would later exploit in the climax of his story "In the Penal Colony," where another apparently inanimate object, the Old Commandant's execution machine, suddenly comes to life only in order to commit suicide by taking itself apart.[10]

We are obliged to read the collapse of the house of Usher the way the narrator reads the story of Ethelred and the way the plot presents the resurrection of Madeline: an act of revivifying reading opens up the possibility of yet more dying. It is the story of Lady Rowena over and over again, who comes to life when her mourning husband thinks about his lost love Ligeia only to die again and again, each time relapsing into a death that seems further and further beyond hope of resurrection. The body of Rowena is now somehow possessed of the "full, and the black, and the wild eyes — of my lost love — of the lady — of the Lady Ligeia," those eyes whose "readings alone [. . .] rendered vividly luminous" (PT 42) the darkest mysteries. Her body oscillates eternally between a terrible death and an even more terrible life. Poe's rhetoric of terror has its beginning in a terror of rhetoric, an anxiety that arises from the realization that signifiers do not possess meaning in and of themselves but are lent significance by a relation to something else. The letters on the page live or die according to how they are seen by the shining orbs that look upon them.[11]

The moon that shines down on the collapsing house of Usher is the figurative repetition of the reading eye. Indeed it almost seems to be the uncanny return of the lustrous eye of Roderick himself. Curiously enough, Poe regularly speaks of Roderick's "eye" in the singular, not of his eyes. This is, of course, a commonplace figure, for we frequently speak of, say, a "sure hand and a steady eye," or, as Poe does in "Berenice," "a startled and ardent eye," in a trope that by no means implies that the person so described has only a single hand or eye. Still, when we read of the radiant moon that looks down on the house of Usher we have a sense of having read about it before, of experiencing what Stanley Corngold calls "prereading" (263). Poe develops the figure of the eye as a proleptic symbol of the moon by means of such rhetorical devices as making "eye" singular and supplying it with epithets appropriate to the moon. Our prereading of the moon takes place when we learn, first, that Roderick possessed a "miraculous lustre of the eye" (PT 66) and then, later, that "the luminousness of his eye had utterly gone out" (PT 73). During the scene of reading the "Mad Trist," the narrator notes "the wide and rigid opening of the eye" that signals (perhaps) Roderick's state of keen attention. The eye that had lost its lustre regains it, though only figuratively, when the radiance of the setting moon bursts through the fissure in the falling mansion. Roderick's eye, through which he had lived a life of reading ("books [. . .], for years, had formed no small part of the mental existence of the invalid" [PT 71]), survives his body's death and even reads life into that death.

The single eye becomes one of Poe's favorite narrative elements. It figures powerfully in "The Tell-Tale Heart" (1843) and even more centrally in "The Black Cat" (1843). In the latter story, a number of tropes receive a literal reading and a release from the contexts that ordinarily connect them to common experience. When the narrator of "The Fall of the House of Usher" speaks of Roderick's "eye," it is a trope and no doubt about it. When the narrator of "The Black Cat" seizes his pet and, for no apparent reason, "deliberately cuts one of its eyes from the socket" (PT 192), the literal meaning of the trope, ordinarily suppressed, undergoes a hideous revivification. It is now all too proper to speak of the "eye" of such a creature. The poor cat is forced into conformity with what we erroneously assumed was an innocent figure of speech that did not mean what it said. But the narrator is not happy with this result, for he did not intend to produce life; he wanted death. He attempts to get it by hanging the mutilated beast, but he succeeds only in transforming it more clearly into a signifier capable of eternally oscillating back and forth between life and death. The cat immediately makes an uncanny return as a cat-shaped mark on the wall of the narrator's burned-down house, then again as another pet, a second black cat with but a single eye. As the first cat had become legible as a mark on the fire-scarred wall, the second becomes legible by possessing an oddly shaped white marking that the narrator reads as "the image of a hideous — of a ghastly thing — of the GALLOWS!" (PT 196). The living body of the cat is for the narrator the living (and all the more effective) vehicle for a sign of death.

In both cases, of course, the narrator does the reading of these marks for us. We, Poe's readers, have no idea what the mark on the wall or on the second cat "really" looked like, and so we cannot say whether or not the interpretations presented here as unquestionable are in fact even remotely plausible. The story itself offers conflicting evidence. On the one hand, the narrator reveals himself to be emotionally unstable in the extreme, very likely quite out of touch with reality. On the other, events as they unfold seem to confirm with supernatural accuracy the propriety of these signs. The cat-shaped mark on the wall suggests the uncanny survival of the dead animal, and indeed it does make a startling reappearance in the form of the second cat. The mark of the gallows prefigures the capital crime that the narrator will commit and later in effect convict himself of. The narrator's readings appear, then, to be absolutely correct even though they may very well be unjustified.

Whether we explain the events of the tale naturally or supernaturally, we find a process whereby events make good on the narrator's readings of the black cat. The only difference between the two explanations is that in the former we suppose that it is the demented but nonetheless consistent structure of the narrator's psyche that compels the congruence of his interpretations and subsequent events, and in the latter we imagine it is the mysterious structure of the physical universe. Certainly the prevalent modern view of the tale is that the narrator essentially writes the script of his own destruction; that he sees the gallows on the second cat because he already (unconsciously) knows that he will kill someone; and that he murders his wife almost as if it were to confirm his own worst fears. What other reason, after all, does he have for this chilling, almost casual act of violence? The wife simply offers a convenient substitute for the cat, since it is clear that the cat and not the woman is the real target of his wrath. And the cat is nothing more than the locus of his overwhelming anxiety.

The narrator, it is true, would have us believe that the source of his trouble is "the Fiend Intemperance," but inebriation explains at best only the mechanism by which his inner demon was set free. It tells us nothing about where the demon came from or why it took the form it did. What Poe's reader would really like to understand is why the narrator's madness seized upon the black cat as the object of its fear and anger. One clue, surely, is all the folklore that associates black cats with death and bad fortune. Another is the name given — by whom we do not know — to the first black cat: Pluto. In one sense it is an innocent enough name. Millions of people find nothing even slightly ominous in the Disney cartoon dog who bears it. But it is, no matter how innocently given, a name that is legible as the trace of death, indeed even the proper name of death itself. Pluto, the ruler of the underworld, belongs to the kingdom of the dead, and his presence in the land of the living can be understood as a contamination, an improper mixing of the two realms. The narrator's troubles begin, not principally because he gets drunk, but because he seems to insist on reading the pet's name as a sign of the creature's nature.

Pluto, in his second incarnation as the cat with the sign of the gallows, returns to the land of the dead in a fashion that turns out to be the worst imaginable for the narrator. After having "buried the axe" in his wife's brain, he buries her body in the masonry of his cellar, inadvertently also entombing the still living cat. It is of course the "wailing shriek, half of horror and half of triumph," produced by the buried cat that betrays the narrator and sends him to the gallows (PT 199). The cat enacts the familiar drama of revivification, of the horrifying discovery of life where there ought only to be death, which closes "The House of Usher" and so many of Poe's other stories. "Pluto" acts out the mythical meaning of its name with hideous punctuality, and with the paradoxical, unwitting assistance of the narrator. The murderer has, albeit unconsciously, produced the most vivid reading of the name "Pluto" imaginable by transforming an otherwise innocent pet into one of the "demons that exult in the damnation" of such sinners (PT 199). This cat that was "Pluto" only figuratively now actually presides over at least one corner of the realm of the dead. The figure of its name is no longer only a figure. It comes terrifyingly close to the literal truth.

By contaminating with its living presence a place where death ought to hold absolute sway, the black cat enacts not only the metaphor of its name but also one of Poe's favorite figures for reading. Often enough in Poe's tales, reading is described as "being buried." The narrator of "Ligeia" describes himself as "buried in studies of a nature more than all else adapted to deaden impression of the outward world" (PT 38). By describing the studies in which the narrator is "buried" as activities likely to "deaden" something, Poe's sentence reanimates the nearly lifeless metaphor and reminds readers that burial implies more than intense concentration. It means death. In "Berenice," too, the trope of burial is used to signify the depth of the narrator's intellectual concentration. After explaining how he had "loitered away my boyhood in books," he speaks of himself as "buried in gloom" (PT 19). Later he tries to convey to the reader the "*intensity of interest* with which, in my case, the powers of meditation (not to speak technically) busied and buried themselves, in the contemplation of even the most ordinary objects of the universe" (PT 20). It is striking that Poe finds the language most fitting to convey the extreme intensity of a living process to be a locution regularly associated with death. How much more striking it is in this particular story, where the living Berenice indeed is buried. We begin to suspect that her living entombment is the narrative analog of the double movement implicit in the trope. Living creatures have already been "buried" in "Berenice" (and in "Ligeia," "Usher," and the rest) long before anyone is actually put into a tomb.

The idea of being buried alive, so central to a significant number of Poe's tales of terror, gathers a considerable portion of its power from its association with the very activity necessary for the reception of tales. The only way to gain access to these fictions is by way of reading and therefore by way of a process that the texts lead us to associate with a form of living death. Berenice, Madeline Usher, and the black cat all live out physically the literal reading of a trope whose figurative tenor we readers act out in the moment of engaging with the text. The hideous drama of revivification taking place in the narrative is doubly chilling because it is repeated, wittingly or not, willingly or not, and to varying degrees, by those to whom the narrative is directed. Life contaminates death and death life as the reader, revivifying the dead letters on the page, buries his or her living psyche in the textual gloom. The uncanny discovery of the living black cat in the dead wife's tomb is therefore frightening not only because the cat's living presence means death for the narrator but also because the cat represents the experience of the reader, buried alive inside a space inhabited otherwise only by actual or prospective corpses.[12]

The scenes of reading that form the climactic moments of both "Berenice" and "Usher" appropriately bring the act of reading to the center of attention just as the issue of live burial takes over the narrative spotlight. "I will read and you shall listen," the narrator tells Roderick Usher, "and so we will pass away this terrible night together" (75). Of course the narrator means this to be reassuring, but the rhetoric allows for a very unsettling reading as well.[13] While the narrator means "pass away" in a transitive sense, it could also be taken as intransitive. Instead of saying "we will spend this terrible night together and get through it" his sentence could say "we will die together during this night." Is the act of reading to bring about survival or "passing away"? The sentence as formulated does not allow us to decide, and the story as it works out answers both ways. The narrator, who does the work of deciphering the written signs, survives the terrible events of the night and lives to tell the tale; Roderick, who interprets the story with a "wild overstrained vivacity," passes away into death. It appears that the act of reading may or may not lead to burial, depending on the nature of one's engagement with the text. Roderick becomes so deeply immersed in the story that he can "read" its import only according to an allegorical scheme in which everything in the text corresponds to Madeline's return from the grave: "ha! ha! — the breaking of the hermit's door [. . .] say, rather, the rending of her coffin," and so on (PT 78).

One might suppose that allegorical reading would be the very procedure necessary to transform the dead letter into the living spirit. Indeed, allegorical readings of the Old Testament have been used for centuries in an effort to follow Paul's advice and thereby harmonize Jewish law with the message of the gospel. Poe's story, however, suggests something else: the lethal result of Roderick's reading indicates how a totalizing allegory mechanically applied can turn one set of dead letters into another set of equally dead letters. Roderick's interpretation of the "Mad Trist" fails to revive the text by applying the living spirit; instead it uses a demented allegorical formula to transform it into a terrifying scenario of destruction.

The narrator does not participate in Roderick's reductive allegory. Because he plays no role in the script Roderick makes out of the "Mad Trist," he manages to escape being buried alive in the collapsing house of Usher.[14] This is the good news of the story's conclusion: "From that chamber, and from that mansion, I fled aghast" (PT 78). His flight is not simply from the building, it is from the scene of Roderick's reading, which the narrator describes as a self-fulfilling prophecy of doom. Roderick dies "a victim to the terrors *he had anticipated*" (PT 78; emphasis added). The narrator, who never anticipated such terrors, has no reason to find them encoded in the text of the "Mad Trist" and can therefore escape becoming their victim. The letter kills. The way to avoid being killed is to avoid both the dead letter itself and the seduction of a demented, reductive interpretation of that letter into an even more deadly allegory.

The reader of Poe's tale may be properly frightened and properly uncertain as to the fate of readers. Even if we readers identify with the surviving narrator rather than the doomed Roderick, as the tale invites us to do, we cannot suppress a genuine anxiety about the power of reading. The narrator barely escapes, and we barely escape with him. But we do come out alive, even though the text of "The Fall of the House of Usher" may be just as threatening as the fall of the house described in the tale. We live on, knowing that we are not obliged to read Poe's tale as the set of deadly letters Roderick finds in the "Mad Trist."

Notes

[1] The narrator would today be diagnosed as having fetishized his cousin's teeth. There may well be sufficient evidence in the story for reasonable medical evaluation

of his psychopathology, but that is not the goal here. My interest in the narrator's condition is focused entirely on its semiology.

2 The importance of this phrase is underscored by the fact that, according to Sloane, the last two sentences of the previous extraction were added to later versions of the story presumably to emphasize the narrator's mad fixation.

3 See Koelb, *Incredulous Reader* 81–83.

4 Berenice's cousin's passion for dismantling existing relationships between signs and then recombining them to create new systems can be seen as the fictional manifestation of Poe's own literary principle. As Renza points out, quoting from Poe's "Peter Snook," "originality is not 'a mere matter of impulse or inspiration' but rather the ability 'carefully, patiently, and understandingly to combine'" (58–89). The related concept of the rhetoric of negation described in the opening paragraph of the present essay is also pertinent to Poe's creative philosophy. This time quoting Poe in "The Philosophy of Composition," Renza writes: "For Poe, literary originality 'demands in its attainment less of invention than negation' — the negation, no doubt, of other textual precedents and the literary norms they give rise to."

5 Williams has made similar observations on what Berenice's teeth represent to her cousin. See especially his fifth chapter, "'Word of No Meaning': Denial of the Symbol" (80–104).

6 Pahl finds that in the Pym story "it is not simply the narrator but the author himself who becomes the chief vehicle through which Poe explores these questions of selfhood and self-presence" (51).

7 See Halliburton for a related treatment of the tales at hand, as well as a discussion of other similarities between Poe and Kafka.

8 Fisher makes some related observations on the narrator's role.

9 See also Griffith's related discussion of the "illuminating" power of Ligeia's eyes.

10 Robinson, in reading Poe's "The Pit and the Pendulum" "deconstructively, as an allegory of reading," makes many interesting observations that remind one both of Kafka's "In the Penal Colony" and of Poe's rhetoric of terror. Robinson writes that the narrator of that story "finds himself strapped to the floor in the center of a dungeon, forcing him to look straight upwards" where one of the ceiling panels, certainly a common object, "'has riveted my whole attention.'"

11 Williams discusses a related aspect of Poe's rhetorical project, what he calls the "contingency of meaning upon conventions of use and context" ("Language of the cipher," 647).

12 It may also be a figure for a nightmare, the events of which were somehow previously buried, or walled up in the unconscious and reemerge sometime later during sleep.

13 Using the example of "The Tell-Tale Heart," Witherington demonstrates yet another of Poe's unsettling devices of rhetorical terror. He shows how the reader is not only terrified by the fact that so heinous a crime could be recounted by so calm and rational a narrator (who is, of course, the murderer himself), but is "seduced" into vicarious participation in the crime by way of such embracing

phrases as "You should have seen me . . ." and "Oh, you would have laughed. . . ." The reader is made "an accomplice after the fact."

[14] A closely related and more expansive treatment of the function of Poe's narrator can be found in Thompson, who in turn is indebted to Abel. See also the exchange between Thompson and Patrick F. Quinn in Thompson and Lokke. E. Miller Budick (40–50) also gives a related account of the narrator's narrow escape.

Conclusion

THE ROMANTIC CENTURY DISPLAYED an abiding interest in exploring the boundary between life and death. The natural philosophy of the late eighteenth century suggested that life might be a fundamental characteristic of all matter. What an observer perceives as life, however, is in fact the presence of a *Geist*, a spirit/intellect that comes into being as a result of matter organized to a particularly high degree. Life inheres in all things, but spirit varies proportionally with the level of matter's organization. When that organization breaks down, spirit breaks down as well, and organisms experience the rupture that we normally think of as death. Such a death is not the departure of life, however; the constituent elements of the body are all still alive, all still capable of reorganization into a being endowed with spirit. According to this model of the natural world, that which is dead is always capable of being revivified.

The foregoing study has examined one cultural paradigm for such revivification: the process of reading, in which apparently dead material objects, letters inscribed on some surface, can return to life as the embodiment of a human spirit. The abiding possibility of such a textual resurrection thrilled and horrified the European intellectual community with remarkable consistency over a remarkably long period of time. The possibility of being "alive again" (as the epigraph to the opening chapter of *Melmoth* puts it) is both exhilarating and terrifying, and we find both emotional extremes explored in the literature of the period. The text most thoroughly saturated with a sense of exhilaration is Gautier's *Spirite*, and that most thoroughly dominated by terror is Poe's "Fall of the House of Usher." These two extremes are, perhaps not coincidentally, the latest of the texts in our sample. By the end of the Romantic century, only the two views at opposite ends of the continuum seemed tenable. Revivifying reading was either a glorious, amplifying transformation away from the literal into a divinely erotic spiritual perfection that could redeem the imperfections of the past; or it was a reductive allegorization that would necessarily lead to further literalization, further entrapment in moribund flesh, and ultimately a more profound death.

Romantic literature generally took a somewhat more nuanced view, one that recognized both what is deadly and what is animating in the process of reading. Consider the following scene of reading from Joseph von Eichendorff's poem "Abschied" (1810):

> Da steht im Wald geschrieben,
> Ein stilles, ernstes Wort
> Von rechtem Thun und Lieben,
> Und was des Menschen Hort.
> Ich habe treu gelesen
> Die Worte, schlicht und wahr,
> Und durch mein ganzes Wesen
> Ward's unaussprechlich klar. (17–24)

[In the forest there is written a quiet, serious utterance about behaving and loving correctly, and about what is most valuable for human beings. I faithfully read these simple, true words, and my whole being was filled with inexpressible clarity.]

The forest itself is presented as a text that not only can be read but also can be understood with perfect clarity — a clarity that surpasses the capacity of language. The basic import of the statement (*Wort*) inscribed in the forest can be expressed, however, and it is summed up in the four lines that precede the ones cited:

> Das mag vergehen, verwehen
> Das trübe Erdenleid,
> Da sollst du auferstehen
> In junger Herrlichkeit! (13–16)

[The dismal sorrows of the earth may pass away and disappear, but you will rise again in youthful splendor.]

The message to be read in the text of the trees is one of both death and revivification, of dismal sorrows and youthful splendor in continuous alternation. The flawed and transitory past will always be redeemed by a new incarnation of spring foliage. Such a text as the forest calls for a spiritual reading, for its "letters" are themselves living organisms that cycle through the seasons, their leaves dying in the autumn only to be reborn in the spring. The idea of spiritual resurrection is implicit in Eichendorff's choice of the verb "auferstehen" to indicate the revival of the forest: the noun derived from this verb, "Auferstehung," is the word ordinarily used to denote the resurrection of Jesus.

Eichendorff's resurrected leaves remind us of Percy Shelley's "Ode to the West Wind," with its invocation of the dead leaves of autumn as the legible leaves of a book: "Drive my dead thoughts over the universe, / Like wither'd leaves, to quicken a new birth" (63–64). Sharon Ruston is surely right to propose that "canonical, familiar poems such as 'Ode to the West Wind' [and Eichendorff's 'Abschied'] are transformed" when placed in the proper cultural context (7). But that context is not simply "the science of life," as Ruston proposes, but rather the whole of the theory of revivification developed by the scientists, philosophers, and poets of the

Romantic century. A genuine appreciation of the ambitions and achievement of such philosopher-poet-scientists can be fully realized only when we see their connection to the Romantic theory of life and their participation in the tradition of the revivifying word.

There is perhaps no better summation of the aspirations of that tradition than Shelley's own definition of poetic transformation in the *Defence of Poetry*, where he expounds in a few words the doctrine of embodied spirit; of literature's power to transmute potentially deadly matter into an organic gold that nourishes the reader; and of the dangerous, miraculous stream that both separates and binds together the land of the dead and the land of the living:

> Poetry redeems from decay the visitations of the divinity in man. [. . .] It transmutes all that it touches, and every form moving within the radiance of its presence is changed by wondrous sympathy to an incarnation of the spirit which it breathes: its secret alchemy turns to potable gold the poisonous waters which flow from death through life. (698)

Works Cited

Abel, Darrel. "A Key to the House of Usher." *University of Toronto Quarterly* 18: 176–85.

Abernethy, John. *Physiological Lectures, Addressed to the College of Surgeons.* London: Longman, Hurst, Rees, Orme, and Brown, 1821.

Abrams, M. H. "English Romanticism: The Spirit of the Age." In *Romanticism Reconsidered*, edited by Northrop Frye. New York: Columbia UP, 1963.

———. *Natural Supernaturalism.* New York: W. W. Norton, 1971.

Asman, Carrie. "'Der Satz ist die Mauer.' Zur Figur der Übersetzers bei Benjamin und Goethe: *Werther, Faust, Wilhelm Meister.*" *Goethe-Jahrbuch* 111 (1994): 61–79.

Augustine. *In Evangelium Ioannis tractatus centum viginti quatuor.* Sant'Agostino: Vita, Scriti, Pensiero, Santità, Attualità. http://www.sant-agostino.it/latino/index.htm.

Bachelard, Gaston. *The Poetics of Space.* Trans. Maria Jolas. 1964. Rpt. Boston: Beacon P, 1994.

Barclay, John. *An Inquiry into the Opinions, Ancient and Modern, Concerning Life and Organization.* Edinburgh: Bell and Bradfute, 1822.

Barfield, Owen. *What Coleridge Thought.* Middletown, CT: Wesleyan UP, 1971.

Bennett, Benjamin. "Goethe's *Werther*: Double Perspective and the Game of Life." *German Quarterly* 53.1 (1980): 64–81.

Bernd, Clifford A. "On the Two Divergent Parts of Kleist's 'Michael Kohlhaas.'" In *New York University Department of German Studies in Germanic Languages*, edited by Robert A. Fowkes and Volkmar Sander, 47–56. Reutlingen: Hultzler, 1976.

Best, Otto F. "Schuld und Vergebung: Zur Rolle von Wahrsagerin und 'Amulett' in Kleists Michael 'Kohlhaas.'" *Germanisch-Romanische Monatsschrift* 20 (1970): 180–89.

Bichat, Xavier. *Recherches physiologiques sur la vie et la mort.* 4th ed. Paris: Gabon, 1822.

Blair, Hugh. *Lectures on Rhetoric and Belles Lettres.* 1885. Rpt. ed. Linda Ferreira-Buckley and S. Michael Halloran. Carbondale: Southern Illinois UP, 2005.

Boccaccio, Giovanni. *The Decameron.* Trans. G. H. McWilliam. Harmondsworth: Penguin, 1972.

———. *Genealogie deorum gentilium libri.* Ed. Vincenzo Romano. Bari: Laterza & Figli, 1951.

Braune-Steininger, Wolfgang. "Ein monströser Leser? Zur impliziten Werther-Rezeption in Mary Shelleys *Frankenstein*." In *Lineages of the Novel*, edited by Bernhard Reitz and Eckart Voigts-Virchow, 93–101. Trier: Wissenschaftlicher, 2000.

Brombert, Victor. *Victor Hugo and the Visionary Novel*. Cambridge, MA: Harvard UP, 1984.

Brooks, Peter. "Godlike Science/Unhallowed Arts: Language and Monstrosity in *Frankenstein*." *New Literary History* 9.3 (1978): 591–605.

Brown, Marshall. "*Frankenstein*: A Child's Tale." *Novel: A Forum on Fiction* 36.2 (2003): 145–75.

———. *The Gothic Text*. Stanford: Stanford UP, 2005.

———. *Preromanticism*. Stanford: Stanford UP, 1991.

Brown, Theodore M. "From Mechanism to Vitalism in Eighteenth-Century English Physiology." *Journal of the History of Biology* 7 (1974): 179–216.

Budick, E. Miller. "The Fall of the House: A Reappraisal of Poe's Attitudes toward Life and Death." *The Southern Literary Journal* 9.2 (1977): 30–50.

Burwick, Roswitha. "Goethe's *Werther* and Mary Shelley's *Frankenstein*." *The Wordsworth Circle* 24.1 (1993): 47–52.

Chaitin, Gilbert D. "Victor Hugo and the Hieroglyphic Novel." *Nineteenth-Century French Studies* 19.1 (1990): 36–53.

Coleridge, Samuel Taylor. *Biographia Literaria. The Collected Works* 7. Ed. James Engel and W. Jackson Bate. Princeton: Bollingen-Princeton UP, 1983.

———. "The Eolian Harp." University of Virginia Electronic Text Center. http://etext.virginia.edu/stc/Coleridge/poems/AEolian_Harp.html.

———. *Hints Towards the Formation of a More Comprehensive Theory of Life*. Ed. Seth B. Watson. London: John Churchill, 1848.

Conger, Syndy M. *Matthew G. Lewis, Charles Robert Maturin, and the Germans: An Interpretive Study of the Influence of German Literature on Two Gothic Novels*. Salzburg: Institut für Englische Sprache und Literatur, 1977.

Corngold, Stanley. "The Curtain Half Drawn: Prereading in Flaubert and Kafka." In Koelb and Noakes, 263–83.

Crook, Nora. "In Defence of the 1831 Frankenstein." In *Mary Shelley's Fictions: From Frankenstein to Faulkner*, edited by Michael Eberle-Sinatra, 3–21. Basingstoke: Macmillan, 2000.

Dawson, Leven M. "*Melmoth the Wanderer*: Paradox and the Gothic Novel." *Studies in English Literature, 1500–1900* 8.4 (1968): 621–32.

Deleuze, Gilles. *Difference and Repetititon*. Trans. Paul Patton. New York: Columbia UP, 1994.

Dietrick, Linda. *Prisons and Idylls: Studies in Heinrich von Kleist's Fictional World*. Frankfurt am Main: Peter Lang, 1985.

Dotzler, Bernhard J. "Werthers Leser." *MLN* 114.3 (1999): 445–70.

Driesch, Hans. *The History and Theory of Vitalism*. Trans. C. K. Ogden. London: Macmillan, 1914.

Duncan, Bruce. "'Emilia Galotti lag auf dem Pult aufgeschlagen': Werther as (Mis-) Reader." *Goethe Yearbook* 1 (1982): 42–50.

Eichendorff, Joseph von. "Abschied." In *Joseph Freiherrn von Eichendorff's sämmtliche Werke*. 2nd ed. Vol. 1. *Biographische Einleitung und Gedichte*, 383–84. Leipzig, 1864. http://de.wikisource.org/wiki/Abschied_%28Eichendorff%29.

Eichner, Hans. "The Rise of Modern Science and the Genesis of Romanticism." *PMLA* 97.1 (1982): 8–30.

———, ed. *"Romantic" and its Cognates: The European History of a Word*. Toronto: U of Toronto P, 1972.

Ellis, John M. "Der Herr läßt regnen über Gerechte und Ungerechte: Kleist's 'Michael Kohlhaas.'" *Monatshefte* 59 (1967): 35–40.

Ferber, Michael, ed. *European Romantic Poetry*. New York: Pearson-Longman, 2005.

Fichte, Johann Gottlieb. *On the Spirit and the Letter in Philosophy*. In Simpson, 74–93.

Fisher, Benjamin Franklin IV. "Playful 'Germanism' in 'The Fall of the House of Usher': The Storyteller's Art." In Thompson and Lokke, 355–74.

Fowler, Kathleen. "Hieroglyphics in Fire: *Melmoth the Wanderer*." *Studies in Romanticism* 25.4 (1986): 521–39.

Gailus, Andreas. *Passions of the Sign: Revolution and Language in Kant, Goethe, and Kleist*. Baltimore: Johns Hopkins UP, 2006.

Gallagher, Catherine. "Formalism and Time." In Wolfson and Brown, 305–27.

Gallas, Helga. *Das Textbegehren des "Michael Kohlhaas": Die Sprache des Unbewußten und der Sinn der Literatur*. Reinbek bei Hamburg: Rowohlt, 1981.

Galperin, William, and Susan Wolfson. "The Romantic Century." In Romantic Circles. http://www.rc.umd.edu/reference/misc/confarchive/crisis/crisisa.html.

Gautier, Théophile. *Spirite*. Works 11: 13–256.

———. *Spirite: Nouvelle fantastique*. Paris: Editions A.-G. Nizet, 1970.

———. *The Works of Théophile Gautier*. Vol. 11. Trans. and ed. F. C. de Sumichrast. New York: George D. Sproul, 1901.

Goethe, J. W. *Die Leiden des jungen Werther*. In *Werke* 6: 7–124.

———. *The Sorrows of Young Werther and Selected Writings*. Trans. Catherine Hutter. New York: Signet-New American Library, 1962.

———. *Werke. Hamburger Ausgabe in 14 Bänden*. Ed. Erich Trunz. München: C. H. Beck, 1996.

Graham, Ilse. *Heinrich von Kleist: Word into Flesh: A Poet's Quest for the Symbol*. Berlin: De Gruyter, 1977.

Griffith, Clark. "Poe's 'Ligeia' and the English Romantics." In *The Naiad Voice: Essays on Poe's Satiric Hoaxing*, edited by Dennis W. Eddings, 1–17. Port Washington, NY: Associated Faculty Press, 1983.

Halliburton, David. *Edgar Allan Poe: A Phenomenological View.* Princeton: Princeton UP, 1973.

Hamann, Johann Georg. *Aesthetica in Nuce: A Rhapsody in Cabalistic Prose.* In Nisbet, 139–50.

Hartman, Geoffrey. *The Unmediated Vision: An Interpretation of Wordsworth, Hopkins, Rilke, and Valéry.* New Haven: Yale UP, 1954.

Hegel, G. W. F. *Lectures on the History of Philosophy.* Trans. E. S. Haldane. Marxists Internet Archive. http://www.marxists.org/reference/archive/hegel/works/hp/hpfrench.htm#robinet.

Hennelly, Mark M. "*Melmoth the Wanderer* and Gothic Existentialism." *Studies in English Literature, 1500–1900* 21.4 (1981): 665–79.

Herder, Johann Gottfried. "Correspondence on Ossian and the Songs of Ancient Peoples." In Nisbet, 154–61.

———. "Shakespeare." In Nisbet, 161–76.

Hess, Jonathan M. "Johann David Michaelis and the Colonial Imaginary: Orientalism and the Emergence of Racial Antisemitism in Eighteenth-Century Germany." *Jewish Social Studies* 6.2 (2000): 56–101.

Highet, Gilbert. *The Classical Tradition: Greek and Roman Influences on Western Literature.* Oxford: Oxford UP, 1967.

Hindle, Maurice. "Vital Matters: Mary Shelley's Frankenstein and Romantic Science" *Critical Survey* 2.1 (1990): 29–35.

Hoagwood, Terence. Rev. of *Shelley's Eye*, by Benjamin Colbert; *Shelley and the Revolutionary Sublime*, by Cian Duffy; and *Shelley and Vitality*, by Sharon Ruston. *Wordsworth Circle* 37.4 (2006): 249–52.

Hoeveler, Diane Long. "Frankenstein, Feminism, and Literary Theory." In Schor, 45–62.

Hölz, Karl. "Der interessierte Blick auf die Fremdkultur: Das Bild der 'Zigeuner' in Hugos *Notre-Dame de Paris*." *Romanische Forschungen* 114.3 (2002): 271–94.

Hugo, Victor. *Notre-Dame de Paris. Les Travailleurs de la mer.* Ed. Jacques Seebacher and Yves Gohin. Paris: Gallimard, 1975.

———. *Notre-Dame of Paris.* Trans. John Sturrock. Harmondsworth: Penguin, 1978.

Kafka, Franz. *The Complete Stories.* Ed. Nahum N. Glatzer. New York: Schocken, 1971.

Kant, Immanuel. *The Critique of Judgement.* In Simpson, 37–67.

Keats, John. *Complete Poems.* Ed. Jack Stillinger. Cambridge, MA: Belknap/Harvard UP, 1982.

———. *Endymion: A Poetic Romance*. Book 1. eBooks@Adelaide (University of Adelaide Library). http://etext.library.adelaide.edu.au/k/keats/john/poems/endymion1.html.

———. *Endymion: A Poetic Romance*. Book 3. eBooks@Adelaide (University of Adelaide Library). http://etext.library.adelaide.edu.au/k/keats/john/poems/endymion3.html.

———. *Hyperion: A Fragment*. Book 1. *Poetical Works*. Bartleby.com. http://www.bartleby.com/126/49.html.

———. *Lamia*. Part II. *Poetical Works*. Bartleby.com. http://www.bartleby.com/126/37.html.

———. *Letters of John Keats*. Ed. Robert Gittings. Oxford: Oxford UP, 1970.

———. "Ode on a Grecian Urn." *Poetical Works*. Bartleby.com. http://www.bartleby.com/126/41.html.

———. "On Receiving a Curious Shell from the Same Ladies." *Poetical Works*. Bartleby.com. http://www.bartleby.com/126/6.html.

———. *Poetical Works*. London: Macmillan, 1884. Bartleby.com. http://www.bartleby.com/126/.html.

Kennedy, Veronica M. S. "Myth and the Gothic Dream: C. R. Maturin's *Melmoth the Wanderer*." *Pacific Coast Philology* 4 (1969): 41–47.

Kessler, Joan C. "Babel and Bastille: Architecture as Metaphor in Hugo's *Notre-Dame de Paris*." *French Forum* 11.2 (1986): 183–97.

Ketterer, David. *Frankenstein's Creation: The Book, the Monster, and Human Reality*. Victoria, BC: ELS Monograph Series, 1979.

Kleist, Heinrich von. *Sämtliche Werke und Briefe*. Ed. Helmut Sembdner. 2 vols. München: Hanser, 1961.

———. *The Marquise of O— and Other Stories*. Ed. and trans. David Luke and Nigel Reeves. Harmondsworth: Penguin, 1978.

Koelb, Clayton. *The Incredulous Reader: Literature and the Function of Disbelief*. Ithaca: Cornell UP, 1984.

———. *Inventions of Reading: Rhetoric and the Literary Imagination*. Ithaca: Cornell UP, 1988.

———. *Kafka's Rhetoric: The Passion of Reading*. Ithaca: Cornell UP, 1989.

———. *Legendary Figures: Ancient History in Modern Novels*. Lincoln: U of Nebraska P, 1998.

Koelb, Clayton, and Susan Noakes, eds. *The Comparative Perspective on Literature: Approaches to Theory and Practice*. Ithaca: Cornell UP, 1988.

Koelb, Janice Hewlett. *The Poetics of Description: Imagined Places in European Literature*. New York: Palgrave Macmillan, 2006.

Koselleck, Reinhart. *The Practice of Conceptual History: Timing History, Spacing Concepts*. Stanford: Stanford UP, 2002.

Kroeber, Karl. *Ecological Literary Criticism: Romantic Imagining and the Biology of Mind*. New York: Columbia UP, 1994.

Lange, Henrik. "Säkularisierte Bibelreminiszenzen in Kleists 'Michael Kohlhaas.'" *Kopenhagener Germanistische Studien*, 1 (1969): 213–26.

Lawrence, William. *An Introduction to Comparative Anatomy and Physiology: Being the Two Introductory Lectures Delivered at the Royal College of Surgeons, on the 21st and 25th of March, 1816*. London: J. Callow, 1816.

———. *Lectures on Physiology, Zoology, and the Natural History of Man: Delivered at the Royal College of Surgeons*. London: J. Callow, 1819.

Leibniz, Gottfried Wilhelm. *La monadologie*. Ed. Claudius Piat. 1909. Rpt. Project Gutenberg, 2006. 15 Aug. 1996 http://www.gutenberg.org/files/17641/17641-0.txt.

Lew, Joseph W. "'Unprepared for Sudden Transformations': Identity and Politics in *Melmoth the Wanderer*." *Studies in the Novel* 26.2 (1994): 173–95.

Librett, Jeffrey S. *The Rhetoric of Cultural Dialogue: Jews and Germans from Moses Mendelssohn to Richard Wagner and Beyond*. Stanford: Stanford UP, 2000.

Liddell, Henry George, and Robert Scott. *A Greek-English Lexicon*. Rev. ed. Oxford: Oxford UP, 1996.

London, Bette. "Mary Shelley, *Frankenstein*, and the Spectacle of Masculinity." *PMLA* 108.2 (1993): 253–67.

Longfellow, Henry Wadsworth. "Evangeline: A Tale of Acadie." *English Poetry III: From Tennyson to Whitman*. Vol. XLII. The Harvard Classics. New York: P. F. Collier & Son, 1909–14. Bartleby.com. http://www.bartleby.com/br/04201.html.

Lovejoy, Arthur O. "On the Discrimination of Romanticisms." *PMLA* 39.2 (1924): 229–53.

Lukács, Georg. "Die Tragödie Heinrich von Kleists." *Deutsche Realisten des 19. Jahrhunderts*. Berlin: Aufbau-Verlag, 1953.

Luke, David, and Nigel Reeves, eds. and trans. *Heinrich von Kleist: The Marquise of O— and Other Stories*. Harmondsworth: Penguin, 1978.

Maturin, Charles Robert. *Melmoth the Wanderer*. Ed. Victor Sage. Harmondsworth: Penguin, 2000.

McFarland, Thomas. *Romanticism and the Heritage of Rousseau*. Oxford: Clarendon P, 1995.

McGann, Jerome J. *The Romantic Ideology: A Critical Investigation*. Chicago: U of Chicago P, 1983.

McWhir, Anne. "Teaching the Monster to Read: Mary Shelley, Education and *Frankenstein*." In *The Educational Legacy of Romanticism*, edited by John Willinsky, 73–92. Waterloo: Wilfrid Laurier UP, 1990.

Mellor, Anne K. "*Frankenstein*. A Feminist Critique of Science." In *One Culture: Essays in Science and Literature*, edited by George Levine and Alan Rauch. Madison: U of Wisconsin P, 1987.

Miller, J. Hillis. *Others*. Princeton: Princeton UP, 2001.

Miller, Philip B., ed. and trans. *An Abyss Deep Enough: Letters of Heinrich von Kleist with a Selection of Essays and Anecdotes.* New York: Dutton, 1982.

Müller-Sievers, Helmut. *Self-Generation: Biology, Philosophy, and Literature around 1800.* Stanford: Stanford UP, 1997.

Nash, Suzanne. "Writing a Building: Hugo's Notre-Dame de Paris." *French Forum* 8.2 (1983): 122–33.

Nichols, Stephen G. "Le Livre tuera l'édifice: Resignifying Gothic Architecture." In *Autobiography, Historiography, Rhetoric*, edited by Mary Donaldson-Evans, Lucienne Frappier-Mazur, and Gerald Prince, 131–59. Amsterdam: Rodopi, 1994.

Nicolson, Marjorie Hope. *Mountain Gloom and Mountain Glory: The Development of the Aesthetics of the Infinite.* Seattle: U of Washington P, 1997.

Nisbet, H. B., ed. *German Aesthetic and Literary Criticism: Winckelmann, Lessing, Hamann, Herder, Schiller, Goethe.* Cambridge: Cambridge UP, 1985.

Ó Dochartaigh, Caitríona. "Goethe's Translation from the Gaelic Ossian." In *The Reception of Ossian in Europe*, edited by Howard Gaskill, 156–75. London: Thoemmes Continuum, 2004.

O'Flaherty, James C. *The Quarrel of Reason with Itself: Essays on Hamann, Michaelis, Lessing, Nietzsche.* Columbia, SC: Camden House, 1988.

Ong, Walter J. *Ramus, Method, and the Decay of Dialogue.* 1958. Rpt. Chicago: U of Chicago P, 2004.

Oost, Regina B. "'Servility and Command': Authorship in *Melmoth the Wanderer.*" *Papers on Language and Literature* 31.3 (1995): 291–312.

O'Rourke, James. "The 1831 Introduction and Revisions to *Frankenstein*: Mary Shelley Dictates Her Legacy." *Studies in Romanticism* 38.3 (1999): 365–85.

Osgood, Charles G., ed. and trans. *Boccaccio on Poetry.* Indianapolis: Liberal Arts Press, 1956.

Oxford Classical Dictionary. Ed. Simon Hornblower and Antony Spawforth. Oxford: Oxford UP, 1996.

Oxford Latin Dictionary. Ed. P. G. W. Glare. Oxford: Oxford UP, 1985.

Pahl, Dennis. "Poe/Script: The Death of the Author in *The Narrative of Arthur Gordon Pym.*" *New Orleans Review* 14.3 (1987): 51–60.

Peckham, Morse. "Toward a Theory of Romanticism." *PMLA* 66.2 (1951): 5–23.

Perloff, Marjorie. *Differentials: Poetry, Poetics, Pedagogy.* Tuscaloosa: U of Alabama P, 2004.

Piper, H. W. *The Active Universe.* London: Athlone Press-University of London, 1962.

Plato. *Phaedrus.* Trans. Alexander Nehamas and Paul Woodruff. Indianapolis: Hackett Publishing Co., 1995.

Poe, Edgar Allan. "Berenice." In *Selected Tales*, 18–25.

———. "The Black Cat." In *Selected Tales*, 191–99.

———. "The Fall of the House of Usher." In *Selected Tales*, 62–78.

———. "Ligeia." In *Selected Tales*, 38–52.

———. "The Masque of the Red Death." In *Selected Tales*, 136–41.

———. *Selected Tales*. Ed. Julian Symons. Oxford: Oxford UP, 1980.

Pollin, Burton R. "Philosophical and Literary Sources of Frankenstein." *Comparative Literature* 17.2 (1965): 97–108.

Poovey, Mary. "My Hideous Progeny: Mary Shelley and the Feminization of Romanticism." *PMLA* 95.3 (1980): 332–47.

Praz, Mario. "An English Imitation of Diderot's *La Religieuse* (C. R. Maturin's *Tale of the Spaniard*)." *Review of English Studies* 6.24 (1930): 429–36.

Profitt, Edward. "Science and Romanticism." *Georgia Review* 32 (1980): 55–80.

Pütz, Peter. "Werthers Leiden an der Literatur." In *Goethe's Narrative Fiction: The Irvine Goethe Symposium*, edited by William J Lillyman, 55–68. Berlin: de Gruyter, 1983.

Quiller-Couch, Arthur Thomas, Sir. *The Oxford Book of English Verse*. Oxford: Oxford UP, 1919. Bartleby.com. www.bartleby.com/101/.

Reill, Peter Hanns. *Vitalizing Nature in the Enlightenment*. Berkeley: U of California P, 2005.

Rennell, Thomas. *Remarks on Scepticism, Especially as it is Connected with the Subjects of Organization and Life*. London: F. C. & J. Rivington, 1819.

Renza, Louis A. "Poe's Secret Autobiography." In *The American Renaissance Reconsidered*, edited by Walter Benn Michaels and Donald E. Pease, 58–89. Baltimore: Johns Hopkins UP, 1985.

Richter, Jean Paul. *School for Aesthetics*. In Wheeler, 162–201.

Rieger, James. Introduction to *Frankenstein*, by Mary Wollstonecraft Shelley, xi–xxxvii. Chicago: U of Chicago P, 1982.

Robinet, Jean Baptiste René. *De la nature*. Amsterdam: Chez E. van Harrevelt, 1761. Rpt. eBooksLib.com, 2004.

Robinson, Douglas. "Trapped in the Text: 'The Pit and the Pendulum.'" *Journal of the Short Story in English* 7 (1986): 63–75.

Rooney, Ellen. "Form and Contentment." In Wolfson and Brown, 25–48.

Ross, George McDonald. *Leibniz*. Oxford UP, 1984. U of Leeds Electronic Text Centre. http://www.etext.leeds.ac.uk/leibniz/leibniz.htm.

Rousseau, G. S. "Science and the Discovery of the Imagination in Enlightened England." *Eighteenth-Century Studies* 3.1 (1969): 108–35.

Ruston, Sharon. *Shelley and Vitality*. Basingstoke: Palgrave Macmillan, 2005.

Ryan, Robert. *The Romantic Reformation: Religious Politics in English Literature*. Cambridge: Cambridge UP, 1997.

Sage, Victor. Introduction to *Melmoth the Wanderer*, by Charles Robert Maturin, vii–xxix. Harmondsworth: Penguin, 2000.

———. Notes to *Melmoth the Wanderer*, by Charles Robert Maturin, 609–60. Harmondsworth: Penguin, 2000.

Sayre, Kenneth M. *Plato's Literary Garden: How to Read a Platonic Dialogue.* Notre Dame, IN: U of Notre Dame P, 1995.

Schiller, Friedrich. "On Naïve and Sentimental Poetry." In Nisbet, 180–232.

Schlegel, Friedrich. *Kritische Friedrich-Schlegel-Ausgabe.* Ed. Ernst Behler. München: F. Schönringh, 1958–.

———. "On Incomprehensibility." In Wheeler, 32–40.

Schor, Esther. *The Cambridge Companion to Mary Shelley.* Cambridge: Cambridge UP, 2003.

Schweitzer, Christoph E. "Who Is the Editor in Goethe's *Die Leiden des jungen Werthers*?" *Goethe Yearbook* 12 (2004): 31–40.

Shelley, Mary Wollstonecraft. *Frankenstein; or, The Modern Prometheus. The 1818 Text.* Ed. James Rieger. Chicago: U of Chicago P, 1982.

———. *Frankenstein, or The Modern Prometheus. The 1818 Text.* Ed. Marilyn Butler. Oxford: Oxford UP, 1993.

Shelley, Percy Bysshe. *Complete Poetical Works.* Boston: Houghton Mifflin, 1901. Bartleby.com. http://www.bartleby.com/139/.

———. *A Defence of Poetry.* In *Major Works*, 674–701.

———. *The Letters of Percy Bysshe Shelley.* Vol. 1. *Shelley in England.* Ed. Frederick L. Jones. Oxford: Oxford UP, 1964.

———. *The Major Works.* Ed. Zachary Leader and Michael O'Neill. Oxford: Oxford UP, 2003.

———. "Ode to the West Wind." Bartleby.com. http://www.bartleby.com/101/610/.

———. "On Life." In *Major Works*, 633–36.

———. "Ozymandias." In *Representative Poetry Online* (University of Toronto English Library). http://rpo.library.utoronto.ca/poem/1904.html.

———. "When the Lamp is Shattered." In *Representative Poetry Online* (University of Toronto English Library). http://rpo.library.utoronto.ca/poem/1894.html.

Sherwin, Paul. "*Frankenstein*: Creation as Catastrophe." *PMLA* 96.5 (Oct. 1981): 883–903.

Simpson, David, ed. *German Aesthetic and Literary Criticism: Kant, Fichte, Schopenhauer, Hegel.* Cambridge: Cambridge UP, 1984.

Sloane, David E. E. "Gothic Romanticism and Rational Empiricism in Poe's 'Berenice.'" *American Transcendental Quarterly* 19 (1973): 19–26.

Smith, David Woodruff. "Phenomenology." In *The Stanford Encyclopedia of Philosophy (Winter 2005 Edition)*, edited by Edward N. Zalta. http://plato.stanford.edu/archives/win2005/entries/phenomenology/.

Spivak, Gayatri Chakravorty. "Three Women's Texts and a Critique of Imperialism." *Critical Inquiry* 12.1 (1985): 243–61.

Thompson, G. R. *Poe's Fiction: Romantic Irony in the Gothic Tales*. Madison: U of Wisconsin P, 1973.

Thompson, G. R., and Virgil L. Lokke, eds. *Ruined Eden of the Present: Hawthorne, Melville, and Poe*. West Lafayette, IN: Purdue UP, 1981.

Tisch, J. H. "The Significance of the Homeric World in Goethe's *Werther* and Moravia's *Il disprezzo*." *Canadian Review of Comparative Literature/Revue Canadienne de Littérature Comparée* 10.1 (1983): 23–30.

Tobol, Carol, and Ida H. Washington. "Werther's Selective Reading of Homer." *MLN* 92.3 (1977): 596–601.

Veeder, William. "The Negative Oedipus: Father, *Frankenstein*, and the Shelleys." *Critical Inquiry* 12.2 (1986): 365–90.

Vuillemin, Marie-Christine. "*Melmoth the Wanderer*: An English Representation of *Faust*." *Mythes, Croyances et Religions dans le Monde Anglo-Saxon* 7 (1989): 143–49.

Vuillemin, Nathalie. "Hypothèse et fiction: les relations complexes de deux discours à l'âge classique." *Comètes, Revue des littératures d'Ancien Régime* 2 (2005). Comètes.org. http://www.cometes.org/revue/numeros/numero-2-sciences-lettres/.

Waniek, Erdmann. "Werther lesen und Werther als Leser." *Goethe Yearbook* 1 (1982): 51–92.

Weissberg, Liliane. *Geistersprache: Philosophischer und literarischer Diskurs im späten achtzehten Jahrhundert*. Würzburg: Königshausen und Neumann, 1990.

Wellek, René. "The Concept of Romanticism in Literary History." In *Concepts of Criticism*, 128–98. New Haven: Yale UP, 1963.

Wheeler, Kathleen, ed. *German Aesthetic and Literary Criticism: The Romantic Ironists and Goethe*. Cambridge: Cambridge UP, 1984.

Williams, Michael J. S. " 'The language of the cipher': Interpretation in 'The Gold Bug.' " *American Literature* 53.4 (1982): 646–60.

———. *A World of Words: Language and Displacement in the Fiction of Edgar Allan Poe*. Durham, NC: Duke UP, 1988.

Witherington, Paul. "The Accomplice in 'The Tell-Tale Heart,' " *Studies in Short Fiction* 22.4 (1885): 471–75.

Wolfson, Susan J., and Marshall Brown, eds. *Reading for Form*. Seattle: U of Washington P, 2006.

Wordsworth, William. *The Excursion*. 1814. Rpt. Oxford: Woodstock Books, 1991.

———. *The Prelude: The Four Texts (1798, 1799, 1805, 1850)*. Ed. Jonathan Wordsworth. Harmondsworth: Penguin, 1995.

Ziegler, Robert E. "Writing in the Hand of Light: The Production and Experience of Art in Gautier's *Spirite*." *Chimères: A Journal of French and Italian Literature* 17.1 (1984): 4–18.

Index

Abel, Darrel, 180 n. 14
Abernethy, John, 35–38, 42 n. 13
Abrams, M. H., xii, 13 n. 2, 13 n. 3, 84
Adam, 7, 25
aesthetic sense, 18
aesthetics. *See* Romantic aesthetics
Agrippa, Cornelius, 129, 131, 133, 137
Albertus Magnus, 129, 133, 138
alchemy, 83, 84, 88, 93–94, 183
ambiguity, of words, 82
animating principle, 14–15, 21
architecture. *See* reading, architecture
Aristotle, 79
ark of the covenant, 85
art: aim of, 3; conception of, x, 19; effects of, 7; living, 18, 87; necessity of, 19; origins of, 17; power of, 15; role of, 4, 8; rules of, 20; theory of (*see* Romantic aesthetics)
Artemis, 53, 54
artist, ix, x, 15, 17, 18, 19, 21; two sorts of, 20
Asman, Carrie, 67 n. 1
audience, ix, x, 20, 21, 26, 72, 136. *See also* reader
Augustine, Saint, 8, 13 n. 3, 22, 24, 25
Augustine, Saint, works by: *In Evangelium Ioannis tractatus centum viginti quatuor*, 22
authority, divine, 6–7, 115–16, 118, 123

Bachelard, Gaston, 77 n. 2
Barclay, John, 42 n. 13
Barfield, Owen, 38, 39
Baudelaire, Charles, 109 n. 1
Bennett, Benjamin, 67 n. 5
Bernd, Clifford, 125 n. 1
Best, Otto F., 126 n. 4
Bible, 4, 5, 13 n. 5, 14, 23, 132, 135; language of, 161–63; parables of, 22; translation of, 116
Bichat, Xavier, 34–36, 37, 42 n. 11, 42 n. 12

Bichat, Xavier, works by: *Recherches physiologiques sur la vie et la mort*, 34–36
Blair, Hugh, 144 n. 9
Blake, William, 144 n. 11
Boccaccio, Giovanni, 22, 25, 161
Boccaccio, Giovanni, works by: *The Decameron*, 127, 161
Bonaventure, Saint, 130–31
Bonaventure, Saint, works by: *Breviloquium*, 130
Bonnet, Charles, 42 n. 6
Braune-Steininger, Wolfgang, 144 n. 10
British imperialism, 144 n. 6
Brombert, Victor, 96 n. 1
Brooks, Peter, 144 n. 9
Brown, Marshall, 144 n. 11, 155, 163 n. 5
Brown, Theodore, 42 n. 15
Budick, E. Miller, 180 n. 14
Burwick, Roswitha, 144 n. 10
Byron, Lord George Gordon, 92, 127, 137, 143 n. 1
Byron, Lord George Gordon, works by: "A Fragment," 143 n. 1

Cain, 79; mark of, 130
Cana, 8
canon, German, 113; literary, 132
Ceres. *See* Demeter
Chaitin, Gilbert D., 29 n. 11, 96 n. 6
Champollion, Jean-François, 26, 88
Champollion, Jean-François, works by: *Précis du système hiéroglyphique*, 88
chaos, 93, 124, 127, 128; Leibniz and, 30; religious, 116
Christianity, 28 n. 1, 116, 160, 162, 171; institutional, 43; and literal reading, 5; preservation of, 6; problem of, 161; and Romanticism, 12. *See also* secularization
chronicle, 120; vs. legend, 114

Coleridge, Samuel Taylor, 11, 77 n. 5; on dead letter and living spirit, 22–23; and theory of life, 36–39, 42 n. 14, 75

Coleridge, Samuel Taylor, works by: "Aids to Reflection," 39; *Biographia Literaria*, 22, 39; "The Eolian Harp," 75; *Hints Towards the Formation of a More Comprehensive Theory of Life*, 36–38

communication, 82; failed, 163 n. 4; of inner mood, 19–20; physical, 107; spiritual, 42, 80, 101–2, 103, 106–7, 108, 152, 154. *See also* poetic medium

Conger, Syndy M., 163 n. 9

contemplation: Fichte on, 17–18; obsessive, 165–66, 177

1 Corinthians, 29 n. 8

2 Corinthians, 5–7, 9, 14, 38, 40, 74, 75, 170

Corngold, Stanley, 174

corpse, 5, 35, 54, 76, 86, 128, 140, 177; reanimation of, 3, 72–73, 74, 127, 137, 146; rhetoric of, 154; text as, 25, 146, 153

creation, 141, 143; of art, 8, 129; by artist, 18; God's act of, 4, 25, 132; of human psyche, 137; and patriarchy, 131; principle of, 128; process of, 73, 128, 179 n. 4

Crook, Nora, 143 n. 2

culture, 3, 7, 30, 86, 171; analysis of, x–xi; Christian, 84 (*see also* Christianity); history of, 83, 87; institutions of, 10; literary, x; medieval, 88; pop, 26

Dante, Alighieri, 60

Dawson, Leven M., 163 n. 5

dead letter, 12, 41, 78, 109, 140, 168; and allegorical reading, 178; ambiguity of, 170, 173; and ancient poetry, 10; and audience, 20; of Bible, 7–8, 161; Coleridge on, 23; in communicative language, 19; contamination by, 61, 62, 171, 172, 177; corpse and, 77, 149; Fichte on, 19–20; Hamann on, 5, 8; Herder on, 9–10; and hieroglyphics, 26, 88; Kant on, 16; meaning of, 78–79; and misreading, 138; paradox of, 152; Paul on, ix, 6–8, 14; person as, 67; in poetry, 14, 21; P. Shelley on, 28; and unsuccessful reading, 25; Wordsworth on, 38

Demeter, 53, 54, 57

destruction: and creation, 131–33; through incorporation, 126 n. 3, 152–53; of legibility, 85, 87, 104; and preservation, 83, 131–33, 152–53; reading as, 93; and reanimation of texts, 73–74; and terror, 178. *See also* dismemberment; mutilation

dialectic, ix; Plato's, 6

dictation, spiritual. *See* writing, automatic

Diderot, Denis, works by: *La Religieuse*, 163 n. 7

Dietrick, Linda, 126 n. 3, 126 n. 4, 126 n. 5

dismemberment, 3, 11, 122, 124, 132, 141, 169; figurative, 104–5; of a text, 73, 147, 168. *See also* destruction; mutilation

Dotzler, Bernhard J., 67 n. 3

doubling, of people, 56, 100, 107–8, 138, 151

dreams: freedom of, 136; structure of, 163 n. 6; world of, 99, 130

Driesch, Hans, 42 n. 15

Duncan, Bruce, 67 n. 3

Eden, 130

Egypt, 27, 85, 88–89. *See also* hieroglyphics

Eichendorff, Joseph von, works by: "Abschied," 181–82

Eichner, Hans, xii n. 1, 41 n. 1

Ellis, John M., 126 n. 6

emotion, 95; as embodiment of spirit, 8; reading with, 62; representation of, 47–48; and Romantic imagination, 11; Romantic intensity of, 50–51, 56, 57, 117, 120, 139; true, 100, 101, 102

Enlightenment: rationalism, 4, 5, 8, 13 n. 5, 14; and science, 30, 41

Exodus, 8

experience: aesthetic, 12, 17; conscious, x–xi; interpretation of, 52; limits of, 15; lived vs. literary, 49–52, 55–59, 64, 67 n. 2; structure of, 95

Eve, 130

faculty, of cognition, 15
Fall of Man, 131, 132
fantastic, 97, 100, 101, 114. *See also* supernatural
fate, 78–79, 81, 95
feminist scholarship, 131, 143 n. 3, 144 n. 6, 144 n. 7
Ferber, Michael, 67 n. 8
Fichte, Johann Gottlieb, 11, 16–21, 29 n. 2, 29 n. 3, 29 n. 4, 29 n. 6
Fichte, Johann Gottlieb, works by: *On the Spirit and the Letter in Philosophy*, 16–21
Fisher, Benjamin Franklin, IV, 179 n. 8
Fowler, Kathleen, 164 n. 12
freedom, limitations of, 136; spiritual, 65
French Revolution, 34
Freud, Sigmund, 117, 144 n. 11

Gallas, Helga, 114–15, 117, 120, 126 n. 3
Galperin, William, ix
Gautier, Théophile, 11, 13, 98, 109–10 n. 2, 110 n. 6
Gautier, Théophile, works by: *Spirite*, 97–109, 109 n. 1, 109 n. 7, 110 n. 4, 181
gaze, the, 57–58
Geist, 67; Fichte and, 18, 19; Hamann and, 8; Kant and, 14–15; Romantics and, x, xi, 181; Schiller and, 24. *See also* living spirit
gender theory, 144 n. 11
Genesis, 50, 75, 79, 87, 132
genius: artistic, 19; Schiller on, 23–24; spirit of, 20, 21
Germany, 3, 53
Gilpin, William, 29 n. 6
God: artist as, 19; and divine authority, 7, 115, 118; knowledge of, 42 n. 16; personal relationship with, 116, 147; as poet, 4, 102–3; as spirit, 25; spirit of, 6, 9, 21, 75; as universe, 39–40; wisdom of, 130; word of, 22, 161
Goethe, Johann Wolfgang von, 9, 11, 30, 98, 137, 138, 139
Goethe, Johann Wolfgang von, works by: *Faust*, 84, 163 n. 9; "Prometheus," 129; *The Sorrows of Young Werther*, 47–67, 67 n. 3, 113,
133, 135, 136, 139, 142, 144 n. 10, 145
Gospel of John, 8, 29 n. 8
Gospel of Mark, 146–47, 152, 155
Gospel of Matthew, 13 n. 6, 22, 70
gothic novel, 41, 145, 146, 150, 155, 163 n. 5
gothic tradition, German, 151
Graham, Ilse, 126 n. 7
Greece, classical, 7
Griffith, Clark, 179 n. 9

Halliburton, David, 179 n. 7
Hamann, Johann Georg, 4–6, 10, 11, 13 n. 2, 16, 21, 41, 163 n. 1; and Enlightenment, 8, 13 n. 5, 14; and hieroglyph, 25, 26; prose of, 15; and Scripture, 9, 13 n. 6
Hamann, Johann Georg, works by: *Aesthetica in Nuce*, 4–5, 6, 13 n. 2, 163 n. 1
harp, 75. *See also* wind
Hartman, Geoffrey, 24
Haydon, B. R., 77 n. 3
Hazlitt, William, 77 n. 3
Hegel, G. W. F., works by: *Lectures on the History of Philosophy*, 32
Hennelly, Mark M., 163 n. 4
Herder, Johann Gottfried, 4, 9–11, 15, 21
Herder, Johann Gottfried, works by: "Correspondence on Ossian and the Songs of Ancient Peoples," 9, 11; "Shakespeare," 11
Hess, Jonathan M., 13 n. 5
hieroglyphics, 96 n. 6, 153, 154; architecture as, 88, 90; imagination as, 25–26; as legible writing, 88. *See also* illegibility; legibility
Hindle, Maurice, 143 n. 2
Hitchener, Elizabeth, 39
Hoagwood, Terence, 42 n. 16
Hoeveler, Diane Long, 144 n. 6
Hölz, Karl, 96 n. 7
Homer: in Goethe's *Werther*, 49–50, 51, 52, 53, 54, 55, 61, 64, 67, 67 n. 4, 67 n. 7, 113, 139; Herder and, 9, 10, 11, 87, 92
Homer, works by: *Iliad*, 87; *Odyssey*, 50, 59, 60, 67 n. 6
Hugo, Victor, 78, 83, 94, 96 n. 2, 109 n. 1

Hugo, Victor, works by: *Notre-Dame de Paris*, 26, 78–96, 96 n. 6, 96 n. 7, 113
human nature, 162

idea, 170; aesthetic, 14–15, 22; possession of, 166–67, 169, 170; recording of an, 84
ideal, vs. real, 108
ideal realm, 107, 109
idealism, 32, 40
illegibility: of Bible, 161; and death, 65, 89, 152; fear of, 25; and life, 152; of objects, (*see* reading, architecture); positive view of, 25–26, 73; of texts, 146–47, 152, 154, 168. *See also* hieroglyphics; legibility
imagination, 21; Fichte and, 18; as hallucination, 62–63; as hieroglyphs, 26; and incorporation, 123–24; Kant and, 14–15; Keats and, 71, 75, 76; modern, 77; Romantic, 11
imitation: artist and, 27; of nature, 4; spirit and, 8, 14
immortality, 68, 69, 71
incarnation, process of, 12. *See* textualization
intellectual revolution, 4
interpretation, 109; ambiguous, 175; of experience, 50, 52 (*see also* experience, lived vs. literary); fallible acts of, 63–64, 123; reductive, 178; of universe, 4
irony, 26, 81; characteristics of, 120
Israel, children of, 7

Jesus, 13 n. 6, 70, 160, 161; covenant of, 7; resurrection of, 3, 147, 155, 182; sacrifice of, 132; and seed analogy, 22
John, gospel of. *See* Gospel of John
justice, 126 n. 8; in Kleist's "Michael Kohlhaas," 113, 117, 118, 119, 120, 121, 123, 124, 126 n. 7

Kafka, Franz, 104, 126 n. 7, 179 n. 7
Kafka, Franz, works by: "Imperial Message," 123; "In the Penal Colony," 173, 179 n. 10; "The Top," 169; "Wedding Preparations in the Country," 98–99, 110 n. 3

Kant, Immanuel, 11, 14–16, 21, 22, 29 n. 5
Kant, Immanuel, works by: *The Critique of Judgment*, 14–16
Keats, John, 25, 71, 96 n. 5, 113; letter to B. R. Haydon, 77 n. 3
Keats, John, works by: *Endymion*, 29 n. 10, 34, 68–77, 146; *Hyperion*, 74; *Lamia*, 33–34; "Ode on a Grecian Urn," 71, 74, 79; "On Receiving a Curious Shell form the Same Ladies," 70–71
Kennedy, Veronica M. S., 163 n. 6
Kessler, Joan C., 96 n. 3
Ketterer, David, 143 n. 2
Kierkegaard, Søren, 144 n. 11
Kleist, Heinrich von, 12–13; literary crisis of, 124–25
Kleist, Heinrich von, works by: "The Beggar Woman of Locarno," 114; *The Broken Jug*, 115; *Die Familie Schroffenstein*, 126 n. 8; "Michael Kohlhaas," 12, 113–25, 126, 145; *Penthesilea*, 117–18, 120–21, 122–23; *Prinz Friedrich von Homburg*, 124; "St. Cecilia," 114
Kleist, Marie von, 118
Klopstock, Friedrich Gottlieb, 56–58, 60, 61
knowledge: absence of, 106; deadly, 134–35; forbidden, 148; of God, 42 n. 16; of past, 129.
Koelb, Clayton, 67 n. 7, 110 n. 3, 110 n. 5, 122, 126 n. 2, 126 n. 7, 130, 163 n. 3, 179 n. 3
Koelb, Janice Hewlett, xii, 29 n. 6, 144 n. 9
Koselleck, Reinhart, xii n. 1
Kroeber, Karl, xii n. 1

Lange, Henrick, 126 n. 3
language: communicative, 15, 19; as defunct, 4–5, 10, 14, 19, 26, 41, 52; of nature (*see* nature, language of); poetic, 19; structure of, 170. *See also* meaning; poetry; text; word
Last Judgment, 3
Lawrence, William, 35–36, 37, 38, 39, 42 n. 11, 42 n. 12, 43 n. 16
Lawrence, William, works by: *An Introduction to Comparative Anatomy and Physiology*, 35; *Lectures*

on *Physiology, Zoology, and the Natural History of Man,* 35, 42 n. 11
legend, 82, 148; vs. chronicle, 114. *See also* mythology; text, legendary
legibility, 83, 88; and culture, 86; and death, 66, 176; destruction of, 85; and emotion, 48, 65; and life, 89; of objects, 25, 28, 69, 73, 79–80, 82, 175 (*see also* reading, architecture); of people (*see* textualization, of people); preservation of, 80; of spiritual text, 25; of text, 21, 27, 87; valorization of, 62. *See also* hieroglyphics; illegibility
Leibniz, Gottfried Wilhelm, 30–31, 34, 35, 37, 38, 41, 41 n. 3
Leibniz, Gottfried Wilhelm, works by: *Monadology,* 30–31
Lemay, Pamphile, 109 n. 2, 110 n. 2
Lermontov, Mikhail, works by: "Ossian's Grave," 67 n. 8
Lessing, Gotthold Ephraim, works by: *Emilia Galotti,* 66–67
Lew, Joseph, W., 164 n. 11
Librett, Jeffrey S., 28 n. 1
Liddell, Henry George, 95
life, boundary to death: Coleridge's, 36–38; Romantic, 12, 28, 183; theory of, 3, 40. *See also* materialism; mechanism; spiritualism; vitalism
living spirit, 12, 41, 109, 140; and allegorical reading, 178; ambiguity of, 170; and audience, 20; of Bible, 161; Coleridge on, 23; corpse and, 77; death of, 79; Fichte on, 19–20; Hamann on, 5; Herder on, 9–10; and hieroglyphics, 26; and materialism, 36, 42 n. 8; and misreading, 138; as organization, 31; Paul on, ix, 6–8; in poetry, 14, 21, 28
logos, 154
Lokke, Virgil L., 180
London, Bette, 144 n, 1
Longfellow, Henry Wadsworth, 97, 103, 109–10 n. 2
Longfellow, Henry Wadsworth, works by: "Evangeline," 97–98, 99–100, 109–10 n. 2
Lord Byron. *See* Byron, Lord George Gordon
Lovejoy, Arthur O., xii n. 1

Lukács, Georg, 114
Luke, David, 113–14, 125, 125 n. 1
Luther, Martin, 116

Macpherson, James, 11, 47
magic, 68, 72–73, 74; as Egyptian science, 88–89, 93. *See also* magical object
magical object: cloak as, 68–70, 73; dress as, 53–54; hammer and nail as, 94; harp as, 75; lyre as, 72; scroll as, 72–73; shell as, 70–72, 73; word as, 94. *See also* alchemy
man: organization of, 42 n. 9; spirit in, 39–40; wisdom of, 93; works by, 17
Märchen, 119, 121, 124
Mark, gospel of. *See* Gospel of Mark
Marlowe, Christopher, works by: *The Tragical History of Doctor Faustus,* 156
Mary Magdalene, 147
materialism: Bichat and, 36, 42 n. 12; Coleridge and, 39; Lawrence and, 36, 42 n. 12; Robinet and, 32, 42 n. 8; Shelley and, 39–40, 42–43 n. 16, 43 n. 17; vs. spiritualism; xi, 31; *See also* mechanism
Matthew, gospel of. *See* Gospel of Matthew
Maturin, Charles Robert, 152, 162, 163 n. 2, 163 n. 8, 163 n. 12; and ambivalence towards writing, 158–59, 160; and genesis of *Melmoth the Wanderer,* 155–56, 158
Maturin, Charles Robert, works by: *Fatal Revenge,* 163 n. 8; *Melmoth the Wanderer,* 145–63, 163 n. 4, 163 n. 7, 163 n. 9, 181
McFarland, Thomas, xii n. 1, 109 n. 1
McGann, Jerome J., xii n. 1
McWhir, Anne, 144 n. 8
meaning, 12, 21, 49, 57, 64, 170, 179 n. 11; absence of, 72, 165, 169, 170–71, 173; abundance of, 52, 165–67; of Bible, 161, 163; construction of, 79, 162; cultural, 87, 89; and death, 81; double, 84; figurative, 91, 118, 166, 176–77; and husk-and-kernel metaphor (*see* metaphor, husk-and-kernel); literal, 118, 168, 174, 176–77, 181; in poetry, 52; real, 100–101; in sign,

meaning (continued)
26, 122; in signifier, 174; spiritual,
5; universal, 169. See also sign;
signified; signifier
mechanism, 12, 31, 34, 41 n. 4. See
also materialism
medieval. See Middle Ages
Mellor, Anne K., 143 n. 2
memorialization, 81; through
literature, 80, 83
memory, as text, 105, 167
metaphor, 106, 130, 131, 151;
biblical, 79; of garden, 29 n. 3; of
horses, 115, 120–21; of husk-and-
kernel, 22–24; of letter and spirit,
20, 23, 29 n. 3 (see also dead letter;
living spirit); literal reading of (see
reading, literal mode of); of
mansion, 172; of name, 176; of
seeds, 22, 23, 29 n. 7, 29 n. 8; of
tree, 132; of unraveling, 73
metonymy, 10, 12, 55, 115, 121, 132,
152, 167
Michaelis, Johann David, 5, 8, 13 n. 5,
163 n. 1
Middle Ages, 41, 78, 79, 82, 88, 92,
94 n. 2
Miller, Philip B., 126 n. 9
Milton, John, 137, 138, 139, 144 n. 11
Milton, John, works by: *Paradise Lost*,
133, 135
miracle, 11, 21, 19; at Cana, 8; of
resurrection, 155; of revivification,
12, 14, 109, 147, 183
mirror, image (*see* double); literature
as, 49, 55, 65
misreading, 130–31, 138–39
modernity, ix–x, xii, 4, 12, 163 n. 4,
163 n. 8
mood, vital, 19–20
Moses, 7
Müller-Sievers, Helmut, 29 n. 8
music, 40, 71, 72, 73, 76; power of,
75. See also song
mutilation, 79–80, 141, 152, 175; of a
text, 142, 146–47, 155. See also
destruction; dismemberment
mysticism, 14, 15
myth, 56, 84; literary, 53
mythology, 20, 53–54, 61, 77, 77 n. 1,
77 n. 6, 80, 129, 176; biblical, 131;
Romantic, 84

name, 176; ambiguous (*see* structure,
reference-); power of, 93
Napoleon, Bonaparte, 88
Napoleonic era, 24
narrative structure: of Kleist's "Michael
Kohlhaas," 113–15, 119–20, 122;
of Maturin's *Melmoth the Wanderer*,
146–48, 151, 153, 156, 158, 163 n.
6; of Shelley's *Frankenstein*, 142–43
Nash, Suzanne, 96 n. 3
natura naturans, 38, 75, 77 n. 5
natural philosophy. See science
nature, 10, 12, 17, 30; actual vs.
second, 15; Coleridge on (see
natura naturans); death of, 4, 11;
as hieroglyph, 26 (see also
hieroglyphics); improvement on,
29 n. 6; Keats on, 34; language of,
4–5, 14, 41; as material (*see*
materialism); Robinet on, 31–33,
42 n. 8; as text, 8; theory of, 31,
168, 181; unified, 31, 32
New Testament, 29 n. 8, 70, 116, 155
Newton, Isaac, 34
Nichols, Stephen, G., 96 n. 3
Nicolson, Marjorie Hope, 41 n. 1
Noakes, Susan, 130
Notre-Dame, 78–93. See also reading,
architecture

Ó Dochartaigh, Caitríona, 67 n. 1
observation, power of, 43. See also
gaze
O'Flaherty, James C., 13 n. 5
Old Testament, 7, 13 n. 5, 50, 116,
132; allegorical reading of, 178;
letter of, 22; power of, 6; rereading,
8, 86. See also Bible; Paul
Ong, Walter J., 13 n. 4
Oost, Regina B., 163 n. 10
organization, 41, 181; Bichat on,
34–35, 36; Coleridge on, 36–40;
Fichte on, 20; Lawrence on, 35;
levels of, 32–33; narrative (*see*
narrative structure); Robinet on,
31–33, 42 n. 6, 42 n. 8, 42 n. 9
Origin, 8, 13 n. 6
O'Rourke, James, 143 n. 2
Osgood, Charles G., 22
Ossian, Goethe and, 47–52, 54–55,
64–67, 67 n. 1, 67 n. 8, 98, 113,
139; Herder on, 9, 10–11

other, 107; vs. self, 108–9
Ozymandias, 27

Pahl, Dennis, 179 n. 6
Paracelsus, 129, 133, 137, 138
paratextual elements, 78, 121
past, 11; books of, 84; Egyptian, 26; imperfections of, 181–82; improving and recovering, 107; vs. present, ix; re-reading, 86; revivification of, 12, 67, 113, 125, 129, 140, 149
patriarchy, rhetoric of, 131
Paul, apostle, ix, 11–12, 61, 125; and Coleridge, 22; and Fichte, 18; and Hamann, 5–8; and Herder, 9–10; and Keats, 74–75; and Plato, 10; and Poe, 170, 178; vocabulary of, 14–16, 21, 38, 40
Paul, apostle, works by: *See* 1 Corinthians; 2 Corinthians
Peckham, Morse, xii n. 1
Perloff, Marjorie, 13 n. 7
Persephone, 54
Petrarch, 137
philosopher: problem of, 12; task of, 4, 5
Phöbus, 120–21
picturesque, 29 n. 6, 82
Pindar, 22
Piper, H. W., 77 n. 5, 77 n. 6
Plato, 6–7, 10, 19, 29 n. 7
Plato, works by: *Phaedrus*, 6–7, 29
Plutarch, 137, 138, 139
Plutarch, works by: *Plutarch's Lives*, 133, 135
Pluto, 54
Poe, Edgar Allan, 12, 113, 179 n. 6, 179 n. 10, 180 n. 14; and Kafka, 179 n. 7; and language, 179 n. 10 (*see also* rhetoric; terror, rhetoric of)
Poe, Edgar Allan, works by: "Berenice," 165–70, 173, 174, 176–77; "The Black Cat," 174; "The Fall of the House of Usher," 171–73, 174, 176, 177–78, 181; "Ligeia," 170, 173, 176, 177; "The Masque of the Red Death," 170; "Peter Snook," 179; "The Philosophy of Composition," 179 n. 4; "The Pit and the Pendulum," 179 n. 10; "The Tell-Tale Heart," 174, 179–80 n. 13

poet: ancient, 11, 65; as divine creator, 129; and ideas, 15; problem of, 12; task of, 4, 5, 24
poetic medium, 19
poetry, 16, 19, 22, 30, 51–52, 56–57, 183; ancient, 9–11, 50, 65, 79, 80; modern, 9; naïve, 23; oral, 10; paradox of, 15, 19; power of, 10–11, 15; reading, 22; and science, 38
Polidori, John William, 127
Polidori, John William, works by: *The Vampyre*, 143 n. 1
Pollin, Burton R., 144 n. 5
Poovey, Mary, 144 n. 7
Praz, Mario, 163 n. 7
prereading, 174
preservation, of Christianity, 6; through consumption of texts, 152–53; of culture, 86; spirit of, 131
printing, 84–87
Profitt, Edward, 41 n. 1
Prometheus, 129, 139
Prussian society, 124–25
psychoanalysis: and castration anxiety, 117; and Oedipal theme, 144 n. 11; and phallic potency, 120
Pütz, Peter, 67 n. 2
Pygmalion, 12, 20, 21

Quinn, Patrick F., 180 n. 14

rationalism, 4–5, 8, 10, 13 n. 5, 14
reader, 67 n. 3; active, x, 22, 56, 70–72, 73, 77, 98–99, 179–80 n. 13; ancient, 27; assimilation of, 117; good, 91; literal, 139, 167 (*see also* reading, literal mode of); medieval, 132; modern, 11, 47, 92, 97, 114, 165; reanimation of, 73–74; self as, 167; skilled, 102–3; woman as, 131
reading: active (*see* reader, active); allegorical, 178, 179 n. 10, 181; architecture, 80, 82–93, 96 n. 3; as burial, 176–77; as communication (*see* communication); as consumption, 113, 116–18, 122, 123–25, 126 n. 3, 152–54; as cultural phenomenon, 83; dark side to, 49, 54, 60–66, 67 n. 6, 79, 80 (*see also* terror); deconstructively,

reading (continued)
179 n. 10; definition of, x; and
eroticism, 48, 53–54, 56, 60,
62–63, 91, 99, 104–5, 106, 181;
experience of, 17, 51; feminine
mode of (*see* woman); hieroglyphics
(*see* hieroglyphics); *in bono*, 82; *in
malo*, 82; incorrectly (*see*
misreading); Lacanian, 114; literal
mode of, 5, 8, 13 n. 6, 23, 90–92,
116, 117–18, 135, 138, 139, 167,
174 (*see also* meaning, figurative;
meaning, literal); necessity of, 129,
162, 177; oblivious, 63, 67 n. 7, 98,
99, 104, 110 n. 3; participation in,
51–52, 54, 60; power of, 60, 68,
178 (*see also* poetry, power of; text,
power of); principle of, 133;
problem of, 3, 54, 60–61, 67 n. 3,
138, 150, 161; process of, x, 5, 22,
60, 96, 147, 161, 163 n. 6, 181;
question of, 16; as reproduction, 27;
Romantic vs. Enlightenment, 4–5;
and self-textualization (*see*
textualization); sophisticated, 23;
spiritual, 182; successful, 117; task
of, 163; transforming power of, 64,
83–84 (*see also* revivification); as
woman, 130–31. *See also* prereading;
text; word
realism, 113, 114, 121, 163;
psychological, 48
realm. *See* ideal realm
reception theory, 67 n. 3
Red Sea, 99
Reeves, Nigel, 113–14, 125, 125 n. 1
Reformation, 115
Reill, Peter Hanns, 33, 41 n. 2, 41 n.
4, 42 n. 6, 42 n. 8, 42 n. 15
Rennell, Thomas, 42 n. 11
Renza, Louis A., 179 n. 4
representation, problem of, 47
repression, 60
reproduction, physical vs. spiritual, 130
resurrection: of Jesus, 3, 147, 155,
182; need for, 84; negative side to,
145, 171–74; textual, 181
revivification, ix; as aim of Romantic
art, 3, 8; through art, 15; of corpse,
73, 74, 109, 146; fictional
depictions of, 12–13, 21; figurative,
146; Gautier's *Spirite* and, 99;
Goethe's *Werther* and, 50; Hamann
on, 4–5, 8; Herder on, 11; Hugo's
Notre-Dame de Paris and, 81; and
hieroglyphics, 26, 28, 88; through
imagination, 75–76; through
incorporation, 113; Keats's
Endymion and, 68, 73–76, 77; of
knowledge, 129; literal, 174; as
miracle, 14; of the past, 113, 125,
182; reading as, x, 21, 25, 27, 77,
140, 168, 181; rite of, 56; terror of,
25, 26, 171, 173, 176; of text, 147;
tradition of, 183
rhetoric: of negation, 165, 179 n. 4;
reversibility of, 170, 173
rhetorical theory, 126 n. 2
Richter, Jean Paul, 26, 120–21
Rieger, James, 143 n. 2, 144 n. 4
Robinet, Jean Baptiste René, 31–35,
36, 37, 38, 39, 40, 41, 42 n. 6,
42 n. 8, 42 n. 9, 43 n. 16
Robinet, Jean Baptiste René, works by:
De la nature, 31–32
Robinson, Douglas, 179 n. 10
Romantic aesthetics, xi, 5, 11, 14, 19,
22, 23, 25, 41, 50, 68
Romantic century, ix–x, xi, 12, 28, 30,
109, 181, 183
Romantic imagination, 11
Romanticism, ix–xi, xii, 30, 97, 131;
British, 96; culture of, x, xi;
feminization of, 144 n. 7; French,
109; keyword of, ix; project of, 41,
84, 125; and science, 41, 143; topos
of, 129
Rooney, Ellen, 13 n. 7
Rosetta Stone, 88, 92
Ross, George McDonald, 31, 41 n. 5
Rousseau, G. S., 30, 41 n. 1
Rousseau, Jean-Jacques, 109 n. 1
Rousseau, Jean-Jacques, works by: *La
nouvelle Héloïse*, 16
ruach, 75
ruin, 93, 134
Ruston, Sharon, 36, 40, 41 n. 3, 42 n.
9, 42 n. 12, 42 n. 16, 43 n. 17, 182
Ryan, Robert, 96 n. 4

Sage, Victor, 163 n. 8, 164 n. 12
Satan, 116, 137, 158, 160, 162
Sayre, Kenneth M., 29 n. 7
Schiller, Friedrich, 11, 23–24, 29 n. 8

Schiller, Friedrich, works by: *On the Aesthetic Education of Mankind*, 16; "On Naïve and Sentimental Poetry," 23–24
Schlegel, August Wilhelm, 4
Schlegel, Friedrich, 4
Schlegel, Friedrich, works by: *Lucinde*, 25; "On Incomprehensibility," 25–26
scholar, task of, 4, 5, 8
Schweitzer, Christoph E., 67 n. 5
science: biological, 11, 12, 30–41, 181, 183; Egyptian (*see* magic); of Egyptology, 26, 28, 182; of electricity, 127, 131–32; of geology, 41 n. 1; history of, xi; Kleist and, 125; of letters, 134 (*see also* reading); and literature, 30, 34; Newtonian, 33, 34, 41; Romantic, 143 n. 3
Scott, Robert, 95
Scripture. *See* Bible
secularization, 22, 84, 94 n. 4, 96, 125; partial, 123
self, 29 n. 4, 113, 134, 179 n. 6; vs. other, 108–9; vs. society, ix; as spirit, 39; as text, 167 (*see also* reading, transforming power of; transformation, into text); true, 101; vs. world, 41
sexuality. *See* reading, and eroticism
Shakespeare, William, 9, 10, 73, 87, 92, 145, 147
Shakespeare, William, works by: *Henry 6*, 145; *The Tempest*, 73
Shelley, Mary Wollstonecraft, 12, 26, 27, 28, 113, 143; and the genesis of *Frankenstein*, 127–29, 137, 140
Shelley, Mary Wollstonecraft, works by: *Frankenstein*, 26, 84, 127–43, 143 n. 1, 143 n. 3, 144 n. 4, 144 n. 6, 144 n. 10, 144 n. 11, 145
Shelley, Percy Bysshe, 27–28, 127, 136–37; and materialism, 39–40, 42 n. 17; on poetic transformation, 183; and religious skepticism, 39, 42–43 n. 16; and spiritual idealism, 40
Shelley, Percy Bysshe, works by: *Defense of Poetry*, 183; "Ode to the West Wind," 27–28, 67 n. 8, 182; "On Life," 40; "On Mutability," 135–36; "Ozymandias," 27; "When the Lamp is Shattered," 40
Sherwin, Paul, 144 n. 11
sign, 144 n. 9, 166; ideal, 169; as ideogram, 26; principle of, 133; recombination of, 179 n. 4; and rhetorical terror, 173; transparent, 24–25. *See also* meaning
signification, process of, 12, 21
signified, and relationship to signifier, 133, 165; Schiller on, 24–25
signifier, 5, 133, 169; and relationship to signified, 165–66; and rhetorical terror, 167, 170, 173–75; Schiller on, 24
silence, 63–64, 72, 76, 95, 150, 154
skepticism, 51; Plato's, 6; P. Shelley's, 42 n. 16
Sloane, David E. E., 179 n. 2
Smith, David Woodruff, x
sola scriptura, 116
song, 9–10, 15, 40, 71, 75, 76
soul, 64–65; Bichat on, 36; vs. body, 139, 155; Coleridge on, 37; damned, 158; dead, 76; Fichte on, 19–20; Herder on, 10; Kant on, 14; living, 109, 154; and materialism, 42–43 n. 16; mirror of, 108; Paul on, 6–7; as perfect reader, 103; Plato on, 6, 29 n. 7; Robinet on, 32; P. Shelley on, 39–40; within a text, 102; and textual spirit, 23
sound, 64, 82, 133; of letters, 10; musical, 72; principle of, 18–19; speech, 13 n. 4
Spiess chapbook, 156
spiritualism: definition of, 42 n. 7; vs. materialism, 31–41; Robinet and, 32; Shelley and, 39–40, 42–43 n. 16. *See also* vitalism
Spivak, Gayatri Chakravorty, 144 n. 6
Sterne, Laurence, works by: *Tristram Shandy*, 131
structure: cultural, xi; of experience, 95; husk-and-kernel, 22–24; of ideas, 12; linguistic, xi, 52, 170; of matter (*see* organization); narrative (*see* narrative structure); of physical universe, 175; reference-, 150–51, 164 n. 11; of thought, 5–6
Stürmer und Dränger, 4
Style indirect libre, 149

subject vs. object, 41
sub-plot, in Kleist's "Michael Kohlhaas." *See* narrative structure
supernatural, 38–39; in Gautier's *Spirite*, 103, 105; in Kleist's works, 114, 118, 123; in Maturin's *Melmoth the Wanderer*, 158; vs. natural, 114, 123; in Poe's works, 175; Romantic interest in, 41. *See also* fantastic
Swedenborg, Emanuel, 110 n. 6
Swedenborg, Emanuel, works by: "Marriage in the Other Life," 109

Temple of Solomon, 85
terror, 163 n. 5, 181; in Maturin's *Melmoth the Wanderer*, 145–46, 148–50, 152, 154–55, 160, 162; in Poe's works, 165, 167–69, 170–71, 173, 176–78; of revivification, 25, 26, 113, 147; rhetoric of, 170, 174, 179 n. 10, 179 n. 13; in Shelley's *Frankenstein*, 129, 138–41. *See also* uncanny
text, ix, 6; ancient (*see also* poetry, ancient), 61; authority of, 6–7, 118, 122, 124 (*see also* authority, divine); as body, 12, 23; communication through, 102, 106 (*see also* reading, as communication; writing, automatic); as corpse (*see* corpse, text as); as dead matter, x, 5, 8, 61, 74, 139, 141, 142; double structure of, 22–24; effects of, 48, 49–50, 52; empty, 123 (*see also* meaning, absence of); figurative, 68–69, 73, 74, 76, 182; illegible, 25, 154, 167, 168 (*see also* legibility); intention of, 63; legendary, 101, 106, 110 n. 5; legible, 27 (*see also* legibility); as letters, 16, 99, 101, 162, 170, 182; magical, 70; of nature, 4; paradox of, 125; as person, 136, 138; person as, 61, 62, 67, 101, 104–5, 107, 122, 141–42; poetic, 14, 51, 54, 57; power of, 12, 21, 25, 41, 72–73, 95, 153, 177, 183; pure, 161; revivification of (*see* revivification, of text); spirit of, 7, 16, 23, 74, 76, 99, 100–102, 141, 170, 182; transcendent, 123. *See also* dead letter; living spirit; poetry; reading; word

textualization: of nature, 55, 57, 58; of objects (*see* reading, architecture); of people, 62, 101, 103, 104, 122, 136, 141; of self, 61, 62, 64, 65, 66, 67, 105, 107
theory of life, 3, 12, 28, 31–41, 41 n. 4, 182; Coleridge's, 36–38; Romantic, 40, 183. *See also* materialism; mechanism; spiritualism; vitalism
Thompson, G. R., 180 n. 14
thought, absence of, 97, 99, 101, 107, 136. *See also* writing, automatic
Thousand and One Nights, 74
time, collapsing of, 152
Tisch, J. H., 67 n. 4
Tobol, Carol, 67 n. 4, 67 n. 6
Torah, 7
Tower of Babel, 87, 89, 115
tragedy, 89–90
transformation: through Christ, 8; into dead letters, 8; of dead matter into living thing (*see* revivification); figurative, 28, 61, 119; through light, 53, 97; literal, 61; magical, 72; mythical, 77 n. 1; poetic, 183; through reading (*see* reading, transforming power of); as Romantic concern, 84; into texts, 55, 83, 103, 120; of word, 85
translation, 79, 116; and construction of meaning, 162; scenes of, 67 n. 1

uncanny, 60, 73, 150, 174, 175, 177. *See also* terror

Veeder, William, 144 n. 11
virgin-mother, 53–54
vitalism, 42 n. 15; Bichat and, 36; Coleridge and, 38; Enlightenment, 41 n. 1; Lawrence and, 36; vs. mechanism, 12, 31–41; Robinet and, 42 n. 8. *See also* spiritualism
Volney, C. F., works by: *Ruins of Empires*, 134
Voltaire, 5
Vuillemin, Marie-Christine, 163 n. 9
Vuillemin, Nathalie, 42 n. 10

Waniek, Erdmann, 67 n. 3
Washington, Ida H., 67 n. 4, 67 n. 6

Watson, Seth, works by: *Manual of Physiology*, 42. n. 14; *On Diseases of the Liver*, 42 n. 14
Weissberg, Liliane, 28 n. 1, 29 n. 2, 29 n. 3, 29 n. 4
Wellek, René, xii n. 1, 41
Williams, Michael J. S., 179 n. 5, 179 n. 11
wind, as spirit, 75
Witherington, Paul, 179 n. 13
Wolfson, Susan, ix
woman, as misreader, 130–31. *See also* reading
word: dead, 113; as divine creation, 4; effects of, 56–57, 95; of God, 22, 156, 161; living, 85; magic, 94; as material, 15, 85; maternal, 122; perished, 80; Ramus on, 13 n. 4; revivifying, 12, 13, 14, 26, 109, 183; of Romanticism, ix; as sign, 79, 144; spoken, 166; structure of, 95, 165; symmetry of, 9; written, 6–7, 10, 12. *See also* language; letter; meaning; poetry; sign; signifier; signified; text
wordplay, 28
Wordsworth, William, 13 n. 2
Wordsworth, William, works by: *The Excursion*, 71, 77 n. 3, 77 n. 4, 77 n. 5, 77 n. 6; *The Prelude*, 38
writing, 110 n. 4; architecture as, 84; as artistic medium, 21; automatic, 100–102, 106, 108; and connection to reading, 5–6, 20, 74; constraints of, 10; illegible, 93, 152 (*see also* legibility); incomprehensibility of, 25; Kleist and, 124–25; legible, 88 (*see also* legibility); living, 87; Maturin and, 159; process of, xi; new notion of, 3; Paul on, 7; skepticism toward, 6; system of, 26. *See also* reading

Ziegler, Robert E., 110 n. 4